Medicine Bags and Dog Tags

Medicine Bags
and Dog Tags

American Indian Veterans
from Colonial Times *to*
the Second Iraq War

Al Carroll

University of Nebraska Press
Lincoln & London

© 2008 by the Board of Regents of
the University of Nebraska
All rights reserved
Manufactured in the
United States of America

∞

Library of Congress Cataloging-
in-Publication Data

Carroll, Al.
Medicine bags and dog tags:
American Indian veterans from
colonial times to the second Iraq
War/Al Carroll.
       p. cm.
Includes bibliographical references
and index.
ISBN 978-0-8032-1085-1 (cloth:
alk. paper)
1. United States—Armed Forces—
Indian troops—History.
2. Indian veterans. 3. Indians of
North America—Government
relations. 4. Indians of North
America—History. I. Title.
E98.M5C37 2008
323.1197—dc22

2007045220

Set in Sabon.

Contents

Acknowledgments . . *vii*

Introduction: *Saint Francis the Soldier* . . *1*

1. "Let's See Some of That Apache Know-How":
Depictions of Native Veterans in Fiction . . *16*

2. "They Kill Indians Mostly, Don't They?":
Rogers' Rangers and the Adoption of Indian Tactics . . *37*

3. Before a Native Veteran Tradition Can Begin:
The Case of Mexico . . *48*

4. Thunderbird Warriors, Injuneers, and the
USNS *Red Cloud: Native and Pseudo-Indian Images
and Names in the Military* . . *62*

5. The Super Scout Image: *Using a Stereotype to Help
Native Traditions Revive* . . *86*

6. "Savages Again": *World War II* . . *114*

7. The Half-Hidden Spirit Guide Totemic Mark:
Korea . . *135*

8. An American Ka in Indian Country: *Vietnam* . . *147*

9. Bringing the War Home: *The American Indian Movement, Wounded Knee II, Counterinsurgency, and a New Direction for Warrior Societies* . . *163*

10. "Fighting Terrorism since 1492": *The Gulf War, the War in Afghanistan, and the Second Iraq War* . . *173*

11. "A Woman Warrior, Just Like Lozen": *The Meaning of the Life of Lori Piestewa to Natives and Non-Natives* . . *207*

Conclusion: *Is It Time for Native Veteran Traditions to End?* . . *223*

Appendix of Tables . . *231*

Notes . . *235*

Bibliography . . *265*

Index . . *275*

Acknowledgments

I WOULD LIKE TO THANK my sisters, aunts, uncles, cousins, grand-parents, and parents for their support and inspiring examples, the professors at the University of Texas–San Antonio (UTSA) who were so invaluable in guiding me, Drs. Antonio Calabria and Yolanda Leyva, the staff at the McNair Program at UTSA (which unfortunately has now been shut down), Dr. Ann Eisenberg and Ruth Terry, the Institute for the Recruitment of Teachers at Andover Academy, my master's thesis committee members (whom I would be thanking even if they were not on my committee) Drs. Donna Akers, Charles Cutter, and Donald Parman, the staffs at Interlibrary Loan at the Purdue librar-ies and the History Department who were always such a great help, Drs. Peter Iverson, Arturo Rosales, and James Riding In at Arizona State University (ASU) (I would be thanking them even if they had not been on my committee), and the wonderful office staff at the History Department at ASU. I would also especially like to thank the veterans and their family members who shared their stories with me, the people at the 45th Division Museum, the Ak-Chin Museum, the annual Sac and Fox Nation Powwow, the annual North American Iroquois Veterans Association Powwow, and the annual ASU and Mesa powwows for their help and the good memories of those gatherings.

Introduction

Saint Francis the Soldier

IT WAS THE IMAGE of the Indian in white minds that tried to set the boundaries for what Natives in the military were allowed to be. Native people used these images, turning these falsehoods against themselves, defining what Native traditions in the military became.

> World War I, World War II
> Vietnam, Korea, Desert Storm
> Soldier boy, soldier boy[1]

The Black Lodge Singers are one of the most popular groups on the powwow circuit. Their veterans honor song "World Wars I and II" is a recitation of all the wars in which Native soldiers fought in the twentieth century, as well as a plaintive call to the individual Native soldier. Though the Black Lodge Singers are Blackfoot, the song is in English. This song is a good illustration of Native veteran experiences, both the wide span of time of the wars in which they fought for the United States and the way military experiences changed Native traditions. American Indians were part of the U.S. and Canadian militaries from the very beginning. Native servicemen often fought in wars that were frankly imperialist in nature or to maintain U.S. global dominance, from the war to conquer the Philippines to the current Second Iraq War. But simultaneously Natives used the military for their own benefit, to hold onto traditions, modifying some, reviving others, inventing new ones, and influencing the military itself.

There is probably no clearer symbol of these mutual changes than how the Yaqui depict San Francisco (Saint Francis). San Francisco

Xavier is not the great missionary risking all to convert others to Christianity, as the church hierarchy depicts, or to any other Western values or belief systems. On the contrary, his role in Yaqui culture is that of a soldier, and not a soldier as Anglo-American culture understands the role to be. He is a defender of indigenous tradition, not assimilation, and his sacred duty is to protect Yaqui lands and culture from outsiders.

The Meaning of Native Patriotism

It is crucial to understand this distinction between Anglo and Native worldviews on the role of the military. One of the central arguments in this book is that the degrees to which Natives regard the military, the nation-state, and a nation-state's wars as something they can support is based on how tenable the claim is that the nation-state is defending Native sacred lands in such wars. If that claim is not sustainable, Native willingness to take part declines. Natives are not foolish or being used by the nation-state; the choices Natives make to be in the military are perfectly rational and in line with longstanding cultural values.

Yet undeniably Native warrior traditions were and are dramatically altered by veteran service. This book looks at the irony of Natives fighting for a nation-state that often sought to dispossess them and at the meanings Native people attach to their service. Why did American Indians join the military in such high numbers? How do Natives reconcile service to nation-states that wrong them repeatedly? The answers are largely cultural motives. American Indians used military institutions to preserve, protect, defend, and revive Native cultures, institutions, and spiritual and cultural practices. Natives took advantage of stereotypes of "the Indian" in the white American cultural landscape and used those odious labels for their own benefit. It is worth repeating, since it cannot be emphasized enough: it was the images of the Indian in white minds that tried to set the boundaries for what Natives in the military were allowed to be. Native people used these images, turning them against themselves and defining what Native traditions in the military became.

Lakota activist Milo Yellow Hair speaks of something similar when describing the American Indian Movement and its members' conception of themselves as a warrior society as groundhog medicine, or the way of the groundhog: something will only seem to be defeated but will rise again in a different place or time.[2] In like manner, Natives first joined the military in the nineteenth century, sometimes to turn violence away from themselves. In both world wars and their aftermaths, Natives used the military to overcome assimilation efforts that tried to eliminate their cultures and religious traditions. But beginning with the Vietnam War and continuing up to the Second Iraq War, Natives increasingly questioned the intent behind U.S. wars. Participation in the military declined, even while the need for honoring and supporting veterans did not change. Many Natives now regard the *purposes* of military with ambivalence or even horror while respecting the men and women who choose to enter it. But are there better alternatives for Natives—other choices? This is a question I shall return to only after discussing the complexity of Native veteran traditions fully.

To understand more fully how Natives regard the military, non-Natives need to be aware that most Natives have an extremely different view of patriotism than do Anglo-Americans (or Anglos, as they are commonly called in the Southwest). After all, most Natives regard themselves as members of a sovereign tribal nation first and foremost and only secondly as either a dual citizen or in a treaty relationship with a nation-state, such as the United States or Canada. Most Natives attach fundamentally different meanings to words and phrases such as *patriotism, our land, fighting for my country*, and *the flag* or *our flag*. There is probably no clearer sign of Natives' different associations with flags than the fact that Native artists take great liberties in their use of flag motifs in their art, alterations that strike some Anglos as offensive. It is not at all unusual for Native artists to alter the colors and the number or style of stars, to use crosses in place of stars, to use golden eagles instead of bald eagles, and above all to change the contexts in which the flag can be used. Flags are used as pincushions, hatbands, pouches, and as capes or shawls; they are also sometimes used ironically, with the bars representing prison bars or barbed wire. The very word *flag* also often means any symbol of a nation or people, such as an eagle staff or other icon with collective sacred meaning. Since government agents often gave flags to tribes during treaty signings, the earliest meaning Native peoples attached to the American flag was the treaty relationship itself: friendship or support for similar political or military goals.[3]

Anthropologist William Powers explains the meaning the flag has for the Lakotas, the Indian nation using flags most frequently in their art. He argues that Lakotas fly or wear flags because their fathers and grandfathers did; this makes them feel more Indian, not more American. Powers argues that seeing conventional patriotism in Lakota flag designs is far-fetched. Thus attributing non-Lakota values to Lakotas makes little sense because there is no evidence of it. Instead, flags are a replacement, metaphor, or substitute for the warrior tradition or prowess of the individual. The National Anthem of the Lakotas is always sung at powwows, never the U.S. one. When Lakotas held dances after World War I with flags, the U.S. flag was just a prop, an adoption of a strategy to utilize elements of a foreign culture to enhance their own culture. Even for Lakotas, less than 10 percent of dancers at powwows have U.S. flags.[4]

Lakota elder Howard Bad Hand agrees, arguing that Lakotas adopted the flag as a symbol of the dominant culture to maintain a sense of being and as a substitute for the older warrior tradition to honor the individual warrior, not as a sign of conventional patriotism. Other Native scholars and leaders are of the same mind. Robert Porter, former Seneca attorney general and director of the Center of Indigenous Law at Syracuse University, said, "Parading the American flag to the tune of traditional Indian music and dance typifies the internal conflict. . . . You will find people who think that is an amazing blend of culture and then there are those like me who view it as a tragedy." Steve Russell, a law professor and Vietnam-era Cherokee veteran, writes, "Indians fight for the Stars and Stripes, the flag that failed to protect Black Kettle's people at Sand Creek . . . the flag that Andrew Jackson dishonored when he removed my great-great-great grandmother (Do you think we forget?) and the rest of the Cherokee in violation of the Supreme Court's order. . . . When Indians raise the American flag over their reburial ceremony, that flag is a symbol that we consider the Indian wars to be over."[5]

In the context described by Russell, the flag becomes a symbol of forgiveness from Native people. But as shown above it can also mean individual warriors or a nation-to-nation treaty relationship, not patriotism, which itself has a very different meaning for most Natives. Gros Ventre veteran George Horse Capture explains Native patriotism this way: "Our devotion and spirit is not for mom's apple pie but for grandma's dried meat. We are dedicated to our country, the physical land, not the country as most other groups think of it. This is *our* country. It makes no difference whose name is on the deed. We are the landlords." Similar views come from Natives in Canada. Stephen Simon, a Micmaq veteran of the Korean War, said, "It's the land I fought for, the land, not the country" or the nation-state.[6]

Writings on Native Veterans

The best writings on Native veterans are for the most part not by historians. The most insightful works and the most accurate depictions come from outside the field and often from within Native cultures. In most of the history books that look at Native experience during the twentieth century's wars, it is apparent that most authors had little or even no contact with or input from Native people, making mistaken assumptions that leave Native readers shaking their heads in disbelief. Most historians on this topic privileged documents from government agencies and white philanthropists over the words and views of Native people themselves, often taking the word of paternalistic policymakers uncritically and at face value.

The central issue at the heart of any look at Native veterans is one of assimilation versus cultural renewal or revival. Since massive Native participation in the military was heavily promoted by assimilationists who saw "war as a civilizer," one has to ask first, to what extent did white Progressives succeed? Is a Native who joins the military abandoning his or her heritage and eagerly running away from his or her Native identity to become an unhyphenated "plain old American"? Did (and do) veterans join the service because they perceived "mainstream" Anglo culture to be superior to allegedly fading Native ways of life?

While the first question is not only valid but also crucial, on the face of it the latter two questions are absurd to anyone Native or to anyone who has any prolonged contact with Native people and cultures. The very questions reflect the worldview of the ones doing the asking and little else. Yet most historians writing about Native veterans naively took the word of self-described Anglo "friends of the Indian" who sought to "kill the Indian, save the man" that the answer was an unqualified yes. The earliest writings on Native veterans were by proponents of assimilating American Indians into "mainstream" America, and up until the end of the twentieth century virtually all the written documents on the subject were authored by the government or white philanthropists. The first attempt at a comprehensive book-length work on Native veterans was by Alison Bernstein in 1991. Of the six books that are general overviews of American Indians during any one of America's twentieth-century wars, five are by historians. Four of them reflect, to varying degrees, the very same troubling privileging of assimilationist propaganda over Natives' own words.

Often this reliance on white reformers' words leads these historians to make outrageous assumptions and assertions. Alison Bernstein and Kenneth Townsend claim *chief* was not an epithet but a compliment eagerly sought by Native servicemen. Diane Camurat has written glowingly of segregationists being "moved by goodwill" rather than racism. Thomas Britten has written that Natives coming into the military were (presumably for the first time) given the chance to learn about hygiene. The insulting inference is that cleanliness was a completely new state of being for Natives and that the stereotype of filthy and ignorant Indians was true. Even more serious than the flights from logic that viewed slurs as sought-after pats on the head and the presence of unintended insults are these authors' lapses in knowledge of Native cultures. Most historians lumped Natives in with other minorities and thus showed an incomplete understanding of how the issue of sovereignty affects Native views on patriotism.

The best work on Native veterans comes from a political scientist and Cherokee veteran of the Vietnam War. Tom Holm's *Strong Hearts, Wounded Souls* should be regarded as a landmark, groundbreaking in its approaches and insightful, the standard by which any writing on Native veterans should be judged. Holm posits that Native veteran traditions are largely adaptations of longstanding Native warrior traditions. To explain this, he revisits Native warrior traditions and how outsiders have misconstrued them. Holm argues that most Anglos examining Native veterans assumed American Indians were utterly dependent on whites for their sense of self-worth. White Progressives and, later, historians viewed Natives as so desperate for white acceptance they would risk life, limb, and sanity while completely and eagerly rejecting their tribal heritages simply to convince any individual whites and Anglo-America in general that they are patriotic, uninterested in seeking anything but acceptance as Americans and not as Natives, and bearing no grudge or desires for redress for past and present wrongs.

I go further than Holm and argue that such widespread misconceptions should not simply be described as inaccurate; they are what must be utterly demolished before we can get any true understanding of the history of Native veteran traditions. As we will see throughout this book, so many Anglos have such a disconcerting habit of seeing only what they wish to see when it comes to Native people, often using Natives themselves to prove their most treasured point whether it fits the facts or not. That most treasured point, whether they are conscious of it or not, is often seeing Native veterans as Tontos, faithful companions and servants to white needs or wishful thinking, the "good Indians" as opposed to those they see as "bad Indians," who demand their rights or talk about topics such as sovereignty and genocide.

This is on display in most books that purport to be about Native veterans. Alison Bernstein's *American Indians and World War II* is largely a study of how the war affected the New Deal for Indians government policy rather than about Natives themselves. To the extent Bernstein looks at Natives at all, her argument is that American Indians showed how eager they were to become "Indian Americans" who thought of themselves as just another ethnic group rather than as separate nations within the United States. Her work is the most assimilationist, Anglocentric, and biased toward white Progressives of all historians who have written on Native veterans. The central thesis of Kenneth Townsend's *World War II and the American Indian* is that World War II and its immediate aftermath were a lost opportunity to assimilate Natives into "mainstream" American society, presumably avoiding those pesky civil rights and Red Power movements. If there is any excuse for the errors in their arguments, it might be that they had just begun their academic careers. Bernstein and Townsend were also handicapped by not having specialists in Native history as advisors.

Other scholars have simply reproduced what was said before or largely avoided any attempts at insight altogether. Diane Camurat's "The American Indian in the Great War" is largely a summary of American Indian history in the nineteenth century, well-trod territory that offers few new insights, though at times the book proves to be a good piece of research into how Europeans perceived Natives and what white Progressives thought about Native veterans of the war. Thomas Britten's *American Indians in World War I* largely fails to include Native voices because he relied on documents biased toward the views of white Progressives. Britten dodges the central question of assimilation versus cultural revival by instead asserting there was such a diversity of Native veteran experiences that no conclusions are possible.

Not every non-Native scholar on the topic did poorly. Jere Franco's *Crossing the Pond* shows how Native servicemen saw World War II as an opportunity much like black Americans' "Double V" campaign to fight against injustice both overseas and at home. Franco is especially good at presenting the issues involved in the sovereignty disputes surrounding the draft and how the newly allowed traditional religious observances played a central part in mobilizing Native communities' support. In *Kiowa, Apache, and Comanche Military Societies* William Meadows demonstrates admirably detailed fieldwork on Native warrior societies and their flag and war songs, limiting himself to three tribes. His approach has a great deal of promise and should be applied to every tribe with a vibrant warrior tradition. Valuable book-length, firsthand accounts from Native veterans are also available, including Lumbee veteran Delano Cummings in *Moon Dash Warrior*, Yaqui/Mexican American veteran Roy Benavidez in *Medal of Honor*, Jicarilla Apache veteran Leroy Tecube in *One Year in Nam*, Cherokee veteran Dwight Birdwell in *A Hundred Miles of Bad Road*, Peter McDonald's autobiography *The Last Warrior*, and James McCarthy's *Papago Traveler*.

Scholars who looked at the American Indian veteran experience in different wars trace its origins back to colonial precedent or economic need. Britten briefly argues for the colonial precedent. Yet after looking at local troops under the British and French colonialists, he concedes that similarities between colonial auxiliaries in places such as India and Africa and American Indian soldiers to be overly broad and superficial. American Indian servicemen were generally not formally segregated. In fact, there was a great effort to ensure they integrated, exposing them to the alleged "civilizing influence" of white soldiers. American Indian veteran traditions are also far more permanent, and American Indian soldiers (outside of the Indian Scouts) were not used to control fellow Natives like India's sepoys, for example. Economic need is the one theory put forth by nearly every scholar writing on Native veterans. Although poverty often explains part of why Natives join, it is insufficient to explain why they usually choose to remain *distinctly* Native and *distinctly* Apache, Cherokee, Lakota, Navajo, and so forth in their military traditions. Other nonwhites as well as working-class and underclass whites also join the military in high numbers to escape poverty. But no other American ethnic groups have distinct cultural and spiritual martial traditions like those of American Indians.

The assimilationist motive of white Progressives clearly explains why many Natives were initially encouraged to go into the U.S. military in World War I in such great numbers. What it fails to explain is how and why an assimilation effort transformed into a means of cultural revival and renewal. As I intend to show, Native traditions in the military are stronger on a cultural and deeply spiritual level than those of any other ethnic group in the United States. This distinctiveness shows up in Native song, ceremony, spiritual practices, and beliefs. In turn, Native example influenced the military (in some cases prior to Native enlistment in large numbers).

American Indian Studies (AIS) often includes the topic of Native veterans but, surprisingly, largely on the margins of other topics. Many AIS scholars utilize decolonization methods, expanding on the works of postcolonial theorists such as Edward Said and Paolo Freire. Under these models, Native veterans are primarily looked upon as a symptom of a colonized people. Ironically, many AIS scholars are themselves Native veterans, and it is likely that the great majority of AIS scholars have relatives who are Native veterans. As deeply as I value and respect AIS scholars and scholarship, and as I often employ their methods myself, I argue that treating Native veterans as symptoms of a colonial system is oversimplified. Worse, that aspect of the methodologies has the potential to alienate Native scholars from their communities. By seeming to (though that certainly is not AIS scholars' intention) devalue Native veteran experience or sacrifice as simply having been used by a colonial system, AIS scholarship on the subject could be misinterpreted as disdaining or hostile to the sacrifices of Native veterans.

Other ethnic studies scholars, most notably Ward Churchill, employ similar theories. I had some online encounters with a Churchill supporter and student who was also an Anglo Vietnam War veteran. She contended that Native veterans were "pimping their traditions" and "complicit in genocide."[7] Churchill himself often makes the latter argument, asking his audiences to consider their own (and his own) role in what he terms "genocide," which he defines as virtually any U.S. military action or foreign policy that dominates other societies. Such an argument cannot be more than rhetorical, since obviously any collaborator in genocide should be charged with war crimes. I have yet to hear of Churchill offering to turn himself in to face charges under the UN Genocide Treaty. His hyperbole on this and other issues obscures more than helps, disrupting and detracting from efforts to make scholarship responsive to Native needs. One would think a Vietnam War veteran such as he, of all people, would know better than to scapegoat veterans. Often would-be revolutionary leftists prove themselves very out of touch with Native communities when they automatically assume or even demand Natives think as they do.

Part of the purpose of this book is to speak truths to everyone I believe has gotten the story of Native veteran traditions wrong, across much of the political spectrum. I also hope this book will help Native veterans and their families and friends understand their service in the largest possible context. As non-Native readers will see, Native veterans routinely turn to Native medicine and oral traditions to cope with the trauma of war, and I hope this book will aid them. I did my best to ensure that this book supports Native oral traditions by listening to and relying on Natives' own words. More than once I had Native veterans and their families tell me this topic is so important and so far from being "academic" that I had better get it right. I hope I have. This book may well be the most important subject I will ever write on, meaning so much to so many people. I also hope to ensure that no other scholars will repeat the errors others have made in the past on this topic. Above all else I hope to explain Native veteran traditions with the needs of Native veterans, their families, communities, and Natives as a whole in mind. Native veterans deserve better than to simply be thought of as servants to white wishful thinking, whether from the political left or right. After all, such categories largely apply to Western societies and have very little use in a Native context.

Elements of Native Warrior/Veteran Traditions

Much of this book attempts to describe Native cultural and spiritual practices that carried over from warrior traditions into veteran traditions. All of the descriptions in this introduction are very general and usually apply to many Native traditions, not all of them. Native institutions called warrior societies have existed since at least the sixteenth century, and their revival in the twentieth century was *not* an attempt to remember a "lost" or romantic past in the form of fabled "good old days." Often non-Natives make the mistake of confusing these societies with historical reenactment groups. Warrior societies were not strictly revivalist in outlook, for it was neither practical nor legal for them to carry on the same practices as in prereservation days. Speaking very generally, traditionally a warrior society carried out an amalgam of the roles of policing and supervising hunts and raids, teaching the young, caring for the elderly and helpless, punishing criminals, and carrying out a wide variety of rituals that varied greatly from tribe to tribe. In the twentieth century, the roles of the warrior societies changed in response to each war. Policing had long since been co-opted by the Indian Bureau, though warrior societies often functioned as informal security at tribal events. Teaching, charitable, and ritual functions continued but with a modern element added. Veterans took the place of traditional tribal warriors. Warrior societies began to have much in common with Anglo-American veterans groups, such as the American Legion.

Natives composed new songs about the contemporary veterans' tradition in the old established styles, with Native performers singing about the meaning of military service to their cultures and peoples. Native songs should not be assumed to have the same meanings or rules as songs from Western cultures. Outside of some social songs, such as the "49s," most songs are thought of as sacrosanct as any sacred object or medicine. Many types of Native songs are meant to be sung only on specific occasions; singing them on other occasions would be profane. Intellectual and cultural property beliefs and practices also tend to emphasize that the author of a song has strict control over who can sing it and when.

For many sacred songs, the usual pattern is to sing the verses four times or more (up to dozens of times in many cases) since the song seeks to invoke or speak to sacred power. The male singers gather around a single drum, which is itself often referred to as having a heartbeat and kept covered when not in use. All the singers/drummers sing the verses and hit the drum simultaneously. Lead singers may interweave with the verses or lead a call-and-response type of style. Often there is a separate group of female singers or female leads who interweave their voices. Until very recently in some cases, women rarely drummed, for the belief in separation of masculine and feminine sacred power is central to the beliefs of many Native groups.

Native war and flag songs differed from Anglo-American patriotic songs in other important ways. The beer hall bragging or individualistic swagger of such songs as "Over There" is absent. If there are any common themes between some of the two types of songs, it would be the display of respect for and solemn honoring of the dead. Yet one element of Native songs differs dramatically from Anglo patriotic songs. There is nothing comparable in Anglo traditions to the ritual preparation and spiritual sanction provided by Native war and flag songs. Anglo-American songs such as "Praise the Lord and Pass the Ammunition" may say that God is on your side, but they do not strive to prepare and warn the individual that war is a dissociative and alienating state. In these and all the Native songs discussed in this study, the actions of the soldier are given cultural and spiritual sanction, usually not the war itself or its purpose. Native flag and war songs also aim for an explicit reintegration of the individual into the community from the unnatural state of war.

Ceremonies and personal medicine for the honoring, protection, and healing of Native servicemen directly continued some aspects of warrior traditions. Contrary to what is portrayed in old Hollywood movies, generally Native spiritual beliefs teach that warfare is an unnatural or disruptive state, one that must be extensively ritually prepared for to survive with mind and body intact. Ceremonies before war protect and prepare the soldier. Ceremonies after the war honor his service and, like the songs, reintegrate him into the community and out of the unnatural state of war. Personal medicine took the form of medicine bags, pouches, or other blessed or sacred items. Often Native servicemen relied on spiritual guides, which could be an ancestor or an animal. Whether these beliefs were literally true is beyond the scope of this study; I focus on the strength and retention of cultural beliefs and practices.

Structure and Outline

Chapter 1 looks at public perceptions of Native veterans by both Anglos and Natives by examining how Native veterans are depicted in fiction, including books (even comics), film, and television, by both Native and non-Native authors with wildly divergent points of view and imagery. Virtually all non-Native authors use (in both meanings of the word) Native veterans as unreal fantasy figures, from Little Sure Shot to Billy Jack to Chakotay. Native authors such as Momaday, Silko, and Louis Owens, by contrast, generally take a reverential approach with great empathy for the pain of the combat veteran.

Chapter 2 examines an instance of how Anglo-American military minds created an image of the Native as a savage warrior so fearsome that Anglo-Americans were often unsure whether to fear him or imitate his fighting style, which led Robert Rogers to adopt Native military tactics as far back as colonial times. No one has taken a sustained look at why distinctively Native military traditions are strong in one country, the United States, and virtually invisible in another, Mexico. Chapter 3 seeks to fill this void. Mexico has both a higher number and higher proportion of Natives than the United States does. Mexicans have very different ideas than Americans about race, and Natives' longer history of integration into the social fabric of Mexico has led to their being far less identified as "Indian" and has resulted in far more violence against those who remain distinctively Native.

Since pseudo-Indian images in the military predate Native enlistment in large numbers by nearly a century, chapter 4 compares Native and pseudo-Indian names and symbols in the military to "Indian" mascots in sports, discusses why there is little protest over these symbols, and shows how their presence both created and indicated a willingness to accept Native people in the military somewhat on their own terms. The use of what were perceived to be Native names or symbolism showed that non-Natives often wanted to take upon themselves what they admired: the Indian's great fighting abilities.

American Indians took advantage of the opening provided by these images and a more separate status to create distinctively Native veteran traditions. Chapters 5 through 9 begin with the backdrop of the Native communities before, during, and after each war. Each chapter then examines how Native institutions and cultures' warrior traditions adapted veteran experiences (or in some cases re-created warrior traditions or created entirely new warrior traditions). Each chapter also looks at how American Indians fundamentally affected military institutions by their example. Chapter 5 deals largely with Native veterans of World War I but also discusses earlier precedents for adapting the military to suit Native needs in the War of 1812, the Civil War, and the Spanish-American and Philippine wars. The Six Nations of the Iroquois, the Five Tribes of Oklahoma, Menominees, Pawnees, and others were some of the first to adapt the U.S. military to suit Native needs. In World War I, most of the Plains tribes found their own ways of adapting the military to carry on or re-create warrior traditions. Many boarding school graduates, however, took the assimilation message to heart and joined out of conventional patriotism. Chapters 6 and 7 deal, respectively, with World War II and the Korean War. World War II saw Native veteran traditions established in virtually every tribal nation, including many that had little or no warrior tradition. The Korean War and its Native veterans played central roles in both the origins of the Red Power movement and the spread of the powwow circuit and warrior societies. By the end of the Vietnam War warrior societies also often took on more overtly political activist functions. The very meaning of a warrior's role was being redefined. Chapter 8 discusses how the Vietnam War ironically had a long-term effect of uniting Indian Country through its influence on the Red Power movement. Chapter 9 focuses specifically on the American Indian Movement (AIM) as a warrior society and how the Vietnam experience expanded the meaning of a warrior to include activism.

Chapters 10 and 11 deal with topics that, so far, have largely been written about by journalists. Chapter 10 discusses Native veterans of the Gulf War, the War in Afghanistan, and the Second Iraq War, seen in the context of Natives taking part in U.S. military interventions in general. Chapter 11 discusses Native women veterans, with a particular focus on the Lori Piestewa story and how traditional beliefs about warrior traditions are being adapted. The conclusion discusses the future of Native veteran traditions and presents final points on decolonization theory and Native veterans.

1

"Let's See Some of That Apache Know-How"

Depictions of Native Veterans in Fiction

The Super Scout Syndrome and Unreal Indians

I REMEMBER QUITE WELL seeing the Arnold Schwarzenegger action film *Predator* for the first time. Shortly after it premiered on cable, I watched it in a hotel the night before my army physical with other would-be recruits, Anglo, black, and Latino. None of them, including those with Native ancestry, found anything outrageous or bizarre about the character of Corporal Billy Bear, an Indian Scout who is part of a modern elite army unit fighting an alien. Take away the alien and the Central American jungle, and Billy Bear is something straight out of old westerns. Stoic and unemotional, he never laughs or even understands jokes and is always seen as fearless by his fellow soldiers. By film's end he fatalistically chooses to die in battle, in hand-to-hand combat with the alien, throwing away his M-16 to fight to the death with his buck knife and, with a grimace, cutting his own chest before his final fight.

I saw the film again at the base movie theater when I was stationed at Fitzsimmons Army Medical Center in Colorado, in an audience solely of my fellow soldiers. I believe many of them would have groaned in disbelief or been outraged by the sight of black soldiers shown as natural mystical warriors. But none of them ever said a thing, either in the theater or to me afterward, about Billy Bear being unrealistic. Throughout my time in the service, I remained amazed that bigger and tougher men than me backed down from fights. Others seemed more than a bit intimidated at the slightest angry look of mine. Officers and

NCOs often assumed I was a far better soldier than I actually was. I do not claim a direct cause and effect, but it strains credibility that one stereotyped depiction after another, both of Native veterans and Natives in general, could not have affected how others in the army saw me and others with Native ancestry.

During World War I, a white army lieutenant named Ray Duncan conducted a series of experiments comparing Native and white soldiers. He tested both groups' abilities to find their way through the woods blindfolded or at night. Duncan concluded from these tests that Natives were not only "natural warriors" but could sense "instinctively" which way north was without a compass and could even see in the dark much like cats. What seemingly never occurred to Duncan was a much simpler explanation than alleged mystical or biological differences. Most of the white soldiers were raised in cities, and virtually all Natives at that time grew up on rural reservations.

Before one condemns Duncan too much, we should recall my own experience in the service and just how much these sorts of attitudes and beliefs persist. One need only look at Hollywood to see that the Super Scout Syndrome is alive and well in the imaginations of white writers and audiences. Hollywood largely regurgitates stereotypes passed on from pulp novels and popular paintings of a romanticized West. Looking at the variety of Anglo written and filmed works dealing specifically with Native veterans is an exercise in the extreme disconnect between the often fantasy-inspired worldview on the fringes of "respectable" fiction from which whites view Native veterans and a reverential approach where veterans occupy a central place in Native narratives, one often filled with an intimate knowledge of pain.

We should begin this look at Native veterans by critically viewing the images of them in popular culture, trying to strip away the many preconceptions most non-Natives have. What becomes immediately apparent is not just how consistently wrong non-Native authors, artists, and filmmakers are on the subject, but also how bizarre the biases they pass along to their audiences are. What looking at Native veterans in fiction reveals is just how far apart Natives and non-Natives are in their perceptions of why Natives join the military and what their places are within these institutions.

I tried to find every instance of a Native veteran depicted in any kind of a fictional setting, including books, films, television programs, and comics. I define a Native veteran very broadly as any indigenous person serving in any formal military organization. I do not include Natives fighting as insurgents or as allies of a formal military. Indian Scouts from the old westerns were also specifically left out, both because it is unclear to what degree they considered themselves allies and simply because depictions of them as fully formed characters (or even as bit players with any dialogue whatsoever) are rare. I will examine how historically accurate these portrayals are, how much they reflect or combat stereotypes, and how they affect how people understand Natives and Native veterans in particular. Where multiple versions of the same story exist, such as book and film, I looked at the more widely known work.

The Pat Boone Reflex: *The Outsider, Veronico Cruz,* and *Windtalkers*

Virtually nothing written about Ira Hayes, best known as one of the flag raisers at Iwo Jima, comes anywhere close to understanding his life or even to rendering a picture of it that avoids being derogatory.[1] A Hollywood film of his life, *The Outsider*, is no exception. Hayes is once again smeared after death as a hopeless drunk, a helpless, passive victim of white society unable to cope with modernity. The crux of the film focuses on the invented friendship between Hayes (played by Italian American Tony Curtis) and the fictional James Sorenson (James Franciscus). *The Outsider* shows Hayes as a shy and easily intimidated loner, a far cry from the popular, friendly, and articulate leader depicted by Hayes's real platoon members. Curtis spends the first half of the film sulking into the camera. Where *The Outsider* shows Hayes as introverted and even afraid of the bigoted members of his platoon, Hayes's own GI buddies in real life remember a gregarious and impassioned man eager to tell jokes or talk about issues dear to him, especially Pima water rights.

One of the most interesting friendships Hayes had in real life, that with Navajo Code Talker Tony Draper, is never shown or mentioned. The film also collapses the many Anglo friends Hayes had in his platoon into the fictional Sorenson. In doing so the film drastically overstates the racism Hayes actually endured in the military. Both Hayes and Native veterans in general faced far more racism from white civilians than from fellow soldiers. The real Hayes had to contend with white crowds heckling him (at war bond drives, no less) with shouts of, "Where's your bow and arrows, chief? How many Japs did you scalp?" None of this is mentioned in the film. Instead, scriptwriter Stewart Stern rather bizarrely focused on creating sublimated intimations of homosexuality between Hayes and the fictitious Sorenson. *The Outsider* is one of three films Stern wrote about alienated veterans, and it is clear that he regarded both veterans and Natives as characters to whom he could attach his own feelings of alienation and conflict over white American gender roles.[2]

After the war Hayes went home to face racism in Arizona that was every bit as bad as it had been prior to his leaving for war. At the same time, he likely suffered the intense pain of combat fatigue and survivor's guilt over the loss of so many friends. Many veterans turned in despair to drinking after suffering one of these traumas, much less all three of them at once. The film shows Hayes spiraling into drunkenness over Sorenson's death and being utterly unable to stop drinking once he first tasted it. In fact, the real Hayes was such an *inexperienced* drinker that a few drinks could cause him to pass out. He did, it seems, resort to what was for him binge drinking. But it was never as frequent or as debilitating as portrayed in *The Outsider* or by white journalists (from whom *The Outsider* likely got its stereotypes). Just as important, Hayes was not as helpless before the bottle as depicted. His death was purely a fluke, and not directly from alcoholism. Hayes died from exposure to the cold after drinking just half a bottle of wine, an amount most alcoholics could have shrugged off. Media reports in the 1950s fell back on white stereotypes about Indians and drunkenness. *The Outsider* repeats these errors uncritically, besmirching a highly decorated man's memory.

Veronico Cruz is, as far as I know, the only Latin American film that portrays an Indian in the military. Other films from or about Latin America, such as *El Norte* or *La Boca del Lobo*, almost uniformly depict a simplistic image of Indians as victims of a military composed of mestizo (mixed-blood) soldiers and criollo (of European ancestry) officers. No film has ever dealt with the complex moral dilemma of Native soldiers' atrocities, largely committed against other Indians, by militaries in Mexico, Guatemala, and Peru. Even the generals were often Indian, as far back as the 1850s.[3]

The film centers on the friendship of a newly arrived idealistic teacher from Buenos Aires and a young boy, Veronico Cruz. Veronico dreams of leaving his village near the Andes to escape the brutal and callous grandmother he lives with. His teacher fascinates him with stories of traveling the oceans but is forced out of the village by authorities on suspicion of teaching subversive ideas. Veronico meets a tragic end when he joins the Argentine Navy at seventeen, only to die in the Falklands War. His teacher mourns the failure of his own idealism and the harm he carelessly brought to the village and to Veronico in particular.

Released in Argentina under the title *La Deuda Interna* (The Struggle Within), the film's intent is revealed. In the same way American films such as *Little Big Man* used the Indian Wars to say something about the Vietnam War, *Veronico Cruz* is really about white Argentina's plight during the Dirty War and the Falklands War. The director and author, Miguel Pereira, is intent on using the Indian as a metaphor for what he sees as Argentina's lost innocence. Pereira thus does not challenge Argentina's mythology of itself as a nation whose past is best represented by the mixed-blood gauchos rather than the sole nation in the hemisphere with an openly declared genocide policy against its Indians for much of its history. *Veronico Cruz* echoes this ideology without question, even reinforces it. The film also, while rightly criticizing the naiveté of idealistic intellectuals, comes close to blaming them rather than the military for the Dirty War. *Veronico Cruz* received numerous awards in Argentina, lauded for being "more subtle" in its criticism than other films on the Dirty War. Because the film was released relatively soon after a horrific period of repression in Argentina, this embrace of the film is understandable. But it does not change the fact that this film actually has little insight about Indians.

Windtalkers was one of the most anticipated and most poorly received films about Natives in recent history. Perhaps what best sums up why Indian Country stayed away in droves from this film is producer Seth Rosenzweig's comment that, incredibly, he did not find the Code Talkers' story very compelling or even very good drama *until* he heard about the white "bodyguard connection and all its moral implications." On that basis, he falsely believed he could sell the film to Hollywood and the general public. Incredibly, he had so little understanding of the place the Code Talkers occupy in Native thought that it never occurred to him the subject demanded fidelity to at least the spirit of their story. Rosenzweig unwittingly further revealed his own mind-set when he had the conceit to brag, "Bringing this knowledge to the world, *I* couldn't be any prouder." Screenwriter John Rice was just as forthcoming: "Our piece was about a man, Joe Enders," the fictional lead white character played by Nicholas Cage, rather than about the Navajo Code Talkers. This mutates the Code Talkers' story from an ironic episode in indigenous struggles and the Navajo people's greatest symbol and source of cultural pride into yet another self-congratulatory paean for whites on their own presumed open-mindedness.[4]

Rice is hardly the first white author, nor is Rosenzweig the first producer, to be unable to see anything in another people's story except how it personally makes them feel. Nor are Natives the only ones to be subjected to this ethnic myopia. Most Hollywood films allegedly about the civil rights movement, for example, are in fact films about *how whites felt* about the civil rights movement. *Dances with Wolves* also is a film not so much about Natives as about a white character congratulating himself on being open-minded about Natives. What nearly all these films have within them is the condescending revelation for the main white character at some point: "Who would have thought it? Natives (blacks, etc.) are people, too!" These films also have an implicit assumption of racism that whites should find insulting but too rarely question: whites are uninterested (perhaps even too racist) in films not about "their own kind."

That such a reflex should still be commonplace among filmmakers at this late date is inexcusable. Perhaps one could make that case back in the day when white teenagers hid their Little Richard records from their parents underneath Pat Boone cover versions. But there has not been an excuse for the Pat Boone reflex to be a part of filmmaking for some time, as Spike Lee and Sherman Alexie could tell

you. Transforming *Windtalkers* into yet another case of whites not
being able to see past their own alleged inner turmoil about race (and
that "turmoil" is usually resolved painlessly and without much real
struggle) and instead learn about other peoples robs the film of its
chance to honor heroes.

Windtalkers was a spectacular failure, both commercially and critically. The tragedy of that failure is that it also stifled a planned movie
by the Navajo nation. Realizing they could not compete with a $100
million film, the Navajo nation opted instead for a documentary, *True
Whispers*. Yet despite the lost opportunity for the Code Talkers' story
to be told accurately to a wide audience, I am extremely comforted by
the reasons *Windtalkers* failed. Both the public and critics panned the
film precisely because it was historically inauthentic and stereotypical.
To my knowledge, this is a historic first for a Hollywood film about
Natives. One can only hope the same fate is in store for any future
Billy Jack remake.

New Age Follies: *Billy Jack* and *Star Trek: Voyager*

John Pope ("Rolling Thunder") was a retired railroad worker who
spent the latter part of his life posing as an "intertribal medicine man."
Pope claimed he was part Cherokee and that he was teaching Seneca
beliefs. This he did, not among either the Cherokee or Seneca but almost entirely among the white hippie counterculture. Pope proselytized
among hippies for the remainder of his life, telling them they were
"Thunderpeople" who would change the world. According to Pope's
own family, his former followers then mercilessly exploited Pope's
name for money beyond all bounds of decency, creating a number of
New Age cults in the process.[5]

Pope played a central role in *Billy Jack*. The movie was very loosely
based on what Pope claimed had happened in his own life, and Pope
had a small part in the film as "Thunder Mountain." Where Pope
claimed to have taken part in the Yaqui Wars in Mexico (the last Yaqui
War was in 1928, when he would have been six to ten years old), Billy
Jack was remade into a Vietnam veteran and ex–Green Beret. Where
Pope claimed to be a part Cherokee "intertribal medicine man" who
taught alleged Seneca beliefs to white hippies, Billy Jack was an "Indian

half-breed" and medicine man-in-training who was taught by a young blond white woman in the films what Indian beliefs "truly" were. The "Indian" beliefs of the fictional "Nishnobie" tribe in *Billy Jack* are a bizarre amalgam of hippie platitudes about pacifism and Christian fundamentalist Holy Roller snake handling.

Pope and the film's author, director, and star, Tom Laughlin, were a perfect match. Laughlin fancied himself a great spiritual thinker and today markets seminars in spirituality as well as T-shirts that depict the pseudo-Indian "snake handling ceremony" from the films. Laughlin claimed his movie was preordained by what he believes were Indian prophecies and other supernatural events. (In less dramatic terms, he saw owls near the movie set. Obviously Laughlin did not know that owls are omens of bad luck or misfortune among most tribes.) Laughlin and Pope shared an apocalyptic and paranoid worldview. Laughlin attributed the spectacular failure of his two sequels to *Billy Jack* to nothing less than a conspiracy by "the Man," the federal government, and "evil forces that tried to keep the picture from being made."[6]

What actually made the first film a success was its blatant attempt to capitalize on both martial arts and blaxploitation films such as *Shaft* by giving the public a pseudo-Indian version of them, one played by a white eccentric and based on the life of an equally dubious person. In all likelihood, the later films flopped because of their preachiness, failure to include martial arts, and Native protests against the films. Even its claim to be sympathetic to Native people and causes comes across as utterly phony. There is not a single word in *Billy Jack* about almost any Native cause. Instead the film invents a fictional issue (the killing of wild horses on reservations to make dog food) that has never happened. The only real issue that *Billy Jack* takes a stand on is that it is wrong to beat someone up for not being white. Coming more than fifteen years after the first wave of civil rights marches, this was not nearly as brave as Laughlin would like us to think. This was a cheap straw man issue that insulted the tremendous pain civil rights marchers went through. The film is hypocritical through and through with its message of "beat people up in the name of peace." Imagine Hollywood making a movie called *Rufus Jack* with Laughlin playing a "half-breed black" who squints to look "more black" with Rufus beating people up in the name of Martin Luther King and showing a phony voodoo or Nation of Islam ceremony that features Rufus being bitten by a snake over and over again to become "a real African."

Billy Jack's status as a veteran tells us nothing about what Native veterans experienced. Billy Jack (both the character and the film) pose as both Native and veteran as merely convenient tropes for the film's author and audience to invent a fantasy (often quite bizarre at that) of what they wish Indians were like, one that bears no resemblance at all to actual Native beliefs, cultures, or history. *Billy Jack* is easily one of the absolute worst films ever made about Natives; quite possibly it is one of the worst films ever made. It fails on virtually every level, from its aesthetic to its technical aspects (a smaller, darker Asian man is clumsily inserted as the stunt double for Laughlin in martial arts scenes) to its utter lack of social responsibility toward Native sensibilities. Too offensive to even be camp, at best the film is a revealing look at the extremes a white filmmaker will go to in order to misrepresent Native cultures. It also is quite revealing of some truly troubling mind-sets among some whites and the counterculture. Who would have expected allegedly peace-loving hippies and New Age followers to wallow in as much gratuitous violence as there is in *Billy Jack*?

The character of Chakotay in *Star Trek: Voyager* (STV) is every bit as much a creature of white fantasies as is Billy Jack. STV's Chakotay is another "faithful companion" or sidekick to a white lead character and in his own bizarre ways far more stereotypical than Tonto. At least Tonto was heroic and rescued the Lone Ranger once in awhile. Robert Beltran actually seemed to imitate the old westerns for his un-flinchingly stone-faced stoic portrayal. The character of Chakotay is a Frankenstein-like patchwork of New Age fantasies and misconceptions. STV's writers deliberately avoided making Chakotay a member of a tribe that existed anywhere outside a screenplay. This enabled the writers to mix and match bits and pieces of New Age clichés about Natives without any regard for accuracy or believability. His fictional "Anurabi" tribe is from the South American jungles, yet they venerate "sky people." Generally, the pantheons of jungle tribes involve forest creatures, not figures from the heavens they could hardly see through the jungle canopy. Chakotay's people also use the sweat lodge, which *STV*'s writers falsely assume is a universal ceremony of all Native peoples.

Chakotay even invites his commanding officer, a white woman in her forties, to take part in a Vision Quest, a ceremony generally restricted to adolescent boys. Chakotay also urges Janeway to try to find her "animal totem" or spirit guide. Again, this was based on New Age misconceptions. Chakotay is not an elder or medicine man but an alienated member of his tribe far from his fictive people. Thus he would likely not even have much knowledge of traditions, nor would he be trusted with the intricate details of ceremonies. His "tribal tattoo" is more of an amusing mistake. Native facial tattoos tend to be far more elaborate, as well as symmetrical and covering both sides of the face. Yet television viewers would likely recoil in horror at an authentic-looking tattoo, so *STV*'s creators settled for a "cute" tattoo in one corner of his face that resembles an incomplete *moko*, not of any Natives in the Americas but of New Zealand's Maoris.[7] *STV*'s writers even completely fabricated a nonexistent ceremony, the "pakra," which resembles ancestor worship as practiced in Asia.

As many errors as the writers for *STV* made, it could have been far worse. In the original script for the episode "Tattoo," writer Larry Brody intended for Chakotay's people to be Mayans and gave them nonexistent "Mayan medicine wheels." Brody's script then began to resemble a *Twilight Zone* episode by making the dubious assertion that the Mayan culture later became the Anasazi, leaping over several thousand miles and enormous cultural differences seemingly without any actual research.[8]

All of these errors would be comical if not for the fact that *STV*'s writers seem to be openly proselytizing their New Age beliefs, in sharp contrast to the usual militant atheist viewpoint of *Star Trek* overall. Even the most cursory Web search shows an overwhelmingly derisive and negative fan reaction to this New Age evangelism. Beltran himself was much criticized for "passing." Beltran identified as Mexican until criticized by Natives, when he suddenly claimed to be Mayan. While his physical appearance leaves little doubt he has Indian ancestry, he has no ties to or understanding of Native cultures, as evidenced by his public defense of the New Age aspects of Chakotay as authentically Indian.[9]

For the purposes of this study, the worst aspect of the Chakotay character was that it gave no insight into either Native peoples in general or Native veterans in particular, being content to spread New Age misconceptions instead. Even Chakotay's name was a clear signal to New Age followers. In the fictional "Anurabi" dialect, his name translates as "Earth Walking Man" or "Man Who Walks the Earth But Only Sees the Sky." In a further instance of New Age homogenizing of all Native cultures into one "generic Indian" framework, STV's writers openly modeled the Anurabi on a composite of Aztec, Mayan, Mixtec, and even Inca cultures. The writers further relied on a number of New Age sites for information and cross-linked to them.

For all of their pretensions to having "enlightened" views of Natives, STV falls back on old stereotypes. The writers show Chakotay's people as trapped or deliberately choosing to live in the past, even in the twenty-fourth century. Indeed, Chakotay's choice to join Star Fleet was scripted as a complete rejection of his Native culture rather than as adaptation. Naturally, STV's writers could not show successful Native adaptation to the military. Instead, they first made Chakotay a mutineer and rebel leader. The writers also show Chakotay seeing the error of his ways thanks to his benevolent white commander, Captain Janeway. The writers also seem to delight in undermining Chakotay by showing him as a bumbler. His commander constantly rescues him or reprimands him for his "rebellious nature," and the principal white male character, Lieutenant Tom Paris, is often beyond Chakotay's ability to command. As with *Windtalkers*, most of the public was smart enough to see through this portrayal and thoroughly rejected it.

More Unreal Indians: Comic Books, Louis Lamour, and Andre Norton

The first time I remember seeing an Indian on television was on Westerns. The first time I remember seeing an Indian in a television story not taking place a hundred years ago or more, it was an animated show based on a comic book. *The Super Friends* was loosely based on DC Comics's *Justice League of America*. But someone at the television network realized with horror that the Justice League were all Anglos. So they hurriedly came up with three minority characters, Black Vulcan, Samurai, and Apache Chief. Even at perhaps ten or eleven years old, I thought it very strange that Apache Chief dressed like it was the 1870s.

Even stranger, one of the first comic books I remember reading, *The Apache Kid*, was a western comic, but its hero had a secret identity. It was never very clear whether the Apache Kid was a white man who dressed as an Apache or an Apache passing as white when he lived in his secret identity. Still, the comic made it very clear to me at a young age that whites harbored some strange notions about Native people. Apparently being white was like being Clark Kent, but being an Indian made you like a superhero.

One might be tempted to ask why anyone takes seriously the images presented by some of the least respected and "pulpiest" or trashiest genres. The fact remains that these genres are often quite popular, particularly with kids and teenagers. Remarkably, one can find more depictions of Native veterans in comics than in any other medium. Thunderbird, Forge, and Dani Moonstar's father of the *X-Men*, Johnny Cloud of *The Losers*, and DC Comics's *Butcher* all are Native veterans. Yet the treatment of veteran experience is less than shallow—it is just the barest mention. As Rob Schmidt, the publisher of Blue Corn Comics, pointed out to me, mentioning that someone is a vet is just a quick shorthand in most of these stories for why the character is obsessed with revenge and is violent, antisocial, and so forth. Such perfunctory treatment is also seen in such characters as the Indian villain John Rainbird in Stephen King's *Firestarter* and many of the characters in the Joe Leaphorn mysteries in Tony Hillerman's works.[10]

One of the few exceptions to this is Tim Truman's comic *Scout* and its follow-up, *Scout War Shaman*. These comics take place in a post-apocalyptic future where the U.S. government becomes crippled after a nuclear war and white racists in Texas secede from the United States. The lead character, Satanta, is an Apache/Navajo U.S. Army veteran.[11]

Truman's other works are primarily westerns, and Truman himself claims to have distant Cherokee ancestry. He also is fond of inaccurately bragging that many Native people love his work. In fact, only one Native scholar, Pauline Escudero Schaefer, has praised *Scout* and uses it in her literature courses. I agree that, compared to all previous works, *Scout* is an improvement, but that is not saying much. Truman does have more knowledge of Apache and Navajo cultures than most Anglo fiction writers, indeed more than some Anglo historians. He depicts Navajo burial customs and Apache *gaan* spirits, for example. It is in his application that I have to disagree with Schaefer, and his accuracy is often lacking, to put it mildly. Truman seems to think *gaans* are identical to spirit guides; they are not. He also shows Satanta inventing his own version of Apache rituals but instead using tranquilizers as part of the ceremonies. This is beyond inaccurate; it is appalling and disrespectful to Apache people. The only semi-accurate portrayals of Native cultures were in the first few issues of *Scout*. Virtually none of it showed up in the later issues. Truman was instead content to turn Satanta into a Rambo-style killer, and *Scout* became yet another addition to the "warnography" genre, except that as a comic it was squarely aimed at teenagers.

In other pulp-style fiction, Louis Lamour's *Last of the Breed* is one of the worst examples of clear-cut racism, a throwback to the very pulp novels that the worst movies in Hollywood's early history imitated. The central character is Joe Mack, a Lakota pilot in the U.S. Air Force who is shot down over Siberia and sent to a forced labor camp. He escapes and flees to the United States across the Siberian tundra and finally the Bering Strait. The majority of the novel concerns how Mack feels himself reverting to the alleged "naturally savage state" of his ancestors. Besides this stereotyping and apologist sanction for racism, Mack refers to himself throughout by the colonial term for his people, *Sioux*, instead of *Lakota*. Lamour basically turned the novel into one long harangue, trying to justify white actions with Natives by depicting a Lakota saying Lakotas were naturally warlike conquerors and barbarians.

Much like Truman and Lamour, Andre Norton wrote about Natives in pulp-type adventure stories. One of her most famous science fiction series is about a Navajo member of the Space Service, Hosteen Storm, in *The Beastmaster*, *Lord of Thunder*, and *Beastmaster's Ark*. Another book, *The Sioux Spaceman*, concerns a Lakota, Kade Whitehawk, in the Space Service (described on the cover as a story of "redskins on the galactic rim"). In all these works Native characters have stereotypical mystical powers or functions. Storm telepathically communicates with animals and has an eagle and a "dune-cat" as best friends. Whitehawk goes on a mission to introduce horses to an alien planet to help a "primitive" race, the Ikkinni, resist the more advanced Styor race. Both characters, naturally, are scouts, shown as alienated but with "racial memories" because of their Native DNA. Norton also wrote another series with the same theme of biological determinism and Natives, the Time Agent series. In perhaps her most bizarre books, she depicts the aftermath of nuclear war as a standoff between Russians who "racially regress" into Genghis Khan's Mongol hordes and Americans who also "racially regress" into American Indians.[12]

Norton's works are the most extreme examples of the bizarre worldview that requires the belief that an apocalypse and "racial memories" are necessary for Natives to regain even a semblance of survival in the future. What is profoundly depressing is how firmly Norton, Lamour, and Truman believe Natives to be trapped in the past, and how much violence, catastrophism, and fatalistic acceptance of a racialized fate they believe Natives should accept as the price for survival in human-kind's near future.

An Unheralded Breakthrough: *The Dirty Dozen*

Lest anyone think it impossible for a non-Native to write sensitively and effectively on Native veterans, and even be entertaining and commercially successful at doing so, *The Dirty Dozen* proves otherwise. The character of a Native soldier and convict, Samson Posey, is a wry and ironic take on just about every stereotype of Natives in film. If not for Clint Walker's appearance not fitting what many people typically think of as Indian, his performance would rank in film history alongside that of Will Sampson's in *One Flew over the Cuckoo's Nest* as a landmark, one that challenges film clichés about Natives on every level. Interestingly, one of the scenes that was edited out had Walker performing an Apache dance. One might suspect that the filmmakers thought Walker's appearance made the dance less believable.[13]

Where Natives had been shown as "naturally warlike," the character of Posey has to be *pushed* and *pushed again*, provoked repeatedly, before he fights anyone. He was a screen first, a Native with a temperament completely unsuitable for violence or warfare. Not only that, where Hollywood Indians had always been stone-faced stoics, Posey's character flaw is that he easily becomes *too emotional*. Where previous cinematic Indians had been either faceless evil or tragic primitives, Posey is very boy-next-door. Indeed, his Southern accent causes the viewer to sympathize with his plight as a man caught up in circumstances beyond his control.

Walker's dialogue in the film probably amounts to less than ten minutes of screen time yet manages to say far more about Native experiences in the military than *Windtalkers* does in two hours. His commander, Major Reisig (Lee Marvin), overflows with bigoted assumptions about Natives, and he does not hesitate to bait Posey with them in front of other soldiers. "Come on, Posey, let's see some of that Apache know-how," Reisig barks right before assigning him duties based on the presumption that Posey has more "natural skill."

The film was also a breakthrough in that it acknowledges how Native people respect the military and how much conflict there is over Natives role in it. Posey's first words in the film are "Reckon my folks'd be a sight happier if I died like a real soldier. Can't say I would." That the film is not recognized as such is probably due in part to the fact that Walker had to compete for screen time with memorable performances from Marvin, Telly Savalas, John Cassavetes, Jim Brown, and Charles Bronson. The fact that Walker does not "look Indian" to many people also kept him from being seen as a Native actor, even though Walker was upfront about it during his entire career.

Native Voices on Film: *Powwow Highway* and *Skins*

Turning to how Natives depicted their own veterans is both welcome and at the same time jarring because such portraits are not only almost always more honest, they are also quite painful and at times cathartic. *Powwow Highway* holds a special place in the hearts of many Native people. It was one of the first films aimed at Native audiences, one of the few to show Native people in a setting after 1900, and one of the few to acknowledge simple Native humanity through such things as showing Indians with a sense of humor and talking about modern-day issues.[14]

Powwow Highway is a road trip film about two mismatched characters, burned-out militant activist and veteran Buddy Red Bow (A Martinez) and comic misfit/philosopher Philbert Bono (Gary Farmer). The film's greatest accomplishment is in letting the viewer see much of Indian Country and its people speaking in their own unhurried way, often humorous but sometimes angry. Red Bow is a very accurate depiction of many Native veterans, seemingly hostile but well-informed as to why he has every right to feel the way he does. He knows all too well what is wrong with his life and the lives of people around him. His frequent inability to do much about it drives his angry nature. A second character (Graham Greene) is much like someone many Native people know all too well in their communities: a traumatized combat veteran unable to speak or express what he has suffered.

Graham Greene's role in *Powwow Highway* is actually better than his later and larger role as a veteran in *Skins*. This movie shows that it is possible for someone Native, even with Chris Eyre's talent, to make a bad movie. It is a film utterly without hope, focused on the worst aspects of reservation life without any clear explanation for why such things are so common, thus reinforcing stereotypes in the minds of everyone not already intimately familiar with the issues involved. For the purposes of this study, the worst aspect of the film is that we never really see why Mogie (Graham Greene) is an alcoholic who can only deal with life through humor and constant drinking. The film only briefly mentions a cause for his drinking, and it is so quick you could literally cough and miss it. Such a conflicted view, simultaneously avoiding discussing the causes of problems while wallowing in the depictions of those same problems, gives the viewer the worst kind of disjuncture.[15]

Native Voices in Literature: *Ceremony, House Made of Dawn, Love Medicine, The Sharpest Sight, Red Earth,* and *Of Uncommon Birth*

> Do anything you have to . . . shoot your big toe off, eat your nuts off, but don't let them bring you here (Vietnam) . . . the stupid bastards think Indians can see at night, that we don't make any noise, that kind of shit.—Louis Owens, *The Sharpest Sight*

It is something of a relief to know that, in spite of the most misguided of Hollywood and pulp fiction efforts, the best-known depictions of Native veterans remain those of the finest and most acclaimed Native authors. Nothing demonstrates the tremendous gap (perhaps better characterized as an outright canyon) between white opinions of Natives and Native self-perceptions than the tremendous differences between *Ceremony* and *Predator*, or between the characters of Abel in *House Made of Dawn* and Chakotay in *Star Trek: Voyager*.

One could hardly do better to describe Native veteran experiences than the first seventy pages of *Ceremony*. Leslie Marmon Silko's justly famous novel is a stunning depiction of the alienation and trauma brought by war and the particular hardships and ironies faced by Native veterans in particular. What both it and N. Scott Momaday's *House Made of Dawn* share are a use of the mixed-blood veteran experience to delineate alienation in modern America and a persistent hammering at the ironies of serving a nation that failed to acknowledge sacrifice and a larger society that gives only temporary acceptance.[16]

Some Native scholars heavily criticized Louise Erdich's novel *Love Medicine* as too negative and ultimately apolitical. Focusing solely on the parts of the novel dealing with veterans, I argue this was clearly not the case. Two of the novel's principal characters, Henry Lamartine and Gerry Nanapush, are veterans. Two more, Henry Jr. and Lipsha Nanapush, mistakenly try to imitate the traditions of their fathers. Henry Jr. meets a tragic death after a long history of bringing the violence of war home with him and abusing one woman after another. Lipsha tries to join, only wanting the approval of the community and to avoid the draft, only to find himself exempt because Nanapush hearts suffer from the "flaw" of loving too much. Erdich and Louis Owens are the only fiction writers, to my knowledge, to deal with the subject of Native draft resistance as well as sensitively explore the ironies around Native veterans of Vietnam.[17]

Louis Owens's *The Sharpest Sight* is the story of the McCurtain and Morales families, respectively mixed-blood Mississippi Choctaws and Mexican Americans who hide being Chumash. Three of the principal characters are Native veterans, Hoey and Attis McCurtain and Mundo Morales. A fourth character, an Anglo veteran named Lee

Scott, served with Natives in Vietnam and liked to use them to walk point. While nominally a murder mystery, Owens's work is far more of an exploration of the meaning of Native military service, perhaps the most angry, incisive, and uncompromising ever committed to paper. Most of the dialogue and inner conflict of the three men involves the irony of their seeking white approval through their service coupled with both families' long denials of being Indian and wishing to be assimilated into mainstream America. This is the argument of every assimilationist, from William Pratt and Joseph Dixon on, thoroughly turned on its head; these families made every effort to assimilate, and it only brought them greater sorrow. The Mississippi Choctaws of Owens's novel suffers terribly because they are denied the peace that their now-lost ceremonies would bring. Ghosts of the dead from Vietnam jungles haunt Attis. Finally, Cole McCurtain comes to understand how the Choctaw way of being a warrior has been utterly warped by the U.S. military from its original intent of not being afraid to die or sacrifice to being willing to kill.[18]

Both stories in Phillip Red Eagle's *Red Earth: Two Novellas* deal with themes of surviving the pain of war through ceremonies. In the first novella, "Red Earth," Lakota soldier Raymond Crow-Belt uses ceremony to break through time and save himself in his own past. While in Vietnam, Raymond dreamt of a woman drawing a circle with a staff of eagle feathers and then disappearing. Raymond follows this dream and goes to the circle pointed out to him in his dream every morning, "mortars and assaults permitting." But Raymond also falls in love with a Vietnamese girl who reminds him of women back home. When South Vietnamese troops murder her, he kills them in turn. Once home, he turns to drinking and fighting to deal with his rage and sorrow. When his grandfather reaches from beyond the grave to save him, giving him medicine in a sacred spot, Raymond steps out of time to see a future in which he is utterly broken by the pain of war. He seeks a way to go back in time to Vietnam to save himself. In the past, Raymond appears as a different soldier to Chippewa nurse Annabelle LeBeaux, who helps him see his inner self. In the present Raymond meets LeBeaux back in the states and thanks her for saving him, "both times."

Ghosts of the children he has killed haunt Lakota veteran Clifford Goes-First in the second novella, "Bois De Sioux." Clifford realizes Lakota warrior traditions were once all about serving people, but the lack of honor in who he was forced to kill in Vietnam dooms him to a spiritual darkness. Much of the novella is also the story of how Clifford's friend James Hailstone learns Dakota ways in Vietnam from him, since James came from a family of apple Indians ashamed of their heritage. Unlike in "Red Earth," there is little resolution in the story. Both stories are very good at pointing out the ironies in Native veteran experience. When an Asian American soldier asks Raymond, "Why do you fight for the oppressor?" Raymond answers, "We don't fight for them. We fight for us . . . we fight for honor." And yet both main characters' lives are torn apart precisely because there is so little honor in the war.[19]

Mark St. Pierre's *Of Uncommon Birth: Dakota Sons in Vietnam* is technically historical fiction, based on the true story of brothers Dale and Billy Jealous of Him. The themes and most of the dialogue are fictitious, but they are based on nearly two decades of research and interviews by St. Pierre. St. Pierre writes almost conversationally, lacking the poetic language of the other works discussed above, but he writes with such conviction the work has more of a slice-of-life feel. The Jealous of Him brothers see the contradictions of the war but join anyway, prayed for by a zealously Christian father who asks, "Promise me you'll remember Jesus and wear this [crucifix]." Neither son has the same faith as their father. Billy says, "In my dreams I often see the white man's devil. . . . Because of that I wonder if there are Indian angels." Later on he observes, "They tell you if you take the Bible that's all you need. I don't believe that 'cause the white man has all the land and the money and he's still trying to get more." Other Dakotas perform ceremonies and honor songs for him before he leaves. Billy feels awkward, not truly believing in Lakota tradition either, but says nothing out of politeness. In Vietnam he identifies more with Vietnamese "growing rice to feed Viet Cong, just like buffalo hunting by my ancestors" than "fighting for the government that fucked [my] people." Shortly before his death he realizes, "Whether I'm fighting for [the government] or just to get back home alive I'm not even sure.

You whiteboys got a world to go back to. If I make it back home it will be to poverty and racial bullshit. Most of you white guys think you're over here protecting the Constitution. I don't. I may look like a dumb Indian, but I came over here on my own, knowing better than any of you what the Constitution is supposed to do, and what it really does." That uncertainty stays with both Jealous of Him brothers, even to Billy's death, as well as with the reader.[20]

Conclusion

Most Anglo works featuring Native veteran characters are not simply inaccurate; they are appalling, leaving a Native viewer with a bad taste in the mouth and a sinking heart. There is such an extremely disconnected fantasy worldview in these examples of less respectable fiction. The contrast with Native approaches could not be more glaring if written with silver glitter. Native authors have a reverential approach in which veterans occupy a central place in Native narratives, one usually filled with the most intimate knowledge of the pain and sorrow, the ironies and frustrations. Veterans are important to Native peoples in ways for which words always seem inadequate. The most talented Native fiction writers place veterans front and center in some of the best Native literature ever written. But to nearly all non-Native fiction writers, Native veterans remain *creatures*, something existing only in flights of the imagination or as a convenient trope with which to create an imaginary setting. "Indians are not real" is the main message of these works. These misperceptions are true of a vast spectrum of non-Native writers and artists, including the politically conservative (Lamour), intellectuals in Latin America (Pereira), gays (Stern), people claiming distant Native ancestry (Truman), would-be revolutionary leftists (Laughlin), science fiction devotees, Latinos (Beltran), and New Age adherents (Laughlin and *Star Trek: Voyager*'s writers). All of them are intent on simply *using* Native veterans, in the ugliest meaning of the word, for their own purposes rather than trying to look at Native veterans' stories honestly.

As pointed out in the introduction, many Anglo historians writing about Native veterans are only slightly better at seeing past their own preconceptions. It should be the task of historians writing on the subject to emulate the very best of Native-authored fiction on veterans, as daunting as that may seem (and indeed is). At the same time anyone, not simply authors, should examine themselves for traces of these pernicious and bizarre attitudes toward Natives that characterize some of the worst works ever written by Anglo authors, not just in terms of accuracy but also aesthetics and prejudices masquerading as insight. The task that I set for myself in the rest of this work is to explain why this chasm in perceptions exists and to show how Natives have used Anglo misconceptions about their military service for Native needs. The themes of Native-authored works on Native veterans are ones to which we will return; as deeply regarded as Native veteran traditions are, Native warrior traditions are (perhaps inevitably) distorted by the contradictions in Native military service. Perhaps Native veteran traditions are, or should be, only a transition. The question then becomes, should we seek to replace Native veteran traditions with ones more true to the ideals of the original Native warrior traditions? But before we deal with this question, we must understand the origins of Native veteran traditions.

2

"They Kill Indians Mostly, Don't They?"

Rogers' Rangers and the Adoption of Indian Tactics

BEFORE NATIVE VETERANS' traditions could become part of the U.S. military, the leaders of the military establishment had to be predisposed to welcome Natives. This admiration and emulation of Native warriors and their tactics caused the military to accept Natives as they were culturally, rather than as white reformers who favored assimilation wished them to become. Ultimately, officers and NCOs who fought both alongside and against Natives became unlikely allies of Natives who wanted to use the military to maintain or reestablish traditions. Natives and non-Natives who admired them decided the Native place in the military, not progressive reformers. Though I do not argue that Rogers' Rangers played the sole or even primary role in the acceptance of Native cultural ways in the military, their example illustrates the manner in which they influenced the U.S. military, especially tactically. The case of Rogers' Rangers also shows the perils of that influence when it interacted with the white images of "the Indian."

The U.S. military partly began with a merging of Native and European ways. This syncretism ultimately became the light infantry martial philosophy used in nearly all modern military units, especially elite ones. Central to the spread of these ways was the process of completely remaking a man named Major Robert Rogers. Rogers was a colonial militia leader who fought alongside, learned from, and adapted his own tactics from his Stockbridge and Mahican allies. A very unusual man of the time, he had a deep admiration and respect for Native people and their ways. He considered his main foes to be other Europeans, the French.

But non-Native authors remade Rogers's image to make him appear to be something very different from who he actually was, someone he would find reprehensible. Two writers, Francis Parkman and Kenneth Roberts, transformed his image into that of an Indian hater. Parkman and Roberts distorted such things as the difference between an Indian fighter and an Indian hater, blurring or erasing Rogers's true image, repainting it to make the image desired. The term *Indian fighter* itself has two interpretations. The first is one who fights Indians. The second is one who *is* an Indian, to varying degrees either literally or symbolically, and is a fighter. The two often overlap in white constructions of Native-European conflict to mean a white man who fights Indians by becoming "more Indian than the Indians." Implicit or explicit in this construction is that the white man (either a particular one, or all white men) could master Native ways simply by virtue of being allegedly biologically superior and from an allegedly superior culture. This construction also has the central paradox of assuming that an Indian fighter must become like those he fights or, even more bizarrely, that he must hate Native people for "forcing" him to be as "savage" as he considers "the Other" to be.

With one grievous exception, Rogers in real life never showed any sign of being an Indian hater. This incident, the attack on the neutral Abenaki village of St. Francis, is the key to seeing how Rogers's image was altered to something directly opposite to his true nature and the way he led his life. Because of the assault on St. Francis, Rogers and his Rangers were reinvented as a group whose principal aim was to "kill Indians, mostly."[1]

The Rogers of Colonial Times: Syncretism and Sympathy

Rogers became a leader of colonial militia at the young age of twenty-six. Before that he was a smuggler of goods between the English colonies, French Canada, and to and from Native peoples. Rogers fought throughout the Seven Years' War in numerous actions. His success in battle won him great fame and many admirers on both sides of the Atlantic. Rogers's methods of fighting had a great influence on both American and British military traditions, eventually earning him his modern-day acknowledgments as the "Father of the Rangers" and

"Father of the Special Forces." His teachings are the cornerstone for all American and British infantry tactics today.[2]

Rogers became famous as much for his "Standing Orders" as for his achievements on the battlefield. His orders used such typical Native tactics as having war parties travel single file and keep a short, uniform distance between members; preventing the enemy from tracking; returning by a different route than the one came by; avoiding enemy fire; dispersing and rendezvousing later when facing a superior enemy; and maintaining secrecy and silence on raids.[3] European warfare of the time insisted on submission to authority and maintaining central control at all times. This was backed up by the use of corporal punishment using floggings and beatings, even death. Rogers, by contrast, followed Native ways of retaining flexible tactics and options at all times, coupled with a desire to keep the troops motivated by respecting and encouraging their individual initiative.

Native allies in Rogers' Rangers were even more essential than in the typical colonial military force. Stockbridge-Mahican and Mohegan companies elected their own officers and practiced their traditional forms of fighting. They were up to one-third of the Rangers at times. Non-Native members held their Native allies up as models to emulate. Anglo-American members "dressed Indian" and carried tomahawks. In modern terms, what Rogers did was syncretic, a selective integration of Native and European tactics. Almost all of his "Standing Orders" were entirely adoptions of Native tactics. The one exception, "Standing Order Number 6," began the innovative practice of having marching columns maintain flanking parties on all sides to give advance warning of attack. Marching columns of troops is a European method. A small scouting party in advance of the main body is a Native one. Combining the two allows simultaneous use of European emphasis on central control and Native insistence on flexibility and mobility.

Anglo colonial America in the mid-eighteenth century largely believed in as strict a segregation of the Native from the European as possible. Most Anglos also saw Natives as an obstacle to civilization. Rogers's way of thinking was startlingly prescient of more modern views. He defended Native rights and abilities in *A Concise Account of North America*. He argued Natives had ingenuity, a capacity for art and science, good mental abilities, strong imaginations and memories, and were so honorable they had no need for coercive laws. He praised "Attawas" for having no poverty and little warfare among themselves. Several centuries ahead of modern scholars, Rogers maintained the Americas were not almost empty lands, but instead once had a population that outnumbered Europe's. Most startling for the time, he understood that Natives traced their succession of leaders and family descent through female lines, and did not express any disapproval.[4]

One particularly interesting aspect of Rogers's writings is how he employs the epithet *savage*. He applies the term equally to both Europeans and Natives and refers more to conduct than any allegedly innate nature. He derides the French as savages in his letter to a French commander, mocking their fear of his reprisals. Natives allied with the French are labeled savage, but he assumes their savagery to be instigated by French orders. Rogers even suggests his own conduct and tactics are savage by dint of ruthlessness dictated by necessity.[5] The two groups he never refers to as savage, significantly, are both his own Native allies and the British. He reserves *savage* for either the ruthlessness of his enemies or his own ruthlessness in having to deal with them. The word was not an epithet for the falsely presumed innate nature of the "inferior." It was a marker of conduct dictated by the circumstances of war.

His most famous action, against the Abenaki village of St. Francis, was also the most highly disputed and the most important for understanding how others reconstructed Rogers as an Indian hater. Rogers's account describes a one-sided attack, a de facto massacre. His troops surrounded the village, surprising its inhabitants. After killing those who tried to escape, the village was set on fire. The fire burned alive those in hiding and lasted the entire night. Rogers wrote clinically and detached, with no hint of enjoyment, only a grim submission to his superior, General Jeffrey Amherst, and his orders to "Take revenge," even though the British gained no military advantage from this attack.[6]

How is one to explain what seemed to be a clear-cut atrocity, the mass murder of the members of a village filled with neutral people and noncombatants? This was completely contrary to every aspect of Rogers's usual character and beliefs. In Rogers's own account, he essentially tries to shift the origin of the actions to his superior, General Amherst. Rogers also tries to maintain, feebly, that he killed no women or children in the attack. Yet this has no credibility, for he states only twenty survived out of the two hundred in the village and clearly says no one was allowed to escape.[7] Rogers also tries to maintain a submissive tone throughout his account, as though what he did was solely dictated by his orders.

But it is his detachment and his attempts to shift responsibility to Amherst that provide the first clues to understanding. Most colonial accounts of massacres of Native people make no attempt to even consider massacres as actions worthy of blame. In many accounts the perpetrators take great pride and even pleasure in describing the brutality. That Rogers felt the need to shift blame or appear unemotional is itself suggestive of something fundamentally suspicious and less than truthful in his account. It also suggests that his own actions likely bothered his conscience.

The truth becomes clearer when one hears the accounts of others, the Abenakis themselves as well as the French that Rogers opposed. Traditional Abenaki accounts say a sympathetic Stockbridge member of the Rangers warned the village residents in advance of the attack. Thus most villagers were absent. The Ranger officers would likely have noted one of their members escaping and the simultaneous absence of so many of the Abenakis. It is hard to believe none of them would have seen the obvious cause and effect. It was thus quite possible that a Native officer of the Rangers, or perhaps even Rogers himself, "allowed" the Abenakis to be warned. Abenaki oral traditions give several different possibilities. One account describes a warning by St. Francis women that wood chips were floating down the river, indicating the building of rafts. Another account by Theophile Panadis describes a "Mahigan" member of Rogers' Rangers warning the village the night before the attack. The women, children, and sick were taken to a nearby place named Siboseck, with the men staying behind to defend St. Francis. Elvine Obamsawin Royce also tells the story passed down by her aunt's grandmother of a stranger warning of an attack. (In her account the warning was not heeded.) Historian Colin Galloway also notes that the Abenakis survived the attack quite well and adjusted fairly quickly, even serving with the same Rangers less than twenty years later.[8] It seems unlikely the Abenakis would serve with men who had committed such an atrocity against their people. If the village had truly been almost entirely massacred, the Abenakis should also not have recovered with such ease.

Yet the fact still remains that Rogers did carry out the attack, one that French colonial authorities said killed thirty members, in contrast to Rogers's claim of two hundred.[9] The fact remains that Rogers, who spent most of his life in the company of Natives and publicly defending their rights and abilities, chose to pose as a leader of an expedition that massacred neutral Natives. His motive might have been to please his superior while hiding his true actions, actions that might have left him open to military punishment for insubordination. Or, since he was already accustomed to enjoying widespread fame at a young age, it might have been to receive the additional approval of Europeans and Anglo-Americans with hostility toward Native people. Historian Stephen Brumwell makes the unlikely argument that he led this massacre to avenge the desecration of his brother's corpse by scalping.[10] His motive is ultimately less important than the fact that this alleged massacre became the incident by which others completely altered the popular view of him.

The Recasting of Rogers as an Indian Hater

Ironically, Rogers's first influence was on the British military establishment. Sir John Moore, the "Father of the Light Infantry," determined to learn from the British loss of the American colonies. He worked to completely alter the British Army, in line with Rogers's philosophy learned from Native people, from one ruled by fear and force to one emphasizing initiative and constant training. Moore ultimately spread these concepts throughout much of the world's western militaries in the concept of the light infantry.[11] Rogers's methods reentered the U.S. military both through the influence of the British military elite units and the severely altered image and legacy of the Rangers.

The memory of Rogers largely faded in the United States after his death until historian Francis Parkman used him in several episodes of *Montcalm and Wolfe*. Parkman intended his book to be as much a "rousing" adventure for young boys as history. Written in 1884, it had assumptions typical of the time. Parkman had the Manichean view of Native spiritual beliefs as forces of darkness: "The devil came at last and told [the medicine men] that the warriors would come back with scalps and prisoners." Parkman even appealed to religious intolerance using anti-Catholic bigotry. Catholicized Natives are described as "zealous and fanatical in their devotion to forms of Romanism." Such devotion could only be nominal, for Parkman assumed Natives were intrinsically incapable of truly understanding Christian belief, for they were "thorough savages in character." [12]

Parkman altered Rogers from an admirer of Natives to one solely defending against them. Rogers's own view was that the French remained the principal and most savage enemy of the English. Natives became dangerous only insofar as they allied themselves to the French. Parkman alters this, in fact almost entirely reverses it. To Parkman, the French and English become cosaviors of civilization by "virtue" of their both being white. Together the Europeans struggle against the savage wilderness, of which the Natives become a part. Parkman remakes Anglo-French warfare into almost a family quarrel. Only the French choice of Catholicism makes them less worthy than the English in his eyes. Parkman never shows Native allies or ways as part of Rogers's life, for that "taints" him.

In the most significant and telling episode, Parkman describes Rogers entering St. Francis just prior to the attack on the village, disguised in Indian dress, surrounded by "unconscious savages yelling and singing." [13] Leaving aside the absurdity of how "unconscious" people could yell or sing, the most striking thing is how Parkman turns Rogers into an Indian fighter in the overlapping sense—a white man who fights Indians by stealing their identity. No other account reports this incident, so it is quite possibly a complete fiction invented by Parkman. Parkman's stories about Rogers influenced a writer of historical fiction half a century later, Kenneth Roberts.

Roberts's version of Rogers in *Northwest Passage* is even more venomous. Written in 1937 and made into a Hollywood movie starring Spencer Tracy, the book revels in turning acts of brutality into folksy jokes and yarns. Rogers' Rangers compete every moment to outdo each other in a kind of joshing viciousness. "Long before anybody else is up . . . Rogers' men have been up a couple of hours, cleaned their muskets, shaved, got their breakfast . . . and maybe shot a few Indians *out of a tree.*"[14]

The final phrase clearly implies that Natives are just one more group of forest creatures to be hunted for sport. But to modern hunters and the Rangers of Roberts's book, hunting was a sport chosen to prove manliness rather than for subsistence as it was for both whites and Natives in colonial times. The Rangers of Roberts's novel thought of themselves as big game trophy hunters, not militia. War becomes a macho sport and killing Indians a source of bragging rights. One Ranger compliments another: "Good shot!" The shooter in turn takes folksy pride in saying, "That's three I got . . . I got a nice one while you was hauling that boy away . . . pretty a shot as I ever made." Another Ranger turns Indian killing into a competition that they all enjoy: "We've got to slaughter five Indians a day, and so far we're about fifty-eight behind!"[15]

Side by side with this laughing at body counts, the virulent hate aimed against Native people equals that done to blacks in *The Birth of a Nation*. Roberts describes Indians as "creatures without property, distinction, religion, humanity, morals, art, or literature." Unlike Parkman, he mentions Native allies but only to show them as beyond hope of being redeemed or civilized. Roberts describes a Christian Stockbridge ally as "a pigsty in need of washing," drunkenly hysterical and crying over Native rites not being observed, and differing only from non-Christian Natives in singing "Onward Christian Soldiers" instead of traditional songs while falling down drunk.[16]

Roberts's assertions of innate white supremacy and biological racism imposed themselves upon the fictional Rogers and his relations with Natives. He turns Rogers into a presumed naturally superior white who "began to chase Indians before he was weaned. . . . In a year's time the smartest Indian couldn't think half as much like an Indian like Rogers could." Roberts was also (ironically, given Rogers's true nature) especially horrified at the prospect of whites being adopted by Natives. A Ranger admonishes white members of the village of St. Francis, "Tisn't good policy to admit white people prefer Indians to their own people." Roberts fails to see that Abenakis *were* those "own people" to the white members of St. Francis. "Besides the Indians would kill 'em if we left," one character falsely asserts. "Anyway, they're white and they got to be white if they get a chance." To Roberts, such mixing becomes inherently wrong, dangerous, and unnatural.[17]

Roberts even replaces Rogers's original twenty-seven "Standing Orders" with his own version of nineteen orders. He heavily alters the language, in an obvious imitation of Davy Crockett or Daniel Boone tall tales. Rogers wrote his original "Standing Orders" in a slightly formal eighteenth-century colonial style. Roberts chooses a more simplified version suited to a fictional nineteenth-century frontier bumpkin style of storytelling. Roberts alters "Order Number 15" from "At first light, awake your whole attachment. This is the time when the savages choose to fall upon their enemies" to "Don't sleep beyond dawn. Dawn's when the French and Indians attack."[18]

In founding the Army Rangers in 1942, army officers looked to both the fictional hater and (unintentionally) the genuine syncretic Rogers as a model. Brigadier General Lucian Truscott recommended a unit formed along the lines of British commandos, units that owed a debt to Rogers and the Natives he learned from. Thus Rogers's use of Native martial philosophy and tactics entered the U.S. military by an indirect route, one that its own founders were unaware of. Truscott named the unit the First Ranger Battalion in honor and recognition of Rogers' Rangers. *Northwest Passage* was such a favorite of an officer with the Ranger infantry school that he wrote Roberts's *fictional* nineteen orders into the Rangers' Field Manual 21-50 rather than Rogers's original and genuine twenty-seven orders.[19] To this day, Rangers study and follow the fictional version of the "Standing Orders."

During the cold war, another author continued the themes of Parkman and Roberts in a biography of Rogers filled with racist overtones. John Cuneo takes obvious pleasure in turning Rogers's assault on St. Francis into a zealous attempt by a committed Indian hater to sate bloodlust. In the attack on St. Francis, according to Cuneo, "[The] Indians [were] in a stupor from the night's orgy . . . [and had] their heads split open before ever waking."[20] Writing in a time of siege mentality in American society, Cuneo's motive in such angry writing is plainly to inspire his readers to defend white civilization from enemies both foreign and domestic. Cuneo regards the most feared domestic enemies as those who had resided in the United States the longest, whom he depicts as stand-ins for Communists, particularly Asian ones.

In the most surreal episode in Cuneo's account, he describes Rangers as being so overcome by hunger while being pursued that they resort to eating Native flesh. Cuneo claims Lieutenant George Campbell and his command came upon "bodies horribly mangled . . . But this was not a season for distinctions. On them they fell like cannibals and devoured part of them raw." Cuneo justifies this, citing such alleged Native brutalities as "squaws . . . skewers thrust[ing] into . . . [a Ranger's] flesh and setting it on fire." Historian Stephen Brumwell also found accounts of cannibalism by both white and Indian members of the Rangers in statements from Lieutenant Campbell and David Evans of Concord, and in Robert Kirkwood's memoirs. Yet none of the original accounts describes this cannibalism with anything but revulsion. Only Cuneo sought to justify and even glorify it.[21]

Even current military hobbyists sometimes choose the fictional racist Rogers over the real one. One hobbyist group described Rangers as "living on the very edge of British civilization on the one side and the dark barbarism of Stone Age Indian tribes on the other." Their description of the Abenakis is straight out of Parkman, "nominal Christians . . . but . . . savages in dress, habit, and character."[22]

What those who tried to remake Rogers into an Indian hater ultimately seek to do is recast the role of the U.S. military in American history. By choosing to single out Rogers, the ultimate source of the military's most elite units and an important man in colonial history, these accounts seek nothing less than to insinuate that pride in white supremacy beliefs is central to the origins of the U.S. military. Yet Rogers himself would have been the most appalled by how his name and life were severely distorted by Parkman, Robert, Cuneo, and many hobbyists. Rogers's high regard for Native people is what informed every part of his life and gave him his success and fame.

Conclusion

The U.S. military has one of the most contradictory histories of any American institution. In popular culture, the military is usually seen as one of the most regressive or traditional (depending on which side of the political spectrum you fall on) institutions around. A more balanced view recognizes that as a caricature. The U.S. military is both the enforcer and proponent of an often unjust status quo, as well as one of the most innovative in its advocacy of social experiments and the progressive outlook of many of its members. These contradictions show up clearly in building the official myths surrounding Rogers' Rangers. Robert Rogers should be remembered as a man every bit as remarkable for his forward thinking as for his innovative tactics. It took great acts of deliberate, willful, and selective blindness from men such as Parkman, Roberts, and Cuneo to remake him into almost an Aryan race warrior.

The image of "the Indian" in the non-Native mind played a powerful part in what role Natives have in the U.S. military. The admiration that Anglo-American military leaders such as Robert Rogers had for Natives became so strong they emulated Native ways and incorporated them whenever possible. However, this esteem and mimicry of Natives ran headlong into other whites' hostility toward Natives. This hostility caricatured the warrior image into that of the savage. Yet even that caricature did not end the admiration many Anglo-American military men had for Native martial abilities. Some military planners sought to channel what they perceived as "savagery" in Indians or hold up Native martial abilities as an image for non-Natives to emulate. Natives in turn took advantage of that image and emulation to turn the service into a means for cultural preservation and renewal, as we shall soon see in the Civil War and especially World War I.

3

Before a Native Veteran Tradition Can Begin

The Case of Mexico

You, soldier leaders
Go ahead
Beautifully
With the mask
And with the headdress[1]

YAQUIS SING OF SAN PEDRO as the *capitán* of the army. He sits at the gates of heaven (in Yaqui song, depicted as almost the same as army headquarters) and advises the soldiers. The San Pedro of these songs is said to have such strength that he broke the bow he received from San Francisco Xavier, who is merely a foot soldier in the ranks. Yet San Francisco comes in for special mention as a great Yaqui soldier who killed a *kupahe*, a powerful bird whose feathers are worn in the coyote dancers' headdress. The verse of the song above is the first sung at every Bow Leaders Society ceremony. It tells of the coyote dancers coming out to bless the four directions to show their special obligation to protect the sacred land of the Yaquis.[2]

The Yaquis believe the first Bow Leader to be Jesus himself, or in some versions San Pedro or San Francisco. They also believe the Yaquis have always been Catholic, even since before Jesus' birth. The spiritual martial ideology of the Bow Leaders Society became central to Yaqui efforts to defend the homeland of the Eight Sacred Towns against Mexican encroachment ever since a Yaqui *alférez* (flag bearer in the Bow Leaders) named Juan Banderas declared himself sent by the Virgin of Guadalupe to restore the sovereignty of Montezuma.

Every Sunday morning in each of the Eight Sacred Towns, the Bow Leaders stand guard while a procession carries a figurine of Our Lady of Guadalupe, to whom they pledge their service. Despite the reference to soldiers, only some of the members are military veterans. A soldier to the Yaquis means one who defends sacred land.[3]

The dramatic differences in the way Native traditions interact with the military of the United States and Mexico are striking. At nearly any powwow in the United States or Canada, veterans carry the American and Canadian flags alongside the eagle staff. Native groups in Mexico have military societies in which Jesuits brought in Spanish military organization and imagery along with the Catholic faith. Mexico's Indians adapted this organization and imagery to suit the cultural and religious need to protect sacred lands against nationalist and expansionist aims of non-Native Mexicans and their governments. In the United States and Canada, virtually the opposite is true. Warrior societies and Natives in the armed forces adapted military service to indigenous cultural ways to defend the nation-state they feel bound to as allies by treaties, or think of themselves as dual citizens. At powwows in the United States, a Christian Indian minister sometimes gives a blessing after the grand entry. But, unlike in Mexico, there is virtually no other sign of Christianity at Native martial religious gatherings.

The comparisons bring up many questions. Why does Mexico, which has the largest indigenous population in the hemisphere and an even higher percentage of people who join the military, seem to have almost no permanent distinctively indigenous tradition within its armed forces? How is it that the United States and Canada, with never more than a small fraction of its members in the military being Native, have such strong traditions? How is it that Mexico's Indians are in many ways integrated into the national fabric not just more than in the United States but more than in most of Latin America? And yet why does Mexico have two extramilitary martial traditions the United States and Canada largely lack, namely an indigenous mercenary tradition and an indigenous revolutionary tradition? The search for answers leads one right away to take a comparative approach to how Anglo and Hispanic cultures view concepts such as race, identity, the question of acculturation versus assimilation, the economic roles of Native people, the roles they played in national development, and the legal status of Native peoples and nations.

One of my main arguments is that for an indigenous veteran tradition to develop that Natives regard as something more than merely a possible escape from poverty, the dominant non-Native society must be willing to deal with Native groups collectively, as people with a legal and social status that marks them permanently distinct from the larger society. At the same time the larger society must regard the indigenous groups as too alien to be easily integrated or that it would be undesirable to do so. This became the case in the United States. In Mexico a societal willingness to acculturate also became a means for Native tribal groups to lose some of their distinctiveness, and the Mexican government refused to deal with these groups on a collective legal basis. Cultural, biological, and especially religious *mestizaje* (mixing) removed both the need and the willingness for distinctively indigenous veteran traditions to emerge.

Legal and Identity Questions

Anglo and Hispanic societies dealt with Native groups in very different ways. One of the first acts after U.S. independence was to seek treaties with Indian nations to secure both their loyalty and their lands while keeping them as segregated as possible from whites. Up until two generations ago, Anglo societies largely offered Native people the "choice" of assimilation or exclusion.[4] Yet the ironic long-term effect of these stark alternatives became the strengthening of tribal-wide identity and the unintentional fostering of Native nationalism.[5] White hostility, an Anglo view of Indians as either too alien or too incapable to take part in the larger society, educational difficulties, and the legal status of tribes kept Natives hemmed in on reservations. Many Native groups that had no previous history of acting in concert except as bands or family groups became forced to do so as tribes. Anglo societies also tended to view racial/ethnic identity as something permanent and biological. This had another ironic effect, that of increasing the numbers who identified or became identified as Native. There was no mestizo "escape clause" where one could escape definition as indigenous as in Latin America. Disease, warfare, and systematic exclusion from territory all left far fewer Natives remaining north of the Rio Grande than below. But the biological view of race and the legal status of Indian people strengthened Indian nations and nationalism in the end.[6]

Spain's colonial policy in its later stages stressed a willingness to co-opt Native resistance by offering concessions to some Native groups and using them as auxiliaries against other Indians. In Mexico, the demand of local *vecinos* (literally "neighbors," but used to mean non-Natives) that Opata troops be disarmed became one of the first signs of the breakdown of relations between the national government and their allied Indian nations after the struggle for independence. These same Opatas fought alongside the *vecinos* against Spanish rule during the struggle for independence. The office of *capitán-general* of the Opatas was also eliminated. A decree in 1828 ordered Indian militias abolished and Indians integrated into regular military units.[7]

While the United States and Canada sought to segregate Native peoples from the white majority as dependent wards, Mexico's Native peoples had citizenship forced upon them from the beginning. With a single extremely limited exception (the Yaquis), Mexico's Native peoples never had legal status as tribal nations nor lands protected on a tribal basis. The basis of identity was much more commonly along pueblo lines, sometimes lines the Spaniards had established.[8]

Historian Alan Knight argues that the roots of this integration of Natives into the national fabric in Mexico go very far back. Aztec rule was far more unpopular than Inca rule in Peru, for example, and was seen as less legitimate by most of the population. Spaniards destroyed Aztec elites far more thoroughly. Intermarriage and acculturation (especially "spiritual conquest") went much further than almost anywhere else in the hemisphere, so much so that the term *Indian* became largely a social construct rather than an identity. Outsiders used *indio* as a label with negative connotations, while Indians themselves identified as *campesinos* and insisted they were patriots. Opatas, for example, preferred to be called Mexicans.[9]

Knight's argument has its strengths and weaknesses. As we saw earlier, Yaquis practice a far different form of Catholicism than that practiced in Boston or even in East Los Angeles. Their constant uprisings also say something very different from what Knight contends. Simultaneously, Knight argues Spain's defeat did bring the removal of the crown as mediator between criollos and peasants (as most Indians insisted being called.) But attacks on Indian cultures were piecemeal and ineffective because of Indian resistance and Conservative support. Indian prophets led the first Indian uprisings against the new state, using Catholic symbols as an ideology of protest. (It is not hard to see parallels between this and Gregory Dowd's *A Spirited Resistance*, in which he details how Shawnee, Delaware, and other Eastern Indians utilized beliefs such as Moravian or Baptist Christianity.) The long-term effects of these conflicts, Knight argues, were that for a time dictator Porfirio Diaz and then the successors to the Mexican Revolution were forced by self-identified peasants (and not as Indians) to institute systems of corporatist mediation, often at the village level. The nation-state of Mexico also mobilized its people through an appropriation of Catholic symbols into a civic public religion, the most famous examples being the Mexican flag and the Lady of Guadalupe.[10]

Anglo and Hispanic societies also had vastly different notions of who could be identified as Indian or white, differences that ultimately go back to the worldview of Protestants and Catholics in the sixteenth century. Catholics saw their faith as a universal church, even for those they regarded as culturally inferior. From this came a much greater willingness to intermingle and intermarry, eventually leading to a cultural definition of ethnic identity. Some Protestant churches saw themselves as members of an elect, with the great majority of humankind preordained to be beyond salvation. Some Protestant sects were also early advocates of the separation of church and state. From these two practices ultimately came a determination to segregate and to see ethnic differences as permanent, biological, and unalterable.[11] The Catholic view and the Jesuit methods of organization came to the Native peoples of north Mexico very early on.

Warrior Societies and Military Societies

Indian nations in the United States and Canada have a long tradition of warrior societies, particularly in the Plains tribes. Tribal nations as diverse as the Cherokees, the Six Nations of the Iroquois, and even the somewhat pacifist Hopis had or have warrior societies.[12] Other groups that traditionally may never have had a warrior society tradition now feature political groups such as the Mohawk Warrior Society that at least claim the title. In Mexico the Mayos, Pimas, Tarahumaras, and Yaquis have or had military societies with roles and ceremonies at first influenced by the Spanish Jesuits in colonial times but adapted to Native needs. Native peoples with a strong martial tradition but who have faced acculturation the longest, such as the Tlaxcalans, show no sign at all of military societies.[13]

For the purposes of this chapter, a warrior society is defined as a Native martial group whose organization springs from indigenous tradition while the meaning and symbolism of its rituals support both indigenous belief and Anglo-American military institutions. A military society is a Native martial group whose organization is Jesuit Catholic while the symbolism and meaning of its rituals are a mix of indigenous and Catholic practices. Many warrior societies revived following World War II and the Korean War as a direct reaction against Termination (efforts by the federal government and conservative politicians to completely end reservations). These wars also saw the spread of the tradition of the veteran assuming the warrior's role even among many tribal nations that previously never had any or much of a warrior tradition. Many tribes that remained indifferent to World War I, such as the Comanches, took part on a huge scale in World War II and in wars since.[14]

The first military societies began as far back as the 1600s in what is now Mexico. Yaqui auxiliaries first adopted Jesuit organization as a way of strengthening themselves enough to keep out the Spanish military and civil authorities. The military society was for local defense as well as ceremonial functions and guarding the governors. Every Sunday at dawn, midday, and sunset the military society procession carried the flags, drums, and statues of Jesus and Our Lady of Guadalupe to the four directions. Bow Leaders with arrows notched at the ready or holding rosaries symbolically guarded the procession. A member of the Bow Leaders served by personal vow or by a pledge from a parent, grandparent, or godparent. The community elected leaders by consensus and acclamation, a practice that clearly did not come from the Jesuits. The Jesuits also did not bring the dress of fox skin and feather headdresses or the coyote dances and songs before campaigns as a ritual preparation and afterwards as a Victory Dance.[15]

The Bow Leaders Society did not spread uniformly. It became strongest in the four Yaqui pueblos that followed Juan Banderas when he led the Yaqui uprising in the 1830s and was weakest among those who joined the Mexican Army to oppose him. By the 1880s the Bow Leaders Society became strong in the tribe as a whole, including in the society's devotion to their patron, the Virgin of Guadalupe. Near Tucson, Arizona, in the 1920s, one of the refugee Yaquis, Lucas Chávez, attempted to bring the Bow Leaders into the United States. With no land base to defend and no military aspects legally allowed, the attempt ended by the early 1940s. In 1971 the Bow Leaders started again after the United States finally legally recognized the Yaquis as a tribe and gave them a title to land they had been occupying since the 1880s.[16]

The Tarahumaras' martial organization is called the Coyote Society. Its members use military titles, such as *capitán*. Jesuits and Franciscans imposed the pueblo style of organization on them, with the Tarahumaras altering the offices for ceremonial and religious purposes. During Holy Week the Tarahumaras stage mock battles of Sontarisis and Pariseos (soldiers and Pharisees).[17]

Pimas of Mexico call their military society the "Pariseos." The Pariseos are all young males chosen by kidnapping during Easter. The titles of the offices are military ones, *henra'ar*, *capitán*, *cabo*, *ma'ar*, and *comisario* (general, captain, sergeant, mayor, and commissary). The Pariseos conduct the rituals for the Lady of Guadalupe and Bantera of the Santisma on December 12, when they celebrate the arrival of new flags. They also act as ritual clowns in sacred places and as ceremonial guards at events where they keep the peace and enforce the rituals of abstinence for Holy Week. The local *blancos* are brought into the ritual in the roles of *judios* (Jews) who wear dresses. Sometimes Pima youths play the roles wearing white cardboard masks. At the end of all the rituals, a mock figure of Judas is taken out of town and shot by a firing squad. Until the authorities stopped them, "Judas" used to be blown up with dynamite.[18]

Not much is known about the Mayo military society other than its association with a Mayo sect. Santa Teresa de Cabora, a young Mayo woman who in the 1870s preached religious devotion as a response to the loss of Mayo autonomy to Mexico, led the Liopaskos. The Liopaskos celebrated a former military society ceremony, the Day of Finding the Holy Cross, and decorated themselves with grain and ribbons where the military society once used military insignia.[19]

What all the military societies have in common is the use of military organization and imagery in ritual religious settings to define themselves as distinctly Native in the context of a larger society that wants to see complete *mestizaje* (the mixing of lineages and cultures). More striking, none of these Native societies chose to bring their customs into the military. In fact, Yaqui who joined the military were not part of those ritual societies. As recently as the 1970s (and thus conceivably today), Yaqui who join the Mexican military were often at odds with the Bow Leaders.[20] Compare this to the United States, where many of the elected tribal leaders and Native activists are veterans. Yet the Indian cultural groups with members on both sides of the border, such as the Apaches, Tohono O'odhams, and Yaquis, do have the tradition of honoring the veteran as a warrior in the United States. Except for the Yaquis, all of these groups in Mexico have no permanent communal land base. That may be a further explanation for the lack of distinctly Indian veteran traditions among them.[21]

Quirquismo and Revolutionary Tradition

Wracked by internal civil conflicts after independence for much longer than the United States, Mexico had a far weaker national government dealing with a recurrent problem the United States did not have—military intervention in politics. As a consequence, civilians in the national government sought to keep the military smaller. The Mexican national government leaders also frequently distrusted state governments because governors were also members of the opposing political factions. This led the state governments to try to deal with Natives using Quirquismo.

James Kirker was a Scotch-Irish immigrant who went to the United States to avoid British conscription. By 1835 he had moved west to Mexico, in New Mexico Territory, where he traded guns, alcohol, and a variety of other contraband across the border and to Native tribes as well. His willingness to make a profit by any means possible led to his being declared an illegal trader. Strapped for funds to maintain state militia and distrustful of the national government, the Mexican states of Chihuahua, Coahuila, Durango, Sonora, and New Mexico Territory revived the colonial-era practice of mercenary warfare against the Apaches by paying bounties for *piezas* (ears and scalps together) of Apaches. Chihuahua and Sonora also gave out *permisos*, the license or contract to raise troops to fight against the Apaches. Stephen Crucier, an American who became a *regidor* and hacienda owner in Chihuahua, knew Kirker from his work providing security on the roads to the local mines and asked him to raise a company of mercenary Sahuanos or Shawnees.[22]

A Moravian Christian Shawnee chief named Spy Buck led the Sahuanos. Buck "dressed Apache and talked American" according to the subprefect of Galeana, Don José Merino. The Sahuanos all came originally from the United States or its reservations, including Delawares, Creeks, Cherokees, and free blacks as well as Shawnees. By 1845 their numbers also included local Mexicans and Tarahumaras, the latter dressed in G-strings and sandals with their hair bobbed and in turbans.[23]

Kirker's tactics were disastrous for the people of northern Mexico. He mostly attacked peaceful groups, such as the Gileno and Mimbreno Apaches, with whom the Mexican states already had peace treaties. He usually attacked Apaches while they were asleep. In several cases he approached Apaches he knew from his trading days and got them drunk before ambushing them. Kirker proved not to be above scalping (or "barbering," as he called it) local Mexicans and even his own dead Sahuanos to collect bounties. With the coming of the Mexican-American War, Kirker's company turned to scouting for the Americans under Colonel Alexander Doniphan. The end of the war saw a flood of mercenaries competing with Kirker, including ex–Texas Rangers and other Americans, Mexicans, Comanches, and even Apaches. Historian John Terrell argues the bounty system turned northern Mexico into "a gigantic field of slaughter" and prolonged warfare while providing little real protection.[24]

Mexican authorities increasingly turned to other Natives as merce-naries. The government contracted out some former Seminole scouts against Apaches and Seris. One thousand Kickapoos were awarded a land grant in Santa Rosa, Coahuila, to protect local Mexicans against the Comanches and Apaches. The ineffectiveness of mercenaries led many military commanders or state authorities throughout the nine-teenth century to turn to old Spanish tactics of bringing in Native auxiliaries and co-opting uprisings by offering concessions. General Corral of Sonora and Governor Torres of Chihuahua used Pima aux-iliaries extensively against the Apaches. General Urrea used Yaqui auxiliaries against the Opatas and Apaches. Father Dávalos, in turn, recruited Opata auxiliaries to use against the Yaquis when Banderas led his uprising.[25]

The Yucatán government gave Mayas who joined in suppressing the independence movement the title of *hidalgo* and rewarded them with tribute and tax exemptions and a promise that they would never be sent to other parts of the country. Breaking that promise became one of the major causes of mutinies, along with low or late pay and inadequate rations. Local *vecinos* encouraged the northwestern Mayas to distinguish themselves from the rebel *cruzob* Mayas by calling them *mestizos de buen hablar*. Most of northwestern Mayas did not fall for this and continued to identify themselves as *macehuales* or *campesinos* (commoners or peasants) and to refer to *vecinos* as *dzules* or *señores* (gentlemen or sirs).[26]

Among the Zapotecs, the Juchiteco and Blaseno regions opposed the French during their intervention while the Hispanicized Tehuano Zapotecs joined the French. For other Indian communities as well, Mexico's war against France solidified an image of criollo elites as identified with foreignness and being Indian with patriotism. Agustin Cruz is remembered as a *maseual* (Indian commoner) from Cuetzalan who organized fellow *maseulamej* to resist the *analtekos* (foreigners) defeating the French-Austrian army at the Battle of Puebla, in their oral histories a blending of the battles on May 5, 1862, and April 2, 1867. *Analtekos* and *koyomej* (non-Indian Mexicans) blend in their stories into a common enemy. This war, rather than Mexico's war for independence from Spain, is remembered locally as their entry into the nation-state.[27]

Insurgents in turn recruited discontented Native groups during civil uprisings against the national government. Refugio Tonori led seven thousand Opatas and Pimas on the side of the French interventionists in the 1860s. Mateo Marquin also led Yaquis on the side of the French. The most famous Native insurgents, the Red Battalions of Mayos and Yaquis, fought under Álvaro Obregón in the Mexican Revolution. Mayos and Yaquis fought on every side in the revolution, often following personal allegiances to a commander rather than political ones. Four battalions of Zapotec soldiers fought for Venustiano Carranza and then Obregón.[28]

Taking advantage of Natives who identified with a village or pueblo, those defending the status quo recruited Native troops to suppress every major civil conflict. Banderas faced four Yaqui pueblos whose members sided with and joined the Mexican Army. In the long Yaqui struggle for independence, loyalties split along pueblo lines. The worst aspect of this is that many times Native troops and leaders took part in the worst kinds of atrocities against other Natives. Little of this can be ascribed to the familiar blaming-the-victim excuse of "old Native rivalries." General Heliodoro Charis, a Zapotec, led the elite 13th Battalion after the Mexican Revolution, a unit that specialized in suppressing revolts. In 1926, ten years before the first carpet-bombing of civilian populations by the Nazis, Charis led a similarly brutal campaign against Yaqui civilians, a people the Zapotecs had had no martial conflict with historically. Later Charis led campaigns against the Cristeros in Nayarit, Michoacán, and Colima, regions that had had no history of conflict with the Zapotecs. General Román Yucipio, a Mayo, also played a great part in the same campaigns, and the Mayos often were allied with the Yaquis, from the days of Banderas up until their time serving together under Obregón.[29]

Certainly there was no reason for Charis to have either regard or hostility for the Yaquis or Cristeros. Yucipio's case is even more striking since the Mayos and Yaquis had had a recent history of serving together under Obregón in the Mexican Revolution. Acculturation likely produced contempt and complete disregard for other Natives, both other tribal cultures and even one's own tribal people. One of Mexico's most admired folk heroes, José Maria Leyva, or Cajeme, showed signs of this. Before he led his famous uprising for Yaqui sovereignty, Cajeme took part in the infamous Bahum massacre. Mexican soldiers burned alive Yaqui women and children in a church, and those who tried to escape were shot. Cajeme did not grow up among other Yaquis but in California during the gold rush days. He did not have contact with Yaquis other than his father until he returned in his late teens. Three years later he volunteered for the campaigns against other Yaquis, where he quickly rose through the ranks to become a captain and alcalde.[30]

The United States had no counterpart to Mexico's Indian mercenary tradition, not even among its Indian Scouts (see chapter 5). The closest to an indigenous revolutionary tradition appears to be some aspects of the Red Power movement during the 1960s and 1970s. The United States holds up the citizen-soldier as an appealing ideal, and it was not until Natives had citizenship, after the state of war between Native and white had long ended, that Natives began joining in their greatest numbers. Indian Scouts in earlier times became enlistees in the regular army and not mercenaries receiving bounties for scalps. Most of the Indian population was too segregated and regarded as too culturally alien for any would-be insurgents to try to recruit. For example, anarchists in the United States made no attempt to recruit Natives while two self-described Zapotecs, the Magon brothers, led the anarchist Partido Liberal Mexicano, which in turn recruited many Tarahumaras and Yaquis. The one exception is the U.S. Civil War, during which Confederate insurgents built an alliance with the Five Tribes. The Five Tribes felt abandoned by the federal government and feared the Confederacy; many of the Confederate Indians switched allegiance back to the United States at the first available opportunity. Some of those who did not switch were the most assimilated mixed-bloods, led by slaveholders with a financial stake in the slavery system.[31] American intellectual thought has always been hostile to both military mercenaries and the idea of revolutions. Without any opportunity, such traditions could not develop. A Native insurgent tradition ironically required a belief in the possibility of acculturating Natives, while a mercenary one was brought by a weak national government.

A Catholic saint such as San Pedro could be at the center of Yaqui belief and be regarded as a central, powerful soldier figure that can break a bow. But having that religious and cultural *mestizaje* and devotion did not bring esteem or even acceptance from non-Native Mexicans. *Mestizaje* brought a strong blending of traditions but it often did not bring respect for the original Native ways of life. Belief in *mestizaje* often bred hostility and even massive violence against Native groups who chose not to merge. *Mestizaje* in some ways became a greater and more successful force for ending Native distinctiveness. *Mestizaje* could even absorb a warrior tradition like that of the Tlaxcalans completely, far better than the bold-faced hostility of complete assimilation or exclusion once in favor in the United States. The cultural definition of Indianness in Mexico achieved a much greater sociocultural integration that ironically made rationalizing indifference to and even violence toward Indian peoples and cultures all too easy.

Besides naming of ships in the Mexican Navy (see chapter 4), the Mexican military uses Indian imagery in other areas as well. One of the most recent and disturbing episodes ironically came from outside the country. During the military's campaigns first against the Zapatistas and then against drug trafficking, one thousand Mexican soldiers received training in Guatemala as Kaibiles. The Kaibiles in Guatemala are an elite anti-insurgency unit notorious for brutality against Native villages. Kaibiles take their name from "Kaibil Balam, a Mam indigenous leader who evaded capture by the Spanish conquistadores under Pedro de Alvarado." A Kaibil is glorified by military trainers as "a man of strategy, he that has force and astuteness of two tigers." The real life Kaibil is valorized in Guatemala's history as "the last Indian chief to fight the Spanish" much the same as Geronimo or Chief Joseph in U.S. history or Cuahtemoc or Cajeme in Mexican history. Guatemala's and Mexico's Kaibiles take as their slogan "If I go forward, follow me. If I stop, urge me on. If I turn back, kill me." More than mere hyperbole, their principal tactic has always been forcibly recruiting local Indian villagers under the threat of death to fight against the guerillas.[32] As we will see repeatedly, Native symbols are adopted by the military to link itself to Indians, to those with the greatest rights to the Americas; this may appear to be patriotism, but it hardly "honors" Natives.

Conclusion

Clearly, valorizing the Indian did not always bring better treatment for *indigenas* of Mexico. It may be that there are other distinctively Native traditions in the Mexican military that just have not been looked at thoroughly enough. Certainly Natives used the institution for economic advantage and advancement into the larger society. Service as auxiliaries became a way to try and shift Spanish and Mexican encroachment away from your own people or pueblo onto other groups. Yet Mexico's need to distance itself from previous colonial Spanish traditions undercut that effort as well. Romanticizing the revolutionary tradition in Mexican history and its flip side, justly laying blame for the lack of social progress on the military, insisted upon showing Natives as victims and the military as their greatest source of hardships. To view Natives as actively choosing the military suggests they took part in their own victimization.

The history of Native soldiers in the Mexican military also brings up the uncomfortable fact that even folk heroes such as Cajeme took part in the worst kinds of brutality against their own people. Cultural definitions of Indianness and identifying with a pueblo rather than a tribe made it far easier for Native soldiers to have a hand in or even direct the worst kinds of atrocities. That disjuncture became something historians of Mexico could not address without disturbing a patronizing worldview of the helpless Native victim.

4

Thunderbird Warriors, Injuneers, and the USNS *Red Cloud*

Native and Pseudo-Indian Images and Names in the Military

> It was the white people who had nothing; it was the white people who were suffering as thieves do, never able to forget that their pride was wrapped up in something stolen, something that had never been, and could never be, theirs.—Leslie Silko, *Ceremony*

> Why do white people work so hard to exterminate the Indians and then turn right around and dress like them? Ain't that the damnedest and most sickening case of necrophilia you ever heard of?
> —Spike Lee, *Huey Newton*

"IT WAS NOT JUST THE COURAGE and brave deeds of Mitchell Red Cloud Jr. that went into the name of the USNS *Red Cloud*, but also the pain and sorrow of his mother." Dressed in traditional regalia, Mitchell's daughter Annita Red Cloud spoke at the dedication ceremony in 1999 for the ship named for her father. Corporal Mitchell Red Cloud Jr. from the Ho Chunk (Winnebago) tribal nation received the Medal of Honor posthumously in 1952. Red Cloud died fighting while partly tied down to show great bravery in the face of death. Too badly wounded to stand up on his own, he ordered his troops to tie him upright to a tree. Red Cloud kept firing until his death, thus allowing his comrades to escape unharmed. At the dedication ceremony, admirals, an army general, the president of the shipbuilding company, and surviving members of his company paid tribute to the man who saved the lives of his fellow Marines. Members of the Ho Chunks performed an honor song before Annita Red Cloud broke the champagne bottle at the ship's christening. In an emotional speech and story for the tribal newspaper, she spoke of feeling both humbled and "like a child waiting for Santa Claus." Still, she "would rather have had a father than a hero!"[1]

Only a few years before Mitchell Red Cloud's death, the 307th Airborne Engineers used an official patch with a cartoon caricature of an "Indian" wearing a loincloth and carrying a tomahawk and machine gun. The 307th called themselves the "Injuneers." By the late 1960s, the patch was no longer in use. Jim Skinner, a white member of the 307th during the Vietnam War, believes the patch "demanded respect from other units" when white soldiers chose to call themselves by this racist epithet and crude attempt at humor. He "doubts seriously the patch was deactivated because of American Indian protest." His explanation for why the patch changed? "Maybe there simply wasn't room [on the uniform]."[2]

These sorts of defenses parallel those offered for racist sports mascots. This paradox, reverence and ridicule side by side, often glibly assumed to be the same, is common when one looks at Native or allegedly "Indian" images in the military. Stereotypes, "generic" Indians, assumptions that Natives are "vanished," and even outright racist slurs are as common in military symbols and names as they are among sports mascots and commercial images. But there are enough important differences to avoid the too easy assumption that since sports mascots are virtually always regarded as offensive by Natives,[3] all attempts at Indian symbolism and naming in the military are offensive as well. Supporters and defenders of sports mascots will be disappointed that the history of would-be Indian symbolism in the military does not clearly support either side's view unequivocally. Like sports mascots themselves, would-be Indian military symbols are complex. Yet a comparison between the two sets of symbols is useful for seeing why sports mascots have remained one of the most heavily debated issues in Native-white relations for over forty years. Would-be Indian symbolism and naming in the military, on the other hand, are only rarely protested. From that initial comparison, we can then proceed to examine how outsiders view the image of "the Indian" through the lens of military symbols and names, whether Natives shaped that imagery, and whether that imagery shaped the place of Natives in the military and the initial acceptance of Native servicemen.

Native and would-be Indian symbolism and naming in the military are older than sports mascots by at least a century and a half. It is a worldwide phenomenon, practiced throughout much of Latin America and such unlikely places as Great Britain, France, and even Turkey. It is also very much a practice of government elites, usually the higher echelons of civilian bureaucracies. Where "Indian" sports mascots owe much of their origin to Indian hobbyists among the general public, such as the Boy Scouts and the YMCA, the blame or credit for would-be Indian symbolism ultimately goes back to the British colonialist belief in "martial races," the notion that certain peoples all over the globe are "naturally warlike." One of the most important questions to ask, then, is: Were other peoples also "honored" in this manner? If so, who and why? And why, then, does this not (with rare exceptions) also happen with sports mascots?

Unlike sports mascots, there are instances of actual Native symbolism and naming in the military. Native symbols have been chosen, designed, or widely approved of by either tribal nations or large groups of Native people of many nations. These symbols and names are very different from their pseudo-Indian counterparts. Why do Native people accept would-be Indian symbolism in the military but not in sports? Ultimately it is because of the different nature of the role of an athlete from that of a warrior. Knute Rockne and sportswriters' clichés aside, an athlete never sacrifices as much as a soldier, and it trivializes *genuine* warriors' sacrifices to claim otherwise. Athletes do not routinely lose their lives, body parts, or sanity, and the manner in which sports are celebrated is very different from that of lost servicemen. There is no Arlington Cemetery for athletes, no memorial walls with flowers left by tearful widows, children, or brothers-in-arms who will always be scarred and haunted by loss. The sense of pride in any final score or championship cannot be compared to that of pointing to a parent who gave his life for the highest of ideals. Many Natives are offended by referring to an athlete as a warrior since a warrior's achievements are celebrated with reverence, not with drunkenness and a cheering squad of scantily clad women.

But even instances of successful honoring, such as the 45th Division "Thunderbird Warriors," have troubling histories of misuse. There are lessons here for both opponents and defenders of sports mascots. It definitely *is* possible to honor Native people through the use of symbols and names. Sports fans could, conceivably, learn how to better pay tribute to the Native people they claim to be theoretically honoring by following the better examples within the military. Yet even under the most ideal circumstances, such honoring can still quickly become as abusive and offensive for many of the same reasons as the worst of the pseudo-Indian sports mascots. Whether from lack of contact, lack of knowledge, or simply wishful thinking, many whites have a very difficult time understanding the difference, and all it takes is one careless or lazy assumption.

One final similarity to be kept mind as we look at both sets of symbols and names is how they affect relations between Natives and non-Natives. The effects of "Indian" mascots on Native children in particular are well documented: a host of issues about self-esteem, shame, and even higher rates of suicide and alcoholism among Native youth can be traced to such mascots.[4] How do Native and pseudo-Indian symbols and names affect Natives in the military? Is it significant that such symbols and names were already widespread before Natives first joined the military in large numbers in World War I, and accelerated afterward? Could pseudo-Indian imagery have even facilitated Native acceptance into the military? Are Native servicemen treated differently because of such images, either for better or worse? Since military insignia and weapon names are little known outside the service except perhaps to military buffs, this is the most important question as well as the one most central to this study of Native veterans. Finally, what does it say about cultural differences when a region with far greater numbers of Native people—Latin America—has far fewer would-be Indian symbols and names than does North America?

Parallels and Differences with Sports Mascots

At first glance, the two practices do appear to be almost the same: both use Indian or allegedly Indian names or images, and both at least seem to promote the image of the Indian as violent by limiting his role to that of a warrior or fighter. (Ironically, as we shall see later, the military actually does acknowledge roles other than as a fighter for Natives in its symbols far better than do sports teams and fans.) There are cartoon caricatures of Natives in both sets of symbols, as well as occasional outright epithets. Sometimes military units take part in practices that are strikingly similar to what goes on at sporting events.

Both practices have elements of the celebration of Manifest Destiny and can be viewed as taking part in the final attempt at colonization of Native people, an effort to take over their cultural landscape.[5] Both are attempts to replace what is actually Native with the white fantasy of an Indian as surely as westerns and the New Age movement try so desperately to do. Both are what Phillip Deloria has explored as cases of "playing Indian," defining one's whiteness in contrast to alleged traits of an Indian. At the same time, those "playing Indian" selectively choose to escape from that whiteness when they find the dominant culture stifling or want to reshape that characterization of whiteness. Playing Indian usually revolves around attempts to define Americanness and seeking to defy or cope with modernity by drawing on an idealized image of the past. Most appropriately for both sports mascots and military symbols, it is also a way to sanction being violent by role-playing as a "savage."[6] People who are not widely thought of as white can play Indian (for example, black athletes) under the guise of losing one's self in something that is defined as simply "American." By playing Indian, a black athlete temporarily has his status as a black person overlooked or negated for what he sees as his own benefit, to win acceptance from whites.

Native servicemen also influenced how would-be Indian symbols were used to define the role of Natives within the military. Sports mascots and military symbolism at times overlapped. In the U.S. Army, members of Company C of the 287th Infantry Regiment of the 45th Division, graduates of the Chilocco Indian School, used a Cleveland Indians doll as their mascot from 1951 onward, nicknaming it "Charlie." When the doll showed severe signs of wear and tear, Specialist 5th Class Taylet Morgan, a Cherokee from Newkirk, Oklahoma, donated a new doll.[7]

Does this mean Native soldiers did not find the Cleveland Indians symbol offensive? Not necessarily, because *Natives* chose and redefined at will this company mascot. Natives engaging in this redefinition should not be seen as approving of the original image anymore than should blacks referring to each other by the n-word be seen as approving of people outside their own group using the epithet. (For that matter, many Natives refer to each other as "skins" and "breeds.") Speculatively, this mascot could also be compared to a popular culture figure such as Tonto, a step forward for that time that was accepted and even promoted by Native people as the best that could be hoped for under the circumstances, even while the character was still understood to be a stereotype.

Even if Natives did not find the Cleveland Indians symbol offensive, there were tangible rewards and protections for Natives who catered to white preconceptions or fantasies. Leon Boutwell, a Chippewa football player for the Oorang Indians, talked about how he used white stereotypes to avoid punishment for his mistakes: "They thought we (the Oorang team) were all wildmen even though most of us had been to college and were more civilized than they were." Boutwell took advantage of the image many whites had of Natives to avoid criminal charges for raising hell while drinking.[8]

Defenders of sports mascots are fond of pointing to the small number of Natives not offended by mascots to justify their use. By doing this, pro-mascot people miss the essential point. In most instances, pro-mascot Natives use their own support, often in sophisticated political maneuvering, to win tangible concessions from the white majority. Seminole chief Jim Billie won better relations with the Florida legislature (many of whom are Florida State University alumni) by his stance on FSU's "Chief Osceola." Arapaho elders won control over how Natives are depicted and how Native history and art are taught in Littleton, Colorado, high schools in exchange for consenting to the use of their name for a team.[9]

Similarly, Native servicemen have long taken advantage of white beliefs that Indians are "natural" warriors to gain acceptance, respect, and admiration in the military, even while learning to cope with the negative consequences of that stereotype. On that matter, I recall how white officers and NCOs assumed that I was a better soldier than I was (when I was actually terribly undisciplined) at the very sight of my Indian features. (The downside of that was dealing with being called "chief," "Geronimo," "Apache," and so on.) In a broader sense, one need only look at Native treatment in the military compared to that of blacks. The question then becomes whether pseudo-Indian symbols and names, including stereotypical ones, cause better treatment or are a result of it.

Historian Raymond Stedman suggests a set of criteria for looking at whether an "Indian" image in commercial popular culture is stereotypical:

1) "Is the vocabulary demeaning?" Are there epithets or insults used?

2) "Do the 'Indians' talk like Tonto?" Are they shown as slow talking, speaking in broken English or grunts?

3) "Do the 'Indians' belong to the featherbonnet tribe?" Is every Native assumed to be a pseudo-Lakota or a generic Indian with no specific tribal identity?

4) "Is there comedy based on depicting Natives as drunk or stupid?"

5) "Are Natives portrayed as extinct or a separate species?" Are they vanishing Indians? Are they shown as incomprehensible, inscrutable, or utterly alien?

6) "Are Natives either noble or savage?" Are they "good Indians" (Tontos) because they like whites and "bad" because they do not?

7) "Is the tone patronizing?" Is there an appeal to pity or an assumption that whites know what is best, disguised as benevolence or sympathy?

8) "Is Native humanness acknowledged?" This can be as simple as giving individual Natives an actual name, one that is not stereotypical.[10]

To these, I add four more that I am surprised Stedman did not include:

9) Are Native religious beliefs or rituals attacked or belittled? Are there mocking or inaccurate versions of rituals being done for inappropriate reasons? This includes the misuse of traditional titles of respect, such as *chief* and *warrior*.

10) Is the history of Native dispossession and genocide trivialized, justified, or even glorified?

11) Are non-Natives profiting from the objectionable images? Is this profit motive driving or distorting the use of the image or name?

The most commonsense standard of all is one regularly invoked by mascot opponents:

12) Do the majority of Native people object?

Applying these standards to sports mascots, absolutely none of the major sports franchises that use "Indian" mascots or names passes. Few of the university or secondary school teams do either. Many fail on every single criteria.

When applying these standards to military images and names, however, many of the criteria are not true. Numbers 2, 4, 9, 10, 11, and 12 are entirely absent. The greatest problem with pseudo-Indian military images is number 3, because they commonly depict a generic Plains "Indian" in a warbonnet. Pseudo-Indian images, surprisingly, started off relatively benign and became more insulting as time passed.

Sports mascots equate Natives with animals, implying a comparison to something subhuman.[11] Military unit symbols, especially early on, usually imitated European heraldry. If Natives were compared to anything in the military, it was to knights and their assumed qualities of nobility and chivalry. (This is hardly a new practice. Europeans, starting with Columbus, commonly referred to Native leaders as "kings.") While this is hardly accurate, since hierarchy is not something valued by most Native cultures, it is not as insulting as being called subhuman. By the early twentieth century, pseudo-Indian military symbols more resembled popular culture depictions, such as the Indianhead penny. Post–World War II military images of Natives show the increasing influence of cartoons, particularly those of Walt Disney. Pseudo-

Indian symbols increasingly became insulting caricatures similar to those found in racist movies such as *Peter Pan.*

Only one use of pseudo-Indian imagery and naming in the military drew the ire of Native people. The air force began using the rank of chief master sergeant in the late 1950s. Groups of NCOs of that rank formed fraternal-type gatherings in 1970 and referred to themselves as "Chiefs." They hold induction ceremonies where they dress up in what are supposed to be Plains Indian "warbonnets." They recite "Chief's creeds," pledging not to "lose their individuality in a crowd," among other things. They also sell merchandise such as coffee cups, coasters, lighters, T-shirts, and buttons emblazoned with a "chief." The "Chiefs" are the only pseudo-Indian image that violates most of the criteria. In particular, the pseudo-religious "ceremony" is deeply offensive, structured as it is to suggest primitive-minded Natives worshiping an air force "Chief" as a god. Even worse from a Native point of view, some of them practice a version of smudging, or use images of ceremony pipes, eagle feathers, and sacred paint.[12]

But the structure of the military hardly encourages protest. Few outside of the most senior NCOs knew about the "Chiefs," which shielded them for decades. In 1998 Native retired air force NCOs began petitioning the air force to disband the "Chiefs." The air force had a mixed response, though it was much better than what most universities and professional sports franchise owners were willing to do.

At their hearing, Native retired air force veterans such as Chuck Dineh explained their objections: "I feel not honored and the twenty-eight years in the USAF is a slap in the face as well as a kick in the ass and they rub their honor crap in our faces. What is 'honor?' Honor by the CMSgts groups is that we are less than they are . . . only a mascot . . . it is like stabbing me in the back and into the heart of my culture and religion and it hurts." Other Native veterans attributed being called by the epithet of *chief* to the air force "Chiefs." The principle chief of the Piscataway and the League of Indigenous Sovereign Nations joined Native veterans in publicly denouncing the "Chiefs." Dineh further argued that "the CMSgts mock and degrade the American Indian heritage . . . [they have] sanctioned and been complicit in disparaging Indian religious leaders . . . [and were] a desecration of things held sacred . . . [this was] a trivialization of their religion. . . . These types of artwork are ridiculing and hurtful . . . subjugating one race to a mere mascot." Dineh further dismissed "self-proclaimed holy men on the Internet (that no Indians have heard of)" who defended the "Chiefs" and claimed to be spokespeople for all Natives.[13]

The air force's officers and senior NCOs claimed to be sympathetic but for a long time did not act. Chief Master Sergeant Dennis Fritz agreed the "Chiefs" were offensive. Yet the air force's official position remained that the "Chiefs" were a private organization beyond their authority. Native activists felt Chief Master Sergeant of the Air Force Frederick Finch in particular sanctioned the "Chiefs" by refusing to act. Finch even defended the "Chiefs" by pointing to the Air Force Academy mascot of a falcon, thus equating Natives to animals, as sports mascots do. Chapters of the "Chiefs" in Andrews AFB, Bolling AFB, Zweibrucken, Germany, and the National Capital Regions Chiefs' Group all disassociated themselves from anything resembling American Indian imagery in their ceremonies. The Andrews Chiefs removed all American Indian images from their Web pages. For these actions, other Chiefs groups ridiculed them while Native activists commended them. I attempted to ask the McClellan AFB chapter of "Chiefs" on their online message board what they thought of the campaign against them. Their somewhat paranoid response ended up censoring not only my question but also that of another person asking for general information. Protests against the "Chiefs" continued until April 2005, when the ranking NCO of the entire air force, Chief Master Sergeant of the Air Force Charles Murray, called for their removal.

Murray called "the use of Native American symbols in an official capacity to signify a rank or insignia inappropriate." He considered such use an abuse of taxpayer dollars, saying "items related to our rank and insignia paid for with appropriated funds should not carry Native American symbols." This was not nearly as clear-cut a victory as it might seem. Murray defended the intent of the "Chiefs" as "to capture the virtues of courage, bravery, and honor associated with the American Indian Chief." Note that he referred to Native cultures in a generic sense. He did go on to denounce the practice in stronger terms as "ridiculing and hurtful and a form of discrimination or subjugating one race." But his letter was nonbinding. Far from discouraging these practices, some "Chiefs" groups immediately denounced Murray's remarks as "unfounded and unnecessary." Protests against the "Chiefs" are ongoing as of this writing.[14]

"Accidentally Indian" Names

Many "Indian" names were adopted by the military unintentionally; often a Native name is also a geographic feature, such as a river, cape, or bay, or a city or state. Naming navy ships after Natives often suggests they are part of the landscape and thus becomes part of the frontier mentality. Equating Natives with the landscape is a deeply ingrained practice in Anglo culture, most famously done by historian Frederick Jackson Turner. It implies (or, in many cases, overtly states) that Natives are something wild to be tamed. However, the U.S. military preceded Turner in this practice by over a century, starting with the uss *Delaware* in 1789.[15]

Even units that do not appear to have Native symbols actually do. In 1921, the 102nd Infantry Division took as its symbol an arc. The 102nd was a reserve unit assigned to Arkansas and Missouri. The French referred to the region as "Terre aux arcs" (bow country), a reference to the Natives who lived there. The unit considered an Indian bow a signifier of good marksmanship.[16] New Mexico's National Guard also uses the Native symbol of the zia, from the state flag, on its insignia.

There are a few military symbols that are ostensibly Indian but their indigenousness seems to count for little. The 26th Infantry Regiment, the "Blue Spaders" previously mentioned, describe their symbol as a "stylized Mohawk arrowhead" chosen by Colonel Hamilton Smith, the regimental commander in World War I, as a symbol of "courage, relentless pursuit of an enemy, and resourceful daring." Yet neither the regimental nickname nor their histories show any identification with Indians.[17]

If an alleged Indian name or symbol is chosen accidentally, or if the symbol evokes little that is Indian even to a non-Native, obviously the claim that Indians are being "honored" or even remembered is false. A symbol whose source and origin are muddy or vague fails as a symbol. If anything, Natives are being implicitly refashioned so they can be ignored. "Indian" symbols and names in these contexts become little more than abstractions, meaning only what others project onto them.

Authentic Native Symbolism and Naming

Canada's military had the first authentically Native symbol for a military unit, chosen during World War I. The 114th Canadian Infantry Battalion selected for its symbol two crossed tomahawks over the motto "For King and Country." The 114th had mostly Iroquois soldiers from the Grand River, Kanahwake, and Akwesasne reserves, and two entirely Native companies. Members of the Six Nations Women's Patriotic League added to the flag traditional symbols with meanings in Iroquois lore, a wolf, a hare, and a turtle.[18] Several other things about the 114th's flag are noteworthy. With a somewhat generic initial symbol, the inclusion of the motto also sought, much like Native service in the military in general, to reconcile indigenous needs with the larger society's version of patriotism and co-opt that patriotism to serve Native people. Adding more authentic symbols also fell to the women, in accordance with their time-honored matriarchal status as keepers of tradition within Iroquoian societies.

The U.S. Army 45th Division began in 1920, made up of units of the Arizona, Colorado, New Mexico, and Oklahoma National Guard, with over one-fifth of its members Native. The 45th originally had a red swastika-like image on a yellow background for its symbol, a Native emblem of the Southwest called the swirling cross. The swirling cross, though, spins clockwise while the swastika spins counterclockwise. In 1938, worried that its symbol would be confused with the Nazi swastika, a board of officers changed the symbol to a figure of Native lore, the Thunderbird, the "bearer of unlimited happiness" in the 45th's official histories. Its members proudly referred to themselves as the Thunderbird Warriors. One can find numerous references to members of the 45th and its officers urging the division to think of themselves as warriors.[19]

Was this use of two symbols from Native lore Pan-Indianism or yet another generic Indian symbol? The official histories certainly leave out the enormous and varied roles the Thunderbird plays in the lore of a wide variety of Native peoples in favor of an oversimplified description of its place in indigenous cultures. The Thunderbird is far from a universal Native symbol since it is not part of the lore of many tribes that had members in the 45th. Yet in choosing that symbol as well the earlier swirling cross, the 45th broke with a number of problems with would-be Indian military symbols. Cultures were represented with a symbol that has meaning for Natives, not an image of an Indian whose meaning is for whites. Thus no caricature or stereotype became possible. The Oklahoma National Guard Officer Candidate School also adopted a Pan-Indian symbol, a Native shield with three crosses and a traditional Native pipe, mixed with an olive branch, a Greco-Roman symbol.[20]

A continuing problem was that side by side with the respectful and authentic symbols of the swirling cross and the Thunderbird came yet more generic and pseudo-Indian images that, with slight variations, seemed depressingly stereotypical. On a positive note, at times one could see evidence of two-way syncretism with other conventionally Anglo symbols, such as shields or Latin slogans.[21]

During World War II, the famous elite jungle warfare unit called the Bushmasters began as an all-Indian unit, Company F, 158th Infantry Regiment, 40th Division of the Arizona National Guard. All the members came from Phoenix Indian School. The unit went to Panama to learn jungle warfare, where the members chose as their unit insignia another Native symbol, this one used by Panamanian Indians, a jungle python wrapped around a knife. Like many of the 45th's members, the Bushmasters chose an indigenous symbol that was not of their own cultures.[22]

In 1970 PFC Michael Burns redesigned the Washington State National Guard's 81st Brigade symbol of a raven, incorporating the traditional designs of three different tribal nations in Washington State. The beak, eyes, and mouth are taken from Nootka art, the lower part from the Kwakiutls, and the top of the head from the Haidas. The raven plays a central part in the creation stories of these tribes. Burns chose to include more of the Nootka style in the design because Nootkas actually live in Washington State, unlike the Kwakiutls and Haidas, who reside in Canada. Burns's design is also reminiscent of older designs that use the family crest of George Washington, a raven on a gold coronet.[23]

Finally, there is the naming of ships after specific Native individuals rather than the use of tribal names. In addition to the USNS *Red Cloud*, the U.S. Navy had ships named *Tecumseh*, *Geronimo*, and *Powhattan*. Like Crazy Horse or Black Hawk, military men admired these three for their skill as leaders and tacticians. By naming ships after them, the U.S. Navy paid tribute to a Native leader's intellectual achievements. This stands in marked contrast to naming a ship after a tribe, which implies the stereotype that an entire people are warlike. Yet some navy ships also had names such as *Canonicus* and *Miantonomah*, Native leaders chosen because of their friendship with early colonists. This falls into the good Indian/bad Indian stereotype.[24]

The only other post-1900 American Indian to have a ship named after him besides Mitchell Red Cloud is Vice Admiral James "Jocko" Clark, the first Native to graduate from the Naval Academy and the commander of the 7th Fleet during the Korean War. The USS *Clark's* symbol is a mix of would-be Native symbolism with heraldic designs including wings, a winged sea horse, stars denoting Clark's part in World War II campaigns, and an arrowhead referring to both Oklahoma and his Cherokee heritage.[25]

Naming after "Martial Races" and Humorous Nicknames: Navies and the Coast Guard

The British (and later the Canadian) Royal Navy gave ships the names of "martial races" beginning in at least 1810. The navy not only had ships with Native tribal names, they also had ships named *Ashanti*, *Bedouin*, *Cossack*, *Gurkha*, *Maori*, *Nubian*, *Zulu*, and, perhaps most interestingly, *Scottish American*. Seemingly any "warlike" group the British came into contact with and either sought to conquer, or had as allies, had a ship named after them in this variation of Orientalism. Both the Canadian and the American navies initially copied their British forebear's practice, choosing to restrict such naming almost entirely to their own most persistent adversaries, Native tribal nations.[26]

The Canadian Royal Navy uses badges, three-dimensional heraldic-style carvings hung in the ship's bridge, rather than insignia. Naval historian Gilbert Tucker and Lieutenant W. P. Wallace of the directorate of Naval Intelligence chose nearly all of the current ships' badges and names. The desire to imitate heraldry, and perhaps the English sense of decorum, produced Native images in the Canadian Navy that seemed more dignified than the U.S. Navy. Only the HMCS *Athapascan*'s badge looks stereotypical, showing a whooping Plains Indian on horseback with warbonnet and warpaint, ready to shoot an arrow. From World War II onward the Canadian Navy made it standard practice to name Canadian warships after a Native tribe or band. Prior to World War II, the Canadian Navy introduced the Iroquois or "tribal class" of destroyers.[27]

The first branch of the U.S. military to use images of the Indian actually had the least amount of contact with Natives. The U.S. Navy began consciously using Native names for their ships as far back as the 1780s. Naming ships has always been the responsibility of the secretary of the navy, who acts on the advice of naval researchers. Researchers chose Native names in an extremely haphazard manner, with a willingness to use any name they could find. Some of the ship names included archaic spellings, Native groups that are not located in what is now the United States, and fictional Native characters. The origin of some names is alternately listed as the name of a Native group or a geographic feature. Often there is no indication of Indianness or any awareness that the ship names are in fact Native on the ship insignias at all. Yet at other times it is clear that researchers chose names and symbols with a purpose, yet often with little understanding of Native peoples. Often they used cartoonlike caricatures. Frequently the regalia of the would-be Indian is wrong. But it is still clear that the use of what were perceived to be Native names or symbolism that showed non-Natives often wanted to take upon themselves what they admired: the Indian's great fighting abilities.[28]

During World War II, the U.S. Navy launched a very unwarrior-like class of ships, tugboats, designated as Powhatan class. Naming ships is an elite practice, one set aside for the highest echelons of the civilian bureaucracy. Yet at least in the U.S. Coast Guard, individual servicemen often subvert that. Individual guardsmen often seem to find the practice ludicrous and deserving of mockery. (See table 1 in the appendix.) The most important point is that it is *not* Natives being mocked. If so, one would expect to find derogatory and racist nicknames. Rather it is the assumption that naming a ship after a tribe, often one that guardsmen have never heard of and have no idea why it should matter to them, that is being poked fun at when guardsmen choose to call their ship the "Pregnant Marshmallow" or the "All Ahead Moped" rather than the *Comanche* or the *Mohawk*.[29] Interestingly, coast guard ships often do have mascots. They are never images of people but always live animals.

The Most Sustained Contact: The Army

The Mexican-American War marked the first time white American soldiers used pseudo-Indian imagery. In 1847 the highest-ranking officers occupying Mexico City formed the Aztec Society, followed in 1854 for a time by the Montezuma Society. Its members included three future presidents (Taylor, Pierce, and Grant), three other future major party candidates for president, and three for vice president. The societies used very triumphalist imagery. Their official symbols depicted an American bald eagle, with the sun's rays streaming behind it, flying over either Mayan or Aztec pyramids shrouded in darkness and jungle vines. After the U.S. Civil War, the Aztec Society revived and partly changed its goal to reconciliation between former Confederates and Unionists, reunited by the celebration of their triumph over the half-Indian people of Mexico. Today the Aztec Society continues as an organization open only to the descendents of the original members.[30]

One of the first units with a symbol every bit as triumphalist as that of the Aztec Society was the 134th Infantry Regiment. Its origins are as a Nebraska volunteer militia designed to *fight* Indians. In 1890, shortly after the Wounded Knee massacre, the unit chose a Pawnee phrase, "Lah We Lah Hs," as their motto. Their regimental history claims it was a "tribute to the assistance of the Pawnee." Less than two decades later, the unit added the Katipunan sun, the symbol of Filipino resistance fighters, to their unit flag as a symbol of their triumph. One has to wonder whether the Pawnee slogan served the same purpose.[31]

Section 1 of the Ambulance Service became the first American unit to take a pseudo-Indian symbol in World War I. The unit members were all Americans who volunteered to drive ambulances for the French prior to the U.S. joining the war. On July 26, 1916, a Frenchman named Jean Tardieu designed the unit symbol of an Indian head from the U.S. five-dollar coin, painting the symbol on the sides of the unit's ambulances.[32]

A truck driver gave the U.S. 2nd Division its symbol from the old Indian penny, an Indian warrior with a Plains warbonnet in a five-pointed white star on a black shield. Members took pride in referring to themselves as the Indianhead Warriors. Unit histories show speech after speech given by commanding officers stressing the term *warrior*. Unlike two other army divisions with Indian symbols, the 2nd Division did not begin as a National Guard unit or have a high percentage of Native members.[33]

The 36th Division, the T-O or Arrowhead Division, began as units of the National Guards of Texas and Oklahoma. An arrowhead with a T in its center represented both states, commonly called the T-patch, Lone Star, or Texas division. Throughout both world wars, frontier imagery played a major part in the unit histories, with much being made of the fact that the unit traced its lineage back to the Texan revolts against Mexico. The U.S. Army Rangers began in 1942 and used both the British commandos and Rogers' Rangers as their models. U.S. Special Forces also began at this time and took as their symbol the crossed arrows and knife of the Indian Scouts.[34] The branch of service that had the most contact with Natives, the army, was also the one that uses images most clearly that at least attempt to compliment Natives by using dignified images. It was also likely not a coincidence that the army initially had, until recently, the highest proportion of Natives of any branch of service.

"Nothing But Indians": Air Forces

White American pilots used pseudo-Indian images before an American air corps even began. The Lafayette Escadrille was a group of American fighter pilots who, like Section 1, volunteered to join the French war effort prior to U.S. entry. Virtually all of the pilots came from well-to-do backgrounds and included lawyers, Ivy League dropouts, and wealthy playboys. In the fall of 1916, the Escadrille chose as its symbol a modified version of the Section 1 symbol. The Escadrille chose to add "war paint" to the Indian head, and depicted a warrior in the middle of a "war whoop." A French officer, Lieutenant Colonel George Thenault, described the effect he deigned the insignia to have: "The wild Sioux, with a menacing look about him, drew everyone's eye to the fuselage where it was painted." After the United States joined the war, the Escadrille integrated into the U.S. Army.[35]

The 169th Fighter Squadron Peoria Illinois Air Guard, an Air National Guard unit, chose as its symbol a "warrior" supposedly of the Peoria tribe shortly before World War II. Yet this "warrior" was cartoonish and Disney-esque. An obese "warrior" wore a pilot's headgear with buffalo horns and a feather attached, his face a snarl with streaks of supposed warpaint on his cheeks. Apparently the artist either did not know or did not care that Peorias were not a Plains tribe and did not hunt buffalo and that warpaint has serious religious meaning. Lieutenant Colonel George O'Bryan, a member of the 169th, confirmed that the symbol was "commissioned by Walt Disney himself," taken from the "Indian chief" from *Peter Pan*. O'Bryan insisted they chose the symbol out of respect and wore it with pride, but he admitted that not only were no Natives consulted about the image but that he did not know of any Natives in his unit.[36]

Many military helicopters and aircraft of the Vietnam era had names of Native tribes or representations of Native warriors. Helicopters such as the UH-1 Iroquois (popularly nicknamed the "Huey") bore the name of tribes admired for their warrior qualities. Fighter planes the F-105 Thunderchief, the A-3 Skychief, and the EA-3B Skywarrior also had names and images perceived to be Indian. All three planes had Indian warriors painted on their sides.[37]

The stated policy of naming army aircraft after "nothing but Indians" became official with regulation AR 70-28 on April 4, 1969. The commanding general of U.S. Army Material Command in St. Louis has responsibility for naming army aircraft, and aircraft names must "appeal to the imagination without sacrificing dignity and suggest *an aggressive spirit . . . confidence . . . mobility, firepower, and endurance*" (emphases added). The only army aircraft without Indian names are ones that were named prior to the regulation. Significantly, they have animal names such as the Cobra or the Bird Dog, creatures also admired for their fighting qualities.[38]

Not only did no Natives ever protest such images, two helicopters received the literal blessing, in the most sacred of ways, from the Fort Apache nation. In 1990 and 2001, White Mountain Apaches celebrated with songs, dances, and warrior ceremonies the introduction of the Apache and Apache Longbow helicopters. (Apache and Apache Longbow helicopter parts are also partly manufactured by a Fort Apache tribal enterprise.) The tribal council and elders gave a warrior blessing "to allow man and machine to become as close as possible . . . so that all . . . will return from battle. Our legends [are] of an energy sent by the Creator to the Apache. . . . to battle evil, Dragonslayer was given a bow and an arrow. It is these sacred symbols of the bow and arrow that we present [now]."[39]

Only one military contractor gave its military aircraft Indian names; all other Indian names came from the military leadership. William Piper founded Piper Airplanes, producing aircraft primarily for the civilian market but also bought by militaries all over the world for rescue duties. After Piper's death in 1954, the company made it their policy to name all their aircraft after Indian tribes or weapons. At the same time, histories of the aircraft emphasize that these tribes are extinct. Comanches are described as people that "*once* roamed the Plains" and Cherokees "*once* dwelled in North Carolina." Naming after Indian tribes, their official company history says, honors what the company alleges is Piper's Indian heritage. However, no mention is ever made of what specific tribe he supposedly came from. In a 1970 speech, his son William Jr. described William Piper as "sober British stock that immigrated to New England," proudly listing his father's Protestant virtues. William Jr. also disparaged some Natives such as Apaches under Geronimo as "renegades slaughtering settlers." If the Pipers actually had any Native ancestry, it was likely quite distant in the past.[40]

Particularly during the Vietnam War, army air combat units, such as the 73rd Surveillance Company, gave themselves pseudo-Indian nicknames such as the "Warriors." During the Vietnam War, soldiers attempted to define themselves using Wild West imagery. Air combat units in the army became designated as either "air cavalry" or simply "cavalry." Helicopters were called "scouts" and had the crossed swords of the cavalry painted on them. One can easily find photos of soldiers wearing old cavalry hats and units with non-Indian nicknames taken from the Wild West, such as "Muleskinners" and "Pony Express" as well as Indian names such as "Comancheros."

Though hardly accurate or flattering, these images at least acknowledged Natives' roles other than as fighters. Some of the unit patches depict Natives as aircraft mechanics and medics. The 45th Aviation Company chose as its symbol a grasshopper man in uniform with an air force insignia over the 45th Division insignia of the Native symbol of the Thunderbird. The Air Force Demo Team chose the Thunderbirds as their name as well. The 60th Troop Carrier Group chose a grinning caricature of an Indian holding a medical bag and an airborne soldier. The 73rd chose a Disney-like cartoon of a plane with a snarling Indian head wearing a Plains warbonnet. When the 73rd was the 23rd Special Warfare Aviation Detachment, their symbol was a dancing "warrior" with feathers, warpaint, a loincloth, and an aviation mechanic's toolbox in hand. The 205th Aviation Company named itself the "Geronimos" in 1967 and had as its symbol a Native warrior with an inaccurate Mohawk haircut.[41]

Much like their coast guard counterparts, air combat unit soldiers often thought the naming of aircraft after Indians far less of an honor than did their high-level commanders. Soldiers, too, apparently thought the claim of "honoring" Indian tribes by naming awkward and frequently malfunctioning war machines after them ludicrous, undercutting the "Nothing But Indians" policy with humorous nicknames such as "Flying Bananas."[42] (See table 1 in the appendix.) Yet most army aircraft with pseudo-Indian names have no such nicknames. Likely soldiers' Wild West image of themselves as cavalry was the cause.

In the 1970s the North American Aerospace Command (NORAD) began using "Indian" terms for their aircraft, notably *warrior, chief, brave,* and *Indian.* In 2005 NORAD officials decided they were offensive and dropped them. NORAD spokesman Master Sergeant John Tomassi explained, "We looked at them and then looked at the regulations and found we shouldn't be using those names, because the regs (regulations) say we shouldn't be using any names that could be construed to be disparaging." NORAD chose to replace the pseudo-Indian names with the names of retired aircraft. In some cases the new names were just as clinical, uninspired, baffling, and even unintentionally comical. Amalgam Fabric Brave and Fabric Indian became Amalgam Fabric Dart and Fabric Sabre, for example. The name changes came shortly after the NCAA decided to ban or alter pseudo-Indian names for sports teams, causing some favoring mascots to complain about political correctness entering the military. Tomassi pointed out the changes had been planned for over a year before the NCAA decision. He took the complaints in stride. "Here we are in the midst of a controversy," but added it was not such a bad place to be.[43] His seeming amusement at the complaints contrasts sharply with the shrill anger pro-mascot people often have when hearing their fantasy images criticized.

Indigenous Naming Worldwide

Latin America's militaries have a history of using indigenous names and symbols as almost as long as those of North America. However, Latin American militaries generally followed the practice of criollo (American-born Spaniard) leaders of their independence movements in using indigenous symbols and names to define themselves. The most famous example is Our Lady of Guadalupe, and indeed *Guadalupe* was one of the earliest ship names used by Mexico's new navy, along with *Montezuma* and *Cuahtemoc*, the last two of the First Speakers of the Aztecs. ("Emperor" came from a misnomer applied to them by the Spaniards.) Peru's navy followed this custom as well, with ships named *Huascar*, *Manco Capac*, and *Atalhuapa*, after the three most famous Inca leaders.[44]

Chile's navy had warships named *Fresiq*, *Glaura*, *Lauca*, *Janequeo*, *Rucamilla*, and *Quandora* after Mapuche Indian women gold panners famous for leading a resistance movement against wealthy elites. Perhaps the closest parallel would be if the U.S. Navy had ships named "Harriet Tubman" or "Mother Jones." One curiosity is that Chile also had a ship named after a tribe that never resided anywhere near Chile, the *Guale*, a tribe once in Florida whose descendants today are among the Seminoles.[45]

The Chilean Navy also had ships named after its most numerous Native tribes. *Araucano* and *Arauco* both share the name of the

Araucanians. However, unlike U.S. and Canadian names that have the name of a tribal nation, Latin American naval ship names usually indicate an individual of that nation. It is the difference between naming a ship "America" or the "American." The Mexican Navy did this as well with ships named *Mexicano*, *Yucateco*, and *Campechecano*. The latter two names should be considered indigenous as well, since the people there are overwhelmingly Native. Other ships named after regions that are largely indigenous include Chile's *Iquique*, Argentina's *Patagonia*, and the Dominican Republic's *Cibao*. The closest things to generic Indian images in Latin America's militaries are the Guerrero Poti (Indian warrior), symbol of Grupo de Avacao 2/8 of the Brazilian Air Force, and the Avazteca of the Mexican Air Force. But unlike the many pseudo-Lakota images from the United States, the Guerrero is stylized and abstract. Grupo 2/8 chose its symbol because of its rescue work with the National Foundation for the Indians. Avazteca is a contraction of the words Ava Azteca (Aztec bird) and is a government program to promote aviation.[46]

Very different from the United States, Latin America's military also often uses *negros* or *morenos* (blacks) in their symbols and names. Argentina's navy had a Moreno class of battleships. Chile's navy had a ship named *Loa*, a spirit in the Voodoo religion. Grupo de Avicao 1/7 of the Brazilian Air Force is named Orungan (the four-armed beast god of the air), its symbol designed by Afro-Bahian artist Mario Cravo.[47]

The only U.S. military symbols involving ethnic groups other than Natives are two Hawaiian National Guard units that have a portrait of King Kamehameha. One likely unofficial symbol also shows up in an air force unit stationed in Japan. Along the lines of cheesecake pinup images of women in World War II, the plane has a depiction of a nude (and seemingly very pregnant) Asian woman in the grip of a dragon. A slogan alongside the painting has the crude double-entendre "The Dragon and Its Tail."[48]

A far greater number of would-be Indian names for weapons came to Latin America through American arms sales. This led to the ugly irony of weapons with names such as Iroquois being used against indigenous people in places such as Guatemala, Colombia, and Peru.

Would-be Indian names and symbols became used worldwide, including in Britain, France (with "Chief" Motorcycles), Turkey, Thailand, and even the Soviet Union during World War II. One of the few exceptions to this is the British-manufactured warplane the Dakotah, an apparent carryover from the "martial races" naming practices.[49]

Conclusion

Between the time of the uss *Delaware* and the usns *Red Cloud*, Natives in the U.S. military went from occasional allies to an ethnic group within conventional military ranks. Whether Natives are romanticized or vilified by white military elite perceptions, pseudo-Indian symbols are an exercise in role-playing by non-Natives who wish to take on what they perceive to be Indian qualities. With extremely rare exceptions, only Indians (or what whites perceive to be an Indian image) are singled out for these practices in the United States, even though other minority groups may collectively possess equally as impressive military or martial records. What this shows is the need of many whites to ameliorate their deeply divided feelings over Natives, as people they both admire and toward whom they harbor deep feelings of guilt and fear. The relatively small size and isolation of Natives from whites, the lack of knowledge about the Native population, and the reinforcement of stereotypes by Hollywood kept many whites from seeing the gaping disjunctures between their stereotyped symbols and real Natives.

Native and would-be Indian symbols and names in the military affect how others perceive Native servicemen. The sheer volume of images and names strains credibility to claim otherwise. If Hollywood images, pulp and romance novels, the New Age movement, and sports mascots all affect Native-white relations, naturally military images do as well. The question then becomes a chicken and egg one, whether these images set the conditions for how the military treated Native recruits when they entered in large numbers in World War I, or simply were a stereotyped response after the fact. That would-be Indian names were already common in the navy suggests the former, but the many new stereotyped symbols in the army suggest the latter.

These symbols and names are both an indicator of how Natives are viewed in the military by their superiors and a factor in how Native servicemen are treated in the service by everyone. Enlisted non-Natives tend to resist these stereotypes from their superiors and take these attempts to "honor" far less seriously. That Natives often controlled the images of themselves or that non-Natives also sought out more accurate and respectful images is a sign of a climate that has gradually improved over time in an institution notorious for resisting change. Even the worst of these symbols showed a willingness on the part of whites to make exceptions for Native servicemen and created an opening other minority groups did not have. It is almost certainly no coincidence that the first unit to be desegregated, the 45th Division, bears the name the Thunderbird Warriors and has both authentic and stereotyped Indian symbols. Native servicemen took these stereotypes and used them to contest the very racism they were designed to reinforce.

5

The Super Scout Image

Using a Stereotype to Help Native Traditions Revive

"We, the Chiefs and Counselors of the Six Nations of the Indians, residing in the State of New York, do hereby proclaim to all the Warrior and Warriors of the Six Nations that war is declared on our part upon the provinces of Upper and Lower Canada. Therefore, we do hereby command and advise all the War Chiefs to call forth immediately their warriors under them and put them in motion to protect their rights and liberties which our brethren the Americans are now defending."—Iroquois Declaration of War, July 1813

IN SEPTEMBER 1812 Iroquois warriors allied with the British took part in rituals to prepare for war. They dressed, painted themselves, and sang purifying songs taunting their enemies and celebrating their own bravery and exploits. They sacrificed pigs with invocations asking for safe return and spiritual protection from enemies.[1]

Shortly after World War I, four Ho Chunk (Winnebago) Indian veterans related tales of their wartime experiences in a traditional ceremony lasting four nights. They spoke to the spirits of the German soldiers they killed in war. In Ho Chunk tradition, a warrior is believed to command the spirits of those he has killed in battle. They told the German soldiers to accompany Hino'nika, one veteran's wife who passed away, to gather wood and food for her and carry her tobacco. The Ho Chunks believed they honored the spirits of the German soldiers, showing they could be trusted because of their bravery in battle.[2]

What had changed in the century between these wars? Two ceremonies took place a hundred years apart, but the latter occurred within the context of veteran traditions rather than warrior ones. Historian Carl Benn believes the Iroquois transformed from allies of the United States to, frankly, subjects to be commanded, soldiers in a formal military, just one more ethnic group. Benn argues the War of 1812 became the last in which the Iroquois truly acted independently. When Benn looked at photos of them from the Civil War and World War I, he mourned their loss of distinctive garb and what he saw as assimilation. In part he turned out to be right, but only in describing what outsiders saw. Iroquois and many other Natives saw (and still see) things quite differently, and continue to maintain and work toward their own assertions of themselves as *still* independent allies.

The Ho Chunk ceremony and many others like it after the First World War became the last thing that white reformers, philanthropists, and self-styled friends of the Indian wanted to see. They thought war should be a "civilizer," a force for assimilation, a way to finally "kill the Indian, save the man." Natives were supposed to naturally fall away from their traditional cultures and practices from prolonged contact with a largely white military. Some Natives did look upon the military as an avenue toward white notions of civilization for themselves, but these ideas usually came from boarding schools, where Natives had already been through an extended "Americanization" effort.

For other Natives who joined the service during World War I, the military became a way to keep or revive traditional ways and at the same time adapt to the larger society and change in general. Many Native communities did *not* take part in the war or even tried to refuse to do so. Many Native people who took part most eagerly in the war were, in fact, the most assimilated. Yet to much of Anglo America, the embrace by many Native people of the military only confirmed all their old stereotypes of "the Indian" as one homogenous group who uniformly lusted for the chance to fulfill their "naturally" bloodthirsty nature.

American Indians went into World War I—and earlier the Civil War and the Spanish-American War—simultaneously weighed down by the burden and lifted up by the images that Anglo preconceptions assigned to them. This burdening and lifting was the culmination of a long historical process based on the old notions of the "Vanishing

Indian," one with an inherently "savage" nature. American Indians tried to use this Anglo image to receive better treatment than that historically given other nonwhites. By using that "savagery" in the service of the military and seeming to harness it to conventional patriotism, many also won the approval of Indian Bureau officials to practice traditional ways a decade and a half before the lifting of the ban on Native ceremonies during the New Deal for Indians. War efforts to enlist the Indian started with the intention of ending Native traditions but wound up reviving old ones or even initiating new ones. The first beginnings of a syncretic adaptation of Native warrior traditions into veteran traditions began in some Native groups as far back as the War of 1812, the Civil War, or as scouts during the Indian Wars of the nineteenth century. Some Anglo proponents of assimilation, such as William Pratt, pushed for the assimilation of Natives into the military during the Spanish-American and Philippine wars much like as in World War I. But Natives often responded to this assimilation push with acts of cultural solidarity and defiance, joining warrior societies, taking part in ceremonies for protection before and honoring afterward, carrying personal medicine, and writing new war and flag songs. Not until World War II did these traditions become widespread among tribal nations all over the United States and Canada, including those that had not previously had a warrior ethos.

Laying the Groundwork for Distinctively Native Veteran Traditions: The Iroquois Experience and the Indian Scouts

The notion of the Vanishing Indian has a long pedigree in American history, going hand in hand with white beliefs in the degree to which Native people could or should be assimilated into "mainstream" American society. The Vanishing Indian goes back as far as 1703, when Baron Louis de Lahontan used the Huron leader Kondiaronk as the model for the character of Adario in his work *Voyage*. (Ironically, Kondiaronk was Christian.) This belief in the Vanishing Indian blamed the victim, shifting guilt away from the actual people who caused the loss of Native life and ways. One of its most famous proponents was no less a personage than Lewis Henry Morgan, the father of American anthropology. Morgan started a secret society called the New Confederacy of the Iroquois. They named their initiation ceremony Inindianation. The (all-white) members donned Indian clothing and listened to someone impersonating the "voice of the Great Spirit" say, "The red men are my children. Long ago, in the future I saw their destruction."[3] To Morgan's credit, contact with actual Iroquois, especially Ely Parker, the future military secretary and head of the Indian Bureau under President Grant, convinced him to stop taking part in rituals designed to appease white guilt. Unlike most other white "friends of the Indian," Morgan took part in activism to defend Native traditions. Nearly all other whites in the eighteenth century wishing to be benevolent toward Native people took the approach consistent with the cultural assumptions of the time: assimilation.

Americans inherited from the British a way of dealing with Native people that stressed physical segregation enforced by military domination. In the earlier stages they had also recognized that, while Native people might have extraordinary martial and woodsman's abilities, these were in no way inborn or intrinsic to their nature. Anglo-Americans understood such abilities to be the result of long practice dictated by environmental necessity. White travelers in Native areas as far back as the early eighteenth century labeled Natives' abilities to hunt and track as "superhuman" but also recognized these abilities were not inborn. Claiming Native skills to be "inherent" was an excuse.[4]

Many Native peoples trace the beginnings of their veteran traditions to older military alliances between their nation and the United States. The most famous of these are the Indian Scouts. The relatively small number of Indian Scouts are written about and memorialized more than all other Native veterans combined, in literally hundreds of history books, novels, and films. Most older works frankly hold them up as Tontos, the "good and faithful companions" against the "bad Indians," with little understanding of their motives or place within their respective Native cultures. Some of the better works of history, such as Thomas Dunlay's *Wolves for the Blue Soldiers*, show a far more nuanced and complicated picture, depicting scouts as neither Tontos nor "sellouts" but as having agency and making rational choices within their cultural context.

For our purposes here, the chief question is whether the Indian

Scouts set a precedent of adapting veteran traditions from older war-rior traditions; some tribal people say yes. Pawnee scouts were one of the largest groups of scouts, even forming their own battalion and fighting as allies of the United States against the Lakota. But the Pawnees themselves are aware of the irony, conflicts, and disjunctures involved. The U.S. Army massacred a group of Pawnee scouts less than a month after their discharge, with their papers still on them. The U.S. military itself took part in gathering bones and ancestral remains on behalf of medical researchers and archaeologists, which to Natives is an act of indefensible desecration. Nevertheless, as Pawnee historian James Riding In points out, "Virtually every living Pawnee traces his or her ancestry back to at least one of the hundreds of men who served as scouts from 1864 to 1876. . . . The scouts established a tradition of military service that continues today." Pawnee drum groups composed special songs to honor their memory. Pawnee heri-tage organizations carried out civic and social functions in their spirit. Some members of the Fort Apache nation similarly memorialized their original Apache scouts, the very ones who helped pursue Goyathlay (Geronimo) and forced his surrender, rather than the Apaches who fought against the United States.[5] In both cases scouts sought advan-tage for themselves and their people. In neither case are they regarded as foolish or unfaithful to their people, though both nations have a strong awareness of the low character of the federal government in its dealing with Indians.

Even before the first Indian Scouts, we can find the case of the War of 1812 and the Iroquois. The Six Nations began the war as allies, not subjects. In the early part of the war, Indian agent Erastus Granger taunted a crowd of Iroquois warriors, telling them that the United States did not need Iroquois support. But, he told them, two hundred warriors could enroll in the army if they gave up their "cowardly" way of war and conformed to U.S. military standards. Benn argues the Iroquois fought as light infantry in the war, which suited them uniquely well. In the War of 1812, many American troops came from local militia without uniforms and went as dictated by their own needs. Iroquois behavior seemed often not so different from white militias. During the war, the British began giving pensions to Iroquois warriors, widows, prisoners, and the maimed, expanding on their earlier practice of gift giving. The United States also began paying formal wages and pensions to the Iroquois, leading to a permanent change: 1814 became the last year the Iroquois fought entirely independently, under their own leaders. In 1814 U.S. Army Major General Jacob Brown organized the Indian Volunteer Corps, with white company officers and Native field officers. We also know that at least five Iroquois women received widow's pensions. Many later Six Nations veterans trace their family veteran traditions to this war.[6]

The earliest written account we have from a Native veteran of the U.S. military comes from Pequot soldier William Apess. Apess has drawn the attention of a number of scholars in recent years, notably Robert Allen Warrior and Jace Weaver. But very little of that focus has been on his time as a soldier. Most scholars in American Indian Studies instead discuss Apess as a survivor of genocide, displacement, and self-hatred, and his conversion to Christianity as a response to these brutal hardships. Other scholars focus on questions of authenticity and his mixed-blood status.

Though his account of his time in the service takes up only five pages of his autobiography, every contradiction involved in Indians joining the military is evident. Far from seeking out the military, Apess literally stumbled upon a recruiting sergeant while drunk, and remained hostile to the institution and people for whom he had no respect: "I could not think why I should risk life and limb in fighting for the white man whom had cheated my forefathers out of their land and become as bad as them." Apess chose to be a drummer, objecting to carrying a weapon. He became more cynical as time went on, witnessing executions for desertion and failing to get the bounty or land promised to him. Apess angrily criticized American society for denying rights, citizenship, and voting to Natives. Yet even he, as a survivor of a tribe that endured some of the most brutal genocide anywhere in what became the United States, seems to have bought into aspects of Americanization. Apess refers to American victories in battle as "a proud day for *our* country" and looks upon American citizenship as a right desperately needed.[7] Apess did not foresee that the War of 1812 would be a turning point, after which Natives would have no

European/white allies of opposing nation-states to play against one another, and no steady source of firearms. But it would be wrong to condemn him for not sharing the sense of dual identity or belief in the treaty relationship most Natives have today. As a member of a nearly annihilated people, he was in an even more desperate position than, say, Pawnees or Iroquois.

The Civil War: Native Veteran Traditions Begin in Oklahoma and the Northeast

Twenty thousand Natives served in the Civil War. Historian Laurence Hauptman has argued that Indians' motives for enlisting ranged from poverty, dependence on or a desire to be integrated into the United States, adventure, alliances, treaties, earlier tradition, gaining status among other Indians, the draft, and, above all, a tenuous existence.[8] For our purposes, we need to look at whether this war set precedents and examine the degree of alleged assimilation, and signs of retained cultures. What follows in this chapter and in most of the succeeding chapters is marshalling the evidence and analyzing the results, looking especially at Native motives for taking part.

Presbyterian missionary Asher Wright influenced Iroquois soldier Newt Parker to join up. Parker spoke of "having God for our shield, our protection, our spiritual advisor." Tuscarora soldier Nicholas Cusick, or War Eagle among his own people, became a Peace Chief and Turtle Clan sachem; there are many stories in Tuscarora oral traditions about him today. Iroquois Captain Emmett Fiske spoke of "warrior soldiers of his tribe." Newspaper accounts accused Iroquois at the Battle of Batchelder's Creek of scalping, but New York state historian Hugh Hastings, writing in 1897, discounted that as propaganda. Cusick described how "300 sturdy warriors took the warpath" after the state petitioned them to join the war.[9]

As Ulysses Grant's military secretary, Ely Parker became the most famous Native soldier of the war, joining the Union army only after asking permission from his father, who then encouraged him when he received his officer's commission. The Senecas held a feast to honor him, and Seneca elders called the Proclaimers of the Law invoked spirits to guard Parker. After the war he described their aid: "I developed the instinct to feel the presence of game or danger. Perhaps I had the goodwill of the spirits." Altogether, three hundred Iroquois joined the Union side, including two who served as army surgeons. Though it did not last or always protect them, for a time Iroquois received concessions from the state government for their service, being declared competent to vote and be citizens.[10]

Already we see a sharp split between what Anglos thought of Indian motives and what Natives themselves often said, along with Natives not being too eager to correct Anglos if the misconception could be used to their advantage. E. M. Pettit, the superintendent of Seneca schools run by the state, claimed Iroquois enlistees to be "truly patriotic, based upon an enlightened view." Trustees of the Thomas Asylum for Orphans and Destitute, who sent many Iroquois into the military, also claimed that Iroquois joined out of loyalty and patriotism. Within the Iroquois, not everyone agreed with some aspects of veteran traditions. After the Civil War some Tuscaroras resented Cusick for fighting against other Indians, while others saw what he did as a warrior's path.[11]

The Oneidas in Wisconsin, fellow Six Nations relatives, came as reluctant latecomers to the Civil War; because they had been subjected to constant land swindles, Oneidas saw less reason to join. The tribe divided over how to respond to white removal efforts. Anglo draft resistance near the reservation may also have influenced them. Some local whites saw the Oneidas as replacements that could be used to avoid having to actually go to war themselves, and bounties for enlistment caused many Oneidas to cynically agree. Forty-three Iroquois asked for discharges because they had never received bounties or because they were underage and wanted out of the service. Samuel George, an Iroquois veteran of the War of 1812, convinced President Lincoln to intervene. Some Mohicans also protested against the draft to the War Department, asserting it to be illegal.[12]

Tuscarora leader Clinton Rickard recalled Iroquois warrior societies had ended by the time he served as a young man in the Spanish-American War. I have seen no evidence of them in the Civil War. This may be part of why so many Iroquois eagerly embraced the Grand Army of the Republic (GAR). The GAR admitted Iroquois and had ceremonial ranks and semi-religious rituals in their meetings. Both Anglo members of the GAR and Iroquois attended the funeral for Ely Parker in Fairfield, Connecticut. Parker was later reinterred in Buffalo, with the GAR sponsoring the headstone. The GAR also appeared at the funeral of Cusick, who was buried at old Fort Niagara. Up until at least the 1920s the GAR held funerary rites for Iroquois veterans. Iroquois ceremonies remained important, however. Seaman William Jones, the day after his return home, took part in the Green Corn Dance, the War Dance, and later the Six Nations council.[13]

For the Delawares, 170 out of 201 of their men in the Union army enlisted. Delawares had different religious traditions, including Baptist, Moravian, Presbyterian, Mormon, and the Delaware traditional religion, Big House. Indian agent Frank Johnson believed Delawares enlisted for "patriotism unequalled" and even the most "wild and untutored" Delaware to be "alive to his own interest, the interest of his own tribe, and the country." Captain Falleaf, or Panipakuxwe, recruited Company D of the 2nd Kansas Home Guard. After the war, Falleaf petitioned the Interior Department so that he and his people could "live as before"; he also argued for communal landholding.[14]

About 125 Menominee enlisted during the Civil War; one-third of them had been killed by war's end. Joseph Gauthier, a nephew of Menominee leader Chief Toma, recruited for the U.S. Army and wrote the "Song of Enlistment" in the Civil War. For all of the claims of many whites that enlisting showed that Indians wanted to abandon their cultures, in the Civil War we already see Natives adopting their songs to the newer veteran traditions. The song is seemingly not too flattering a picture.

The white man came and took the Indians[15]

Like the Iroquois, both traditional beliefs and newer veterans' groups remained important to the Menominee. One Menominee, Cawunipunas, asked that photos show his Grand Army of the Republic badge. Cawunipunas attributed his safe return to carrying the tail feathers of a striker bird as directed by his dream. Another Menominee, Kapo'sa, carried the feathers of a white eagle and a buzzard for protection and wrote the "Song of Protection during the Civil War."

All the powerful birds like me and gave this song[16]

On the insurgents' side, while memorialized by Confederate apologists as "Cherokee cavaliers," many of the Five Tribes who allied with the Confederacy did so out of fear or a feeling of abandonment by the United States. Other Cherokees decried Stand Watie, the leader of pro-Confederate Cherokee units, as un-Cherokee, assimilated, and out of touch with tradition. According to a Cherokee delegation to Washington, Watie was "disaffected" and E. C. Boudinot, the other prominent leader of Confederate Cherokees, was Cherokee by birth but not education, a New Englander at heart and never a Cherokee citizen. The great majority of Cherokees were pro-Union and saw Boudinot's paper the *Arkansian* as "consecrated to . . . the sacrificing of the Cherokee people . . . upon the altar of . . . Southern avarice and Southern hate."[17]

The Eastern Cherokees were an interesting paradox, often insisting they were American citizens but fighting for the Confederacy. William Thomas recruited two hundred Eastern Band as a home guard, the Junauska Zouaves. Similar to the case of New York State and the Iroquois, the state of North Carolina conceded the Eastern Band the right to live in the state in recognition of their service. Zouaves came from an interesting phenomenon of the time, European/white soldiers dressed in imitation of Middle Eastern fighters. This led to the interesting situation of Indians dressing much the same way as Anglo soldiers who "played Arab" as part of the fad popular in many army units in Europe and the United States. This was not too different from "playing Indian," as many U.S. servicemen did (see chapter 4).[18]

Ritual and tradition remained important to Eastern Band soldiers as well. Anthropologist James Mooney described a ritual of Cherokees consulting an "oracle stone" prior to battle and also seeing a War Dance at the town of Soco. Oosawih, a Cherokee herbal doctor, used traditional medicine to cure Cherokee soldiers who had measles and mumps.[19]

Many other Indians living in the South, particularly the Pamunkeys and Lumbees, joined the Union side to preserve their communities in the face of long conflicts with white Southerners. Lumbee guerilla bands worked with escaped black slaves and white Union soldiers from Confederate prison in Florence, South Carolina. The most famous leader of these guerillas, Henry Berry Lowry, is still honored today by the Lumbees with plays, pageants, and annual awards bearing his name.[20]

Ojibwes and Ottawas in Michigan who joined the Union army chose a unique "battle flag" for their unit, a live eagle perched on a pole on a platform. An Anglo officer, Colonel Deland, described Company K of the 1st Michigan Sharpshooters as a "company of civilized Indians" led by Garrett Graveret as "educated a half breed as a band as ever struck a warpath." At the Battle of the Crater, Lieutenant Freeman Bowley of the 30th Colored Troop recalled, "Some of them were mortally wounded and drawing their blouses over their faces, they chanted a death song and died, four of them in a group."[21] These and many other incidents point to a strong cultural retention of identity and tradition throughout the many Indian units in the Civil War.

Manifest Destiny Marches On: The Spanish-American War and the Filipino Uprising

Little of this cultural retention affected the long-term treatment of Natives within or outside of the military. Anglo-American approaches toward and beliefs about Native people changed dramatically with the case of *Standing Bear v. Crook* in 1871. The cause of Standing Bear, an elderly Ponca man imprisoned for leaving the reservation, was taken up by Thomas Tibbles, a white journalist married to a Native woman. Tibbles successfully filed a writ of habeas corpus on Standing Bear's behalf. This case had two major effects. For the first time Anglo law recognized Indians as legal persons. The case also marked the first time Native people successfully challenged the government's ability to impose reservations upon Native people using the law. In the aftermath, Standing Bear went on a tour sponsored by Tibbles and Susette and Joseph Laflesche, famed mixed-blood Native proponents of assimilation. From the tour came a public outpouring of demands for a solution to Native peoples' marginal status.[22]

Most whites of the time believed assimilation was the solution to the "Indian problem." That belief found concrete expression in the Dawes Allotment Act. Allotment started as a severely misguided reform scheme. Only later with the increased demand for private farmland did it become a naked land grab. Anglos assumed that Native people, unlike other nonwhites, were capable of being "civilized." These assumptions clearly had an overpowering cultural bias but were not based on biological racism. While these assumptions stopped far from calling for full equality, they did have strong underlying implications of a much more limited equality. This belief in assimilation not only allowed for at least economic self-sufficiency for Natives, it actually committed Anglo-American society to achieving this while assuming political and social equality to be unattainable and undesirable.[23]

Yet as white demands for the remaining Native lands grew toward the end of the century, biological racism overtook cultural racism. Policymakers had begun to give up on achieving Native self-sufficiency by the 1890s, being either unwilling to invest the resources needed or unable to convince others of the necessity to do so. With the advent of U.S. adventures in imperialism around the turn of the century, reservations became openly treated as internal colonies, primarily a source for cheap natural resources. Theodore Roosevelt's openly hateful belief that Natives were psychologically incapable of even having a culture stood as the most obvious instance of the newer belief that the Indian's biology or "race" was his destiny and any attempt to uplift him was wasted effort.[24]

Such a belief did not keep Roosevelt from utilizing Native abilities for his own aims in the Spanish-American War. The most famous Native soldiers of the war served in the Rough Riders. William Pollock, a Pawnee, carried the regimental flag. Pollock described his own motives: "In the memory of our brave fathers, I will try and be like one of them." But he conceded, "Some folks at home thought I was very foolish to put myself into such a situation." Pollock spoke further of his "duty as a soldier under the service of the U.S. government." At least one account describes Pollock's "war whoops." "Black Jack" Pershing celebrated the famous charge up San Juan Hill as an incident of racial reconciliation "unmindful of race or color . . . mindful only for their common duty as Americans." Pershing remained in the minority among Anglos. Newspaper accounts luridly trumpeted stereotypes with Buffalo Bill's claims that he had six hundred Lakotas ready to fight the war. No such group ever appeared.[25]

Two Yaqui brothers, Joseph and Frank Brito, also served in the Rough Riders. Roosevelt gave Frank the nickname "Monte" (short for Montezuma). Joseph went on to take part in crushing the Filipino struggle for independence and went missing in action, presumed dead. After the war Frank became something of a rarity off reservation, a Native law officer, at different times a deputy, sheriff, town constable, city jailer, and game warden. He also joined the National Guard, taking part in the pursuit of Pancho Villa. Cherokee soldier Thomas Isbell served as one of four point men for the Rough Riders. Of the thirty-four battle casualties suffered by Oklahomans during the war, more than half came from Indian Territory. At least this far back Natives were already being put into battle at high rates.[26]

George Bird Grinnell, best known as a painter and naturalist, proposed raising regiments of Native soldiers, ironically because of his bigoted opinion of some immigrants: "I do not trust these dagos to fight, nor how much dependence is to be placed on them, whereas I know the Indians will fight." The most famous of the Indian boarding school superintendents, Richard Pratt, asserted that Native wartime service vindicated his assimilation approach to education. But simultaneously he betrayed an assumption of Natives as "naturally" suited for warfare: "The interest they show suggests that . . . *universal enlistment* can be made . . . for the welfare of the nation."[27] The first known Native women veterans, the Congregation of American Sisters, an order of Lakota Catholic nuns from Fort Berthold Reservation, joined the U.S. Army as nurses, pushed by a strong belief in assimilation by their leader (see chapter 11).

In the brutal crushing of the Filipino independence movement, white racists depicted Filipinos as racially and culturally "Indian," their conquest thus justified by the same rationale. Indeed both the leading opponents and supporters of the United States against the Philippines used the Indian Wars as examples when stating their case. The Anti-Imperialist League's first act was to adopt a resolution urging the United States to cease conquest of foreign populations until "we have shown we can protect the rights of men within our own borders,

like the colored race of the South and the Indians of the West." Teddy
Roosevelt, in his letter accepting the nomination as vice president,
argued giving self-government to Filipinos "would be like granting
self-government to an Apache reservation under some local chief."
The *Portland Oregonian* argued in an editorial, "The Manifest Destiny
idea of the 40s has been surpassed by the actuality of 50 years later."
A front-page headline in March 1899 proclaimed Filipinos "Worse
Than Indians." U.S. Army Philippine scouts fought "Filipinos Filipino
fashion" and were taught to "sneak up Indian fashion." Corporal
Chriss Bell described a local tribe, the Kanakas, as "lazy good natured
folk not unlike our Indians."[28]

These racialized descriptions varied according to the need to justify the war. Filipinos became "Indians" when seen as primitive or
when their land needed to be taken, "black" or "nigger" when their
killing had to be justified, and Hispanicized when white racists saw
race mixing. Manila became filled with "natives and mestizas" in
descriptions in *The Soldier's Letter*. Soldier William Platt described
the son of Anglo officer Captain Wilkinson and his Filipina wife as
"look[ing] like any Mexican boy, very cute." Soldier George Telfer
similarly found Filipino "manners are enough of the Latin race to be
pleasing," though their children were "like the darkey babies, only
smarter." Another soldier, Albert Southwick, described going "nigger
hunting" after insurgents, but claimed the Macabebes allied with the
United States to be "probably the most civilized." George Telfer worried about "standing off any stray party of Indians." But when fighting
face-to-face, Telfer called Filipinos "niggers." "It is great fun to for the
men to go on nigger hunts. The air would be delightful were it not for
the odor from dead niggers. . . . We received some Krg Jorgenson rifles
today. So now we can reach Mr. Nig at his own distance."[29]

But unseen attackers always became "Indians." Private Chriss Bell
described how he and his fellow soldiers "shoot on sight all Natives.
Natives will not or cannot understand kind and civilized treatment."
A fellow soldier named Telfer compared the Spanish former elites to
Filipinos: "These Spaniards are really our best friends . . . the natives
have not a single virtue to redeem them. They are infinitely lower and
viler than our own Indians." Segregated all-black units were some of

the few to try to identify with Filipinos or support their cause. In a letter in the *Cleveland Gazette*, a black soldier wrote, "I should class the Filipinos with the Cubans . . . some of the best mulatto people I have ever seen in my life." In a letter home black soldier Arthur Peterson described tribal Filipinos as "only semi civilized," but "the most moral people I ever saw. Our civilized brethren . . . could learn something in that line. . . . They are something like our North American Indian."[30]

Tuscarora soldier Clinton Rickard fought in the U.S. war of conquest against the Philippines from 1901 to 1904. Just prior to that he served as part of the guard detail for, ironically, then Vice President Roosevelt. Rickard's great-uncle fought in the Civil War. His great-great-grandfather fought in the Revolutionary War. Rickard sincerely believed that the aim of the war was to "bring order" to the Philippines for Filipinos' own good and defended that belief to the end of his life. But the racialized view of the war affected him, too. Once, when called in to his new commander's tent, his captain thought him to be Filipino and called frantically to his guards, "For God's sake, pacify this wild Indian!"[31]

Like his ancestors, Rickard relied on traditional teachings to cope with war. He recalled in his autobiography how his grandmother prophesied for him as a young boy that he would go into battle, seeing two flags, an American and one she did not recognize. She told Clinton he would be fired upon by one side, then the other, and would almost lose his life but would come back and devote himself to helping his people, living a long life. Rickard also saw his grandmother's spirit visit him in the Philippines on the day of her death. Rickard thought of veterans' organizations as similar to the old warrior societies; after the war he joined the Army and Navy Union, the United Spanish War Veterans, and a Masonic lodge. Rickard himself played the lead role in organizing Tuscarora Post 8242 of the VFW. Throughout the remainder of his long life, he led struggles against the loss of land, Termination, and registration of Iroquois as aliens, and, most important for this subject, he led the struggle *against* drafting Iroquois in both world wars. In 1999 the North American Iroquois Veterans Association honored Rickard at their annual powwow.[32]

"America's Cossacks": "Friends of the Indian" and Native Response to World War I

U.S. entry into World War I brought a rush of many Native people to volunteer for the military, but this became by no means as universal or "natural" as many Anglo-Americans assumed. Volunteering turned out to be the greatest, in some cases 100 percent, among Natives from government boarding schools. Tribes with a strong martial tradition had lesser, though still high, enlistment. Isolated tribes, or those with little or no martial tradition, had an enlistment rate of less than 1 percent.[33]

Anglo-American philanthropists seized upon the war as a way to save the Indian by utilizing his "natural savagery." This belief—that Indians would otherwise vanish—became central to the arguments of those pressing most strongly for Native people to be not only allowed but *required* to take part in the military as their sole life's work and the only thing for which their "natural" abilities suited them. In his address to the Congressional Committee on Military Affairs on June 25, 1917, one of the most famous self-appointed "friends of the Indian," the eccentric Joseph Dixon, called for military schools for all Native male youths from ages eight to eighteen. Once they completed schooling, all Native males would then be drafted into military service. Their permanent position in U.S. society would become "America's Cossacks." Dixon's argument relied on a wide variety of biased assumptions, ones that even a lifetime around Native people failed to alter in him. He saw the Indian as a "born scout from the cradle up . . . a natural soldier [and] a good hater." He argued that all young American Indian males must be forced into the military before the rest of America stopped hearing "the dying echo of moccassined feet." Sending Natives off to war, he claimed, was what they were suited for, because "by no stretch of the imagination can we conceive of the Indian as a pacifist."[34]

Dixon ignored massive amounts of readily available data and subsumed over five hundred Native peoples and traditions into one homogenous mass. No one need "imagine" that Natives could be pacifist; many Native traditions *are* in fact historically more peaceful than warlike, and in a few cases they are largely pacifist. The most famous examples are the Hopis and the Zunis. After a prolonged struggle with authorities, both tribes achieved religious conscientious objector status like the Amish or Quakers. None of the Native peoples of California, the Great Basin, or the Arctic and sub-Arctic had any known history or tradition of warfare prior to European arrival.[35]

Even for traditions that had a warrior ethos, Dixon's argument assumed these traditions to be just a more "savage" version of European warfare. But Native martial traditions generally taught that war was an unnatural state, one requiring extensive ritual preparation to enter into and even more extensive purification to return to a normal and balanced spiritual and mental state afterward. Dixon also ignored that the aim of warfare in most Native cultures was fundamentally different. The aims tended to be raiding for sustenance, prestige, or revenge rather than total warfare designed to conquer territory or political subjugation. To find a Native tradition of political conquest, one must go to Mesoamerica, or to Native nations allied to Europeans in the colonial period.[36]

Dixon was not alone in his belief. Western historian Frank Lindemann also used the war to argue for assimilation and depicted Crow leader Chief Plenty Coups as simply *American* in his biography of the same name. Lindemann argued, "No white man has ever thoroughly known the Indian," and in any case, "The real Indians are gone." Lindemann claimed in his books that Plenty Coups spoke to the spirit of George Washington, asking for help to save his people, and stressed Plenty Coups's urging Crow men to fight in the world war. Officials in the Department of the Interior concurred with views like Dixon's and Lindemann's. A bulletin after the war described how "one Cheyenne typical no-account reservation Indian with long hair" changed into a "square shouldered, level-eyed, courteous, self-reliant [man] and talked intelligently."[37]

Massive draft resistance among Natives proved to be the most dramatic contradiction of Dixon's and Lindemann's beliefs. Some Navajos and Utes threatened draft register employees. The Goshute engaged in a tribal-wide protest that involved the majority of their members. The National Guard had to be called in to forcibly register members of the tribe. The Pamunkeys and Mattaponis of Virginia successfully petitioned to have their members exempted from the draft.[38] In most of these cases the root of the resistance proved not be an aversion to war per se, as the violent nature of almost all of the protests shows. The roots of Native dissatisfaction came from the denial of citizenship, land rights, or the violation of treaties in which the United States pledged to never require tribal members to fight in America's wars. Yet the fact remains: many Native peoples proved *not* to be eager to go back to their allegedly "warlike" ways at the first chance.

Most scholars tried to downplay or dismiss Native draft resistance as aberrations. The usual explanation historians gave is that Native draft resisters failed to understand the registration process because of language difficulties or lack of contact with Anglo ways. Where this explanation is somewhat lacking is that two of the most notable cases came from among the Five Civilized Tribes, the Creeks, and the Seminoles. The Iroquois were another. These Indian nations had over a century of continually dealing with white legal and governmental systems. Like the Five Tribes, Native tribes of Virginia also had a long history of sustained contact with whites and a high proportion of English speakers. The assumption by some scholars that Native draft resisters acted out of ignorance had a counterpart among the Indian Bureau during the war. Bureau employees often derided Indian draft resisters as mentally unbalanced.

Virtually alone among scholars, historian Erik Zissu has argued that Native draft resisters did in fact understand the draft as well as their white counterparts did. Zissu took a look at the Creek and Seminole cases and found a clear understanding of registration and a sophisticated response to it. Their Green Corn Rebellion involved several hundred Natives who planned to march on Washington to join a mass movement of farmers and workers opposed to the war. Mass arrests by the Home Guard and local vigilantes prevented this. Further east, the Cherokees of North Carolina remained indifferent to the war. When reservation superintendent James Henderson tried to get Cherokee to enlist or register for the draft, David Owl questioned whether the draft applied to them.[39]

Historian James Sherow also found a great deal of evidence of draft resistance even among one Native group with the strongest of martial traditions, the Lakota on Rosebud Reservation. Camp Funston at Fort Riley had to deal with many Lakota who sought to be discharged and sent home. At least in part, an awareness that this was the same base where those who took part in the Wounded Knee massacre were trained added to their resistance. But citizenship remained the major issue for most of them. Most Lakota at the camp asked for temporary exemptions or deferments until the government settled their citizenship status. Pierre From Above wrote to the agency, "This doesn't mean that I am backing out of the Army, but I'd rather be a citizen before I go." In another tribe with a strong martial tradition, Chippewa elders argued the draft violated treaties and urged the young not to fight. The Chippewa of Sucker Point, Minnesota, drew up a petition to protest the draft. The editor of the White Earth newspaper, *The Tomahawk*, led public calls for Chippewas to stay out of the service.[40]

Even those who joined the military did not do so primarily to fight. A Tohono O'odham, James McCarthy, joined the Arizona National Guard at the start of the war. His unit, 1st Infantry Regiment, Company F, came entirely from Indian recruits from reservation boarding schools. McCarthy volunteered for service overseas. Almost all of his fellow Native soldiers in the unit called him "foolish" for taking such a risk. Only two out of the entire company joined him.[41]

In Canada the strongest draft resistance came from Iroquois bands. They were not the only resisters. A letter from the chief of Fairford, Little Saskatchewan, and Lake St. Martin bands argued that treaties exempted them. The chief of Keatzie Indian Reserve in Port Hammond, British Columbia, also petitioned for exemption, arguing, "We have no full rights of citizenship. We have no rights to vote; Nor have we our Franchise. Therefore we object to the Registration of our Race." The Iroquois especially objected to a question on the draft cards that required one to mark whether one was a British subject by birth or by naturalization. With no other alternative on the card, to most it seemed the cards could be used to set a precedent to deny treaty rights. Two-thirds of the chiefs at Six Nations Reserve rejected registration. Superintendent Annis at Brantford Reserve blamed K. C. Bowlby, a defense lawyer, for encouraging Natives to desert. While Annis could not bear to admit that Natives acted on their own volition, Bowlby did suggest Six Nations leaders register their own people and secured printed forms stating the bearer to be a member of the Six Nations, with the question of status as British subject deleted. A few Iroquois did register and became shunned by their own people. After the war, the Six Nations filed a claim with the League of Nations at Geneva stating their position as allies and not subjects. The governments of Ireland, Panama, Persia, Estonia, and the Netherlands officially supported their position.[42]

Assuming Natives had a naturally warlike character had a dual effect. Native servicemen were never formally segregated, outside of one failed experiment in the 1890s. Native people historically had far better treatment in the military than other nonwhites as a result of the awe, or at least respect, inspired by notions of "savagery" that their presumed military prowess gave them. During the war this notion of savagery became widely used for propaganda. One article had the title, "Lo, the Rich Indian Is Eager to Fight the Savage Hun." (Apparently the author confused the Cherokee with the allegedly "rich Osages.") The article alleged that a Cherokee soldier named Jess Fixon gave his reasons for going to war as: "Kaiser killum papoose and killum squaw, so Jess Fixon will find this Kaiser and stickum bayonet clear through." The German public, given a steady diet of lurid stories about Native people through pulp novels, were shielded as much as possible from the knowledge that their soldiers faced American Indians in combat. Some German military commanders even ordered their snipers to make a special effort to shoot Native soldiers whenever they could be identified.[43]

Combat for Native soldiers had other special dangers brought by their perceived "natural" abilities. Anglo officers and NCOs frequently pushed Native soldiers into the most dangerous situations in combat. One white soldier recalled how officers in the 167th Infantry Regiment ordered a Native soldier to be a courier for messages during a battle every night for twenty-one nights in a row until he was finally killed. Native soldiers had a far higher casualty rate than that of any other group: 5 percent of Natives died in combat while less than 1 percent of all other members of the American Expeditionary Force in France died.[44]

In Canada the war brought a very brief and temporary halt to demands for assimilation. In the popular press Indians were seen as patriotic or shown as great soldiers with a mix of surprise and praise that they could "act like white men." The public talked of rewards for Natives after the war, a hope that was never fulfilled. In fact the assimilation effort worsened. As in the United States, many Indians in Canada remained unaware of the war because of their isolation.[45]

Warrior Societies

Warrior society roles changed in response to each war. After World War I, warrior societies began to have much in common with Anglo-American veterans groups such as the American Legion. The Ponca Heyoshas say they are the oldest warrior society in continuous existence in the United States. It formed in the 1830s in the aftermath of a battle with Mexican soldiers. The members strived, and continue to strive, to be the most traditional of all the warrior societies. Only Ponca or other Native languages can be spoken at their powwows. The Heyoshas never allow vendors, contests, masters of ceremonies, or sound systems. In the aftermath of World War I, more contact with other Native groups caused some younger Heyoshas to learn and dance a Northern Plains–style dance called the Fancy Dance. The older Heyoshas at first strongly opposed it and derided it as the "Crazy Dance." By the mid-1920s, however, the older Heyoshas accepted that the young would not stop fancy dancing any time soon. Since then the Fancy Dance has become a regular part of the Heyosha powwows.[46]

The Ohomah Lodge or Hethuska of the Kiowas began in the 1880s and stayed active through the 1920s. Membership was inherited. The Kiowa Gourd Dancers held Sun Dances in secret both on and off the reservation from the 1890s through the 1930s. The Kiowas were one group that had little interest or involvement in World War I, and these two societies were the only cases I found of groups carrying on warrior traditions without having new veterans coming in. It is not clear why either group ceased being active; perhaps its members were simply dying out. Korean War veterans revived the Gourd Dance Society in the 1950s. Vietnam veterans brought the Hethuska back in the 1970s.[47]

The White Horse Brigade became one of the few groups to give ceremonies for new recruits prior to their leaving for war. In December 1917, they honored seven men at Standing Rock Reservation with a parade, songs, and speeches. The Brigade rode horses alongside the recruits and chanted the "ancient Indian warriors' parade song."[48]

After the end of World War I most warrior societies seemed to be still dormant or had not yet adapted the tradition of the veteran as a warrior. Not until after Native women's societies in World War II helped prepare the way, and after the threat posed by Termination in the 1950s, did most warrior societies reconstitute themselves. Historian James Dempsey found a different picture in Canada. He attributes Canadian Natives joining in high numbers to the warrior societies that carried on despite five decades of being officially discouraged by the Canadian government.[49]

Flag Songs and War Songs

Lakotas sang a war song at the first Victory Dance seen since Little Bighorn. Notice the way the song refers to World War I as though it was much like the old Indian Wars of thirty to forty years earlier. The first and last lines are an open taunting of the German soldiers.

> The Germans retreat crying
> The Lakota boys are charging from afar
> Lakota boys, the Germans
> Whose many lands you have taken
> Are crying like women over there[50]

Andrew Blackhawk and Jim Carimon, two veterans of the war, composed this Ho Chunk flag song. Flag songs began partly as a surreptitious way to get around the prohibition on ceremonies. Bureau of Indian Affairs bureaucrats loathed suppressing a ceremony with what seemed to be visibly patriotic elements, the flying of flags and Native songs paying tribute to those flags. Yet the flag's integration into songs and ceremonies was not just a cover or intended to deceive. What most outsiders did not understand at the time were the multiple meanings most Indian nations attached to the word *flag*. A flag can be symbolic of a deceased veteran. It can also stand for the service of all veterans. A flag can also mean the emblem of the tribal nation, the eagle staff or other feathered staff that is a locus of collective medicine for a Native people.

> I love my flag
> So I went to the old world to fight the Germans
> If I had not loved my flag
> I would not have come back[51]

A Pawnee, John Luwak, composed this song describing a dream of a skull or helmet on a pole, which he took as a sign of the defeat of the Germans.

> At this
> Whoever you may have belonged to
> You are now hung on a pole[52]

The "Song for Returned Pawnee Soldiers" seems to have a similar theme.

> You are coming
> You are the ones I am looking for[53]

The "Women's War Song" was performed at a Victory Dance after the war. The Lance Society was a warrior society of men proclaiming their bravery by staking a lance in the ground, obliged to defend the position with their lives.

> They are coming yonder
> The men who belong to the Lance Society[54]

An Iroquois soldier in Canada named Simeon Gibson described doing War dances in English pubs, along with singers George and Joshua Black.

> Now we two shall sing the War Dance of olden times
> As when they used to be fighting in ancient times

This was followed by three stanzas of vocables (sounds that have no meaning but are sung for the feeling, such as "hey ya hey"). The same War Dance may have been performed as medicine or during the Iroquois Declaration of War.[55]

The "Arapahoe Song of the World War," written by Yellow Horse, described taunting a German soldier.

The German got scared and ran and dragged his blanket along

A second song by Yellow Horse taunted Germany's navy in a similar way.

Germany, why didn't you put your ships in our way?
(In the way of the navy, to be destroyed.)[56]

Ceremonies and Personal Medicine

From the data available, it appears that ceremonies were generally either not practiced prior to soldiers leaving for war or only done in secret. "Pagan or heathenish" practices, including dances or ceremonies, remained specifically forbidden on reservations under threat of withholding rations from whole families. Largely in the aftermath, after Native communities and elders petitioned Indian Bureau commissioner Cato Sells to allow ceremonies with patriotic elements, traditional ceremonies began to be openly celebrated once again. Even then some restrictions stayed in force. Bloodletting or "self-torture" remained specifically forbidden, along with "reckless giveaways" and "immoral relations." The Lummis' Sequehealous Dance, for example, remained banned as a "reversion to paganism" and "nothing but evil."[57]

White institutions often put wartime necessity above any concern for "pagan" practices and played a leading role in reestablishing some customs. Indian dancers went on tours to raise money for war bond drives, even dancing in towns hostile to Natives before the war. The YMCA organized "Indian nights" for Native soldiers to sing their own songs and speak in their own languages. Interference from authorities and the war's atmosphere of patriotism brought many changes in ceremonies. Authorities banned chest incisions and skewers during the Sun Dance, so some dancers fulfilled their vows by having the Red Cross painted on their chest and giving to the Red Cross instead. The Yumas, like many other groups, incorporated the American flag into rites in the aftermath of the war, flying the flag above their Temple of the Dead.[58]

The Lakotas also combined flying the flag with traditional symbols, such as the sacred tree and the wolf. Victory dances featured an effigy of Kaiser Wilhelm that the veterans counted coup upon and shot at. Lakota elder Frank Fools Crow described Lakota veterans being cleansed and renewed through sweats and elders talking to them about their wartime experiences "for days on end" to try and heal them of the trauma of war. The veterans then feasted, followed by the traditional giveaways. Many of the Lakotas adopted a new custom: only veterans who had served honorably in wartime could give Indian names to children in naming ceremonies.[59]

An Omaha, Bacon Rind, sponsored two dances in honor of his son George, who was in the army. At the first, Rind gave away presents of pipes, horses, and blankets. The second had singing, dancing, and more presents. On Rosebud reservation, one official reported seeing a funeral ceremony for a veteran who had died of influenza at Camp Dodge, Iowa: "In front of the procession rode a young brave carrying Old Glory. . . . It was so impressive in its complete demonstration of loyalty that I could not hold back the tears."[60] What continued to bother many agency people, however, was the many ways some veterans tried to bring back old practices.

Lakota soldier Richard Fool Bull, for example, wrote to tell his agency that he would bring back a German scalp. Some Cheyenne Scalp dances featured actual German scalps. Pawnee veterans, dressed both traditionally and in uniform, carried German helmets and knives on scalp poles in Victory dances. The Comanches recognized their veterans as warriors in a dance for them by the older warrior society members on the banks of a creek near Indianoma, Oklahoma. Most of the Comanches near the towns of Indianoma and Cache attended. Others farther away could not make it because of the distance. The welcoming was "the biggest they [ever] had."[61]

F. D. Smith, an Anglo, described the Skidi Band holding dances north of Pawnee, Oklahoma in honor of Pawnees in the world war. Two hundred attended, including about forty Pawnees in the U.S. Army. A German helmet was carried like a trophy, along with a scalp and a captured German knife. They said prayers at every public gathering and at a second dance to which whites from the local town were invited.[62]

Accounts of Native soldiers carrying personal medicine into battle during World War I are rare. This does not necessarily mean the practice had vanished. Accounts describe Apache soldiers in the Rough Riders and those with Pershing in pursuit of Pancho Villa as very devout, praying and singing traditional prayers and songs, and taking sweats on a daily basis. Naishan-Apache Ray Blackbear confirmed some Native soldiers carried peyote with them into battle in World War I for protection.[63]

In World War I the most famous story of a Native carrying personal medicine came from Francis Pegahmagabow, an Ojibwa soldier in the Canadian Army known as the "Indian Sgt. York." Pegahmagabow recalled his ship being pulled into port near a reserve. Purely by chance, an elder spotted him and pressed a medicine pouch into his hand: "I have no idea what was in it. Sometimes it felt as hard as a rock, other times it seemed to be empty. At night it seemed to be rising and falling like it could breathe. I kept it with me at all times and I don't think I could have survived the war without it." Pegahmagabow attributed his most famous action, capturing three hundred German soldiers, to the protection his pouch gave him.[64] The furtive way the elder gave him the pouch is very striking. It suggests many Native soldiers and elders wanted traditional medicine but feared that outsiders would misunderstand the practice or even try to confiscate the pouches.

Seeking Proof for "Natural" Native Abilities

The belief in a biological origin for Native fighting abilities spread beyond the educated easterners who made up white philanthropist circles. Questionnaires collected after the war showed such notions filtered down to many white officers and NCOs. Some claimed Native soldiers never needed compasses because of their "instinctive" ability to sense true north. Officers from the 142nd Infantry Regiment tested that alleged Native ability against white soldiers in a competition with both groups crawling while blindfolded. Lieutenant Ray Duncan of the 142nd claimed "the Indian has demonstrated his keenness of sight to us on many occasions. He can see at night like a cat." People of other countries also believed the myths. A British officer, Major R. Glyn, commented on Indians' "characteristic quiet and stealth."[65]

Native soldiers discovered that no matter how assimilated they became, they remained trapped within the natural warrior image by white attitudes. A boarding school graduate like Private Johnson of Company I, 4th Artillery Regiment, was still regarded as an instinctively good tracker and scout for being Blackfoot. Joseph Dixon praised "Chief Strong Wolf," the first Native to enlist in the war, as speaking "the call of a dying race . . . [in] a romantic drama." Neither Strong Wolf's impeccable suit and short hair nor his studies at Stanford and the University of Pennsylvania altered Dixon's view.[66]

Unlike the case with black Americans, few attempted to disprove Native abilities as inherent in their biology. One army officer, Lieutenant John Eddy of the 39th Infantry Regiment, became the leading advocate for a scheme falling somewhere between Dixon's "America's Cossacks" and the Indian Scouts. Eddy had been an Indian Bureau employee for nine years prior to joining the army and worked at both the San Xavier and Northern Cheyenne agencies, serving as superintendent of both the agency and its school at his last post. In 1919 Eddy conducted a highly biased survey of officers who commanded Native soldiers, one designed to elicit stereotypes. Eddy used the results of his survey to argue for the creation of Indian Ranger companies commanded by white officers, with Southwestern tribal members recruited for their running abilities and Plains tribal members recruited for fighting abilities. The army gave his study three years of serious consideration but never followed up on his recommendations.[67] Likely the shrinking military and a more isolationist stance following the war made Eddy's proposed units seem unnecessary.

Conclusion

Seventy years later, little had changed in the public mind. In the 1988 Arnold Schwarzenegger film *Predator*, an Indian Scout named Billy Bear can see and sense things no white soldier can. Alternately shown as stoically unemotional and unsmiling, or fatalistic and in love with the idea of dying in combat, as a character he would not have been out of place in the silent movie era or a Karl May novel. Most strikingly, the image of the American Indian as a natural warrior changed little in the public mind even long after the discrediting of "scientific racism."

Many Anglo-Americans just replaced the biological racist notions with the original culturally biased ones, but such biological determinism has not died out. In the spring of 2004 one of my own students repeated the same stereotype in her essay exam, describing Navajo Code Talkers as "respected because of their instinct to fight."

The paradox is that these stereotypes and images allowed many Native traditions to be reestablished or newer traditions to begin. The awe of or at least curiosity about the image of savagery undercut the aims of assimilationists, especially when that alleged savagery could be useful for the military and national leaders as propaganda. Native people did not have nearly the same degree of struggle for just treatment within the service that other nonwhites did precisely because they were able to use a stereotypical image to their own benefit. This warrior image continued into all the other wars Natives fought in and likely will continue as long as Native people feel the need to draw on the military as a source of strength and cultural renewal or until that tradition is superseded or replaced.

6

"Savages Again"

World War II

SHORTLY BEFORE THE BATTLE of Okinawa, eight members of the famous Navajo Code Talkers held a traditional ceremony. They danced and prayed for a safe and easy landing. Three thousand non-Native Marines watched. The Code Talkers ended the ceremony by singing their own version of "The Marine Corps Hymn" in Dineh, the Navajo language, but still using the original melody. As the other Marines started to recognize the tune, a few cheered. But most remained quiet, fascinated and moved, and reserved their loudest shouts and applause until after the song ended.

The landing went very well. Later, when the battle turned much more ugly and brutal, a white Marine skeptically asked one of the Code Talkers, "Well chief, what do you have to say about your ceremony now?"

"It worked like it was supposed to," the Code Talker replied with a smile. "We only prayed for a safe landing."[1]

Far more than just another war anecdote, this story has virtually every element of Native experience in World War II embedded in it. This account shows the paramount importance of ritual and tradition, Native faith and reliance on such practices, and the defense of it against white skepticism. The view of the Anglo-American, alternately fascinated and appreciative when such a tradition seemed to flatter him or could be useful, easily turned to disdain and even an unthinking use of a stereotypical slur to try to deal with what seems alien even after a lifetime (or centuries) of intimate contact.

A few years after the war's end Manuel Holcomb, the president of Santa Clara Pueblo, said, "During the war we were accepted as equals. But now that the war is over we are savages again."[2] Wartime necessity temporarily allowed some advancement and even relatively equal treatment. To take what the Pueblo leader said even further, to an extent the Indian remained a savage in Anglo eyes, but one that could be put to good use with the alleged "savagery" properly channeled or exploited. Outside of the campaign that killed Custer, no other war in American history left so many indelible images of Natives put to canny use by white propagandists. Yet in spite of the best intentions of many, some images, such as that of Ira Hayes and the flag raising at Iwo Jima, became undone by whites asserting old stereotypes.

Others images, such as the famous Code Talkers, became examples of how Natives learned to control the public vision of themselves in the military and used that view to win recognition. To Native people World War II became an opportunity to use the institution widely thought of as the source of their defeat, the military, as the means to strengthen old traditions and start new ones. In World War II, Native veterans brought their traditions into military service in unprecedented numbers. The war greatly expanded the opportunity to continue, revive, or establish warrior traditions in which the veteran took the place once accorded the tribal warrior, a process that had begun in World War I for some, and went as far back as the Civil War, the Indian Wars as scouts, or even the War of 1812 for others. A newer practice also began as a part of Native veteran experience in World War II, that of intertribal syncretism, where tribal nations without any or much of a significant warrior tradition first began to imitate the warrior ethos of other tribal nations. Native women's societies also played a role in reviving traditional ways.

The Social Backdrop of Native Communities

Historian Gerald Nash argues that World War II affected Native people more than any other event since Columbus landed. Within four years, American Indians went from the most isolated of all ethnic groups in the country to the most mobile. Up to one half of all Natives left the reservations, either to join the service or to work in war industries, especially as migrant farm laborers where they competed with Latinos.

This is a pattern that still holds true today. In no other war did Native communities become so united or eager to take part in the struggle that now faced them.[3]

Just eight years earlier newly elected president Franklin Roosevelt had declared a New Deal for Indians, an effort led by FDR's controversial and contradictory Bureau of Indian Affairs (BIA) commissioner, John Collier. Collier fought hard for the protection of Native cultures, yet insisted only a paternalistic approach could keep alive the "Red Atlantis" he so admired. Collier, by canny politicking, deception, and outright threats, imposed upon most Native peoples "tribal" governments more distinctly Western than Native. The new reservation governments often resembled corporations far more than any traditional Native ways of governing. Culturally assimilated mixed-bloods often dominated the new reservation councils. At the same time Collier allowed (and in a few cases imposed) religious freedom on reservations for the first time, setting off yet another source of conflicts between traditionalists and the new councils.

Up to one half of American Indians did not have the status of citizens in World War I.[4] By the time of Pearl Harbor, all Native peoples of the United States had American citizenship forced upon them by legislative acts in 1919, 1923, and 1940. The authors of this last act specifically designed it to *not* give Natives legal rights but to take them *away*. With all Natives legally citizens, the main legal basis that tribal leaders used to argue against the draft vanished. Citizenship acts had nothing to say about the legal domination the BIA had over Native lives and did not give Natives the right to vote. Eleven states specifically barred Natives from voting until the late 1940s or 1950s. Citizenship acts also did not settle land claims, protect religious or civil rights, or do anything about the widespread discrimination and poverty Natives faced.

Forcibly imposing citizenship worked to a very limited extent in that tribal protests now had no hope of winning in courts. Some groups still engaged in mass civil disobedience for the same reasons as they had in World War I—dissatisfaction with the treaty relationship between themselves and the United States and the frequent failure of the government to honor its agreements. Eleven tribal nations argued for draft exemption and pointed to treaty provisions to support their positions. The Hopis claimed conscientious objector status because of their pacifist tradition. Officials responded that Hopi objections were considered nationalism, not religious objections. Twenty-one Hopis went to prison for draft evasion. The Hopis formed a lobbying group called Hoping Hopis and drew their funding from other pacifists, such as the Quakers. Hopis finally received conscientious objector status long after the war in 1953, when tribal spokesman Thomas Banyaca finally convinced President Eisenhower. The Zunis asked for (and got, thanks to Collier) missionary exemptions for those in tribal religious roles. Some Pueblos also argued, unsuccessfully, for religious exemptions because their beliefs did not allow haircuts.[5]

A few Navajos and many more Seminoles resisted the draft by simply disappearing into territory not frequented by outsiders. One Navajo headman argued that Navajos should not fight unless Hitler invaded, pointing out that the U.S. treaty with the Navajos in 1868 stated that Navajos would never have to fight in U.S. wars. The Seminoles based their case on a still-official state of war between their nation and the United States. Seminoles still in Florida had never been defeated and finally agreed to peace in 1943 on their own terms. One band of Tohono O'odhams maintained they were Mexican citizens since their nation had not been consulted on nor had they recognized the Gadsden Purchase. Their leader, Pi Maccuddam, also known as Pia Machita, led a yearlong resistance campaign that drove away federal marshals and tribal police at first, before Maccuddam and several of his followers finally went to prison.[6] Finally, as shall be shown toward the end of this chapter, the Iroquois used a very clever ruse to avoid submitting to the draft or conceding a loss of sovereignty.

Yet in spite of these conflicts, almost all Native nations remained uniquely energized by the expansion of their political freedoms and their new economic and military roles in "mainstream" America. Even when split by questions of Christianity and assimilation versus traditionalism and the need to maintain sovereignty, such conflicts now played themselves out in newer arenas such as tribal elections, where the issues often wound up being defused or deferred until after the war. Native peoples also recognized the very real and pointed threat the

Axis posed to nonwhites and to the United States, a nation-state they relied on for protection as much as they resented its dominance.

Some Natives also identified very much with the lives and struggles of subject peoples who fought against the Axis, including the Filipinos against the Japanese. Athapascan soldier Richard Frank recalled, "The native people of the [Philippines] . . . didn't rely on any government. Their food was provided by the sea and land. That was really very interesting, same as home. . . . They were a group that exercised the same method as we do to make our living." It pleased Frank to take part in the Filipinos' fight against their newest invaders.[7]

Aboriginal Canadians saw the Axis threat in much the same way as Natives in the United States did, as a menace to both nonwhites and to the British Commonwealth bound by treaty obligations. Historically, in terms of violence and treaties, Canada treated Natives far better than Natives were treated in the United States. Paradoxically, with each twentieth-century war their situation worsened because of the incredible strength of that society's longstanding presumption of slow assimilation being in Natives' best interests. Natives leaving the reserves, including those joining the military, lost all tribal or band rights, leading to dramatic population declines in their homelands. Considered officially "de-tribalized" and presumed to be partly or completely assimilated Métis (mixed-blood or mixed culture), nearly all Métis and non-status Natives chose to live apart from the Anglo-Canadian majority and kept a strong sense of either tribal or Pan-Indian identity. Métis and non-status Natives eventually outnumbered Natives on the reserves and often led Native political activism in the late 1940s and 1950s.[8]

Ceremonies and Personal Medicine

World War I saw the beginnings of a tradition among the Plains tribes where the veteran carried on the tradition of a warrior. World War II saw these traditions spread to many tribes that had been indifferent to World War I. Ak-Chin, south of Phoenix, Arizona, stood out as one of the most striking examples. This farming community of less than six hundred O'odhams and Pimas did not have a single member serve in World War I. But nine of the seventeen tribal members who served in World War II died in combat.[9]

Native and Inuit (Eskimo) peoples of Alaska had little history of warfare prior to the coming of Europeans. In World War II they became the first Americans to fight the Axis after the initial surprise attacks and the only soldiers to fight on U.S. soil. The Alaska Territorial Guard organized itself prior to World War II, with militia organized down to the village level, including a village captain. Later they became the Eskimo Scouts, a special unit of the Alaska National Guard, using surplus World War I rifles to defeat the invasion of the Aleutian Islands by the Japanese. They did so without receiving recognition or even pay until the 1950s. Alaska governor Ernest Gruening personally recruited half of the three hundred enlistees and attributed their enthusiasm to a desire to keep their sacred homelands safe from further outside invaders. That turned out to not always be true. Draven Delkittie was drafted. He mournfully recalled the recapture of Attu: "We won this time, yet there was a feeling that was not too good. And today the way I feel, it's just the same feeling that, 'Why did we do this?'" With no tradition of warfare to tell them how to cope, many Alaska Natives were at more of a loss than other Native groups. Delkittie remembered a fellow Athabascan who drank himself to death at the memory of killing twelve Japanese.[10]

During World War I few Native servicemen took part in ceremonies until after the war had ended. In World War II, thanks to the policy of toleration by Collier, not only did ceremonies become common before and after military service, many Natives eagerly took part in them while in the service on a scale not seen since. The medicine men of the Santa Ana Pueblo prayed at their secret shrine for a month following the start of war. Rosebud Reservation held the Yuija ceremonial to give strength and encouragement to men going off to war. Standing Rock Reservation held a battle Sun Dance to pray for the destruction of the Axis and the victorious return of servicemen. The Zunis held a Eutakya blessing ceremony.[11]

The Zunis became one of several tribes rumored to have a contest to see who could bring home the most scalps. While the media certainly exaggerated or possibly even manufactured such rumors, scalp taking by Native soldiers was far from unknown. Native soldiers recognized that the fear of them as "savages" could be put to good use to strike terror into the hearts of their enemies. Cherokee sergeant John Fulcher was the leader of a ten-man sniper squad, half of whom were Natives. In combat in Italy, the squad made a practice of scalping the German soldiers they killed and leaving the corpses formally seated by the road with arms folded.[12]

Native scalping practices should not be confused with the angry mutilation of corpses by American soldiers of all backgrounds, which was all too common in the Pacific theater. Scalp dances or purification dances using actual scalps were a solemn part of the welcome home ceremonies of many tribes. Women relatives and not the veterans themselves often performed the dances. The dances generally had the intent of reconciling the spirits of the deceased soldier and the one who killed him in battle, not to celebrate.

Ceremonies did not become universal, nor were they always successful. In his autobiography, Code Talker (and later tribal chairman) Peter McDonald laments how the rejection of the old ways became common among most Navajo veterans. Many turned to alcohol to deal with their difficulties. In Evon Vogt's study of Navajo veterans after the war, Vogt found a rather ironic correlation between how likely a veteran was to have gone through healing or honoring and how much combat he had been in. Of the fifteen veterans he interviewed, only one did not attend numerous ceremonies. All but one had the ceremonies done to please their parents or grandparents but with little belief in their efficacy. Many Navajos wound up pulling menial duties because of a lack of English skills and felt very isolated, having no chance to fulfill the role of a warrior. Even their more famous counterparts, the Code Talkers, had some difficulty. Their part in the service remained classified until 1968, forcing many to make the choice between breaking military protocol by talking about their experiences in the Enemy Way healing ceremony, or ignoring tradition and embracing a chance to purge themselves of the stress of combat. Thus some may have been forced to turn to alcohol.[13]

By 1977 researcher Broderick Johnson found a very different picture when he interviewed Navajo veterans. All his subjects talked with a great deal of pride about their experiences and stressed the importance of ceremony to them in surviving the war with mind and body intact. Johnson interviewed the most highly decorated and recognized veterans for the Navajo Community College. His interviews should also be read to understand what Navajos thought was important at the time of his study.[14]

An alternately curious and mystified Anglo public eagerly accepted reports of practices of Native ceremonies. Famed correspondent Ernie Pyle described seeing Native dances prior to battles in Sicily, Normandy, the Philippines, and Okinawa. Just as in World War I, Natives performing traditional dances became commonplace at war bond sales and blood drives. The titles of articles aimed at the general public have a less dignified approach. A typical title was "The Indian Takes the Warpath Again." Far fewer knew that one of the most famous and most cynical images of the war, cartoonist Bill Mauldin's two haggard soldiers Willie and Joe, was modeled on Sergeant Rayson Billie, a Choctaw that Maudlin served with in the 45th Infantry.[15]

White appetites for a more lurid view of Native traditions even extended to a famous symbol of coexistence between Natives and Anglos, Ira Hayes. Hayes, fresh from the battlefields of Iwo Jima and an instant celebrity because of the flag-raising photo, suffered the indignity of people demanding, "Where's your tomahawk at, chief? Where's your bow and arrows? How many Japs did you kill, chief?" at public appearances. Hayes was one of many Natives who performed traditional dances while he was in the service, as well as before and after the war. A devout Presbyterian, like most Pimas, his Christian beliefs did not preclude him from having a going-away ceremony that combined Christianity with a syncretic mix with older practices. Tribal elders, church leaders, and a choir gave a dinner in his honor before he left that included hymns and prayers for his safety.[16]

Few cases of personal medicine use have been documented for World War I. But a lack of recorded cases could simply show the great need to keep these practices secret. That need for secrecy ended, however. During World War II accounts of personal medicine are easy to find. Navajo elders gave Navajo servicemen sacred corn pollen and holy water. Zunis carried sacred prayer meals and fetishes (carved amulets of small animals). Chippewa servicemen asked for protection from their guardian spirits and had totemic spirit marks tattooed on their right forearm. Apache servicemen carried peyote buttons. Sometimes Native ceremonies reconciled servicemen to their fates. Private Daniel Garneau of Dinorwic, Ontario, had a vision of his own death in the war during a sweat lodge ceremony prior to his leaving for Italy. He took time to visit all friends and family to say good-bye, repeating to everyone what he saw in his vision.[17]

Sometimes traditional teachings could be both omens and a means to cope with new realities. Nez Perce veteran Horace Axtell believes elders of the Seven Drums religion foretold the bombing of Hiroshima and Nagasaki, and compared the bombings to the massacre of his people at Big Hole: "When our ships pulled into Hiroshima harbor, I could see bodies still floating, killed by the atomic bomb. I saw all the Japanese, the children, the women and elders. I went to the crater where the bomb had landed and the devastation, the carnage, brought me back to the feelings of the Big Hole Massacre. When I saw what happened [in Japan] and when I got back, it was almost a vision of what had happened from the stories that I had heard from my elders."[18]

But traditional teachings were not universal. Many Native servicemen were either "conventionally" Christian or had long ago been forced to pass as white, Latino, or black and had lost touch with their Native heritage. The Miami Nation of Indiana are a tribe that has been forced to pass since the mid-nineteenth century. The daughters of two Miami veterans interviewed for this study did not know about the practice of personal medicine. Their families had long been conventionally Christian. Some Native servicemen carried items of both religious traditions in a syncretic blend of the two. Chaplain Charles Richmond noted that a blending of the two was common in the 45th Division, a unit with one-fifth Native members. Native soldiers attended mass in high numbers and then went to Native meetings that had songs and dances in their own tongues.[19] Outside observers who lament the "impurities" brought into Native cultures and spiritual beliefs miss the essential point. Native servicepeople and their communities voluntarily adapted newer elements for use in ways that aided them.

War Songs and Flag Songs

Native songs became one more way the old traditions adapted to new realities in a syncretic manner. In war songs the serviceman and the war against an enemy of the United States or Canada took the place of the warrior and the raids on another Native enemy. Flag songs began as a surreptitious way to get around the prohibition on Native ceremonies after World War I. Most outsiders did not understand at the time the double meaning many Indian nations attach to the word *flag*. A flag could also mean the emblem of the tribal nation, the eagle or other feathered staff that was also a locus of medicine for a collective Native people. As famed Pueblo singer and flutist Robert Mirabal wrote in the introduction to his song "Bataan Death March," "It was not the flag which kept the Native soldier going, it was the thought of the dances and voices of his people which were his strength."[20]

William Meadows and Louis Lassiter both collected a great number of War Mothers songs about World War II and noted that many others remain unknown to outsiders. Louis Tayebo, a prolific and highly admired Kiowa, composed the great majority of War Mothers songs. The "Kiowa War Mothers Song" is an invocation and prayer set to drumbeats. The translator's choice of "God" instead of "Creator" or "Grandfather" may say that either the translator or the singer is Christian, or both.

> Our young soldiers are somewhere
> Wherever they are, day or night
> God, take care of them for me[21]

The "Kiowa Veterans Song" below is unusual in being one of the few to mention women as warriors. The third line does not mean that men and women fought side by side. "Together" refers to being reunited with the Kiowa community.

> Our sons and daughters went overseas
> They fought the Germans
> They returned safe, together[22]

Tayebo also wrote "Kiowa D-Day Invasion Song," reproduced below. The song describes the actions of the soldiers, with great attention paid to their having followed the example of what a warrior is supposed to be, unafraid and willing to sacrifice for others.

> Young Kiowa men, they are said to be brave, they are said to be brave,
>   news of them appears
> And then, they were said to be coming together, (established a base) in
>   the midst of the smoke and
> They were reported to have charged at the approaching, charging
>   enemy and
> They were reported to have been unafraid (without hesitation) and
> It is worth telling[23]

Jeanette Berry Mopope wrote the following song for her nephew Gus Palmer, the brother of Lyndreth Palmer mentioned in the first song. Mopope presented this song to Gus at his homecoming celebration. The first half of the first line talks of the dangers of artillery shells, while the rest relates the family's and community's relief at the return of the warrior/veteran.

> The enemy bounces as they are hit, he came home for us again
> And we were elated (or very happy), and we felt good, and
>   we were elated[24]

Martha Doyeto composed this next song to honor the return of her younger brother, Roland Whitehorse. It is important to understand that a chief, unlike the racist slur often unthinkingly given to all Natives, is in fact a position to be earned by specific acts of bravery in wartime. Most Kiowa warriors/veterans would never earn this title, so a genuine chief is someone highly respected.

> Unafraid of danger, he is a chief
> Unafraid of danger, he is a chief
> Unafraid of danger, he is a chief
> Because he is strong hearted, he is a chief[25]

An unknown Dakota wrote the untitled piece that follows, one of the first Native songs about World War II. At first glance it may appear to be a more formal, Nativized take on an Anglo-American flag song until one recalls the different meaning of the word *flag* to many Natives. "My country" also has a different meaning; it is a reference to the traditional lands of the tribal nation rather than the United States as a political entity. Even the reference to the president can be misinterpreted. The president is the symbol of a treaty relationship between the United States and tribal nations, not an elected leader to whom one is loyal. Many Natives did not have the right to vote in state or national elections until the 1950s.

> The President, the flag, and my country
> These things I stand for
> So saying the Lakota boys went as soldiers[26]

The "Lakota World War II Veterans Song" below mentions the enemy by name. Hoksila translates roughly as "boy," "adolescent," or "teenager." Perhaps the most precise meaning is "male who is changing from a child into a man."

> The War is a hard time
> The Japanese are charging
> Lakota Hoksila you are in the
> Middle of this battle[27]

"Six Islands" is a reference to the major island battles against the Japanese. Notice that the second and third lines assume that the sacred significance and meaning of land would be the same for the Japanese, and its loss would trigger the same trauma for them that it had for Lakota in the past.

> You have taken the Six Islands
> The Japanese are crying because
> You have taken their land[28]

Lakota singer Fire Shaker composed another song about war against the Japanese. The final line tells us that white racism was filtering into Lakota society. The Lakotas were not unique in that; Collier's bringing two Japanese American internment camps to reservations was very unpopular.

Lakota boys, you went over there
And you took the Japanese prisoners
When the soldiers came back
They told us the Japs were crying![29]

Thomas Tyon and Henry White Calf wrote this honor song for General MacArthur. This song was also in the form and style of the Omaha songs. "Wise Eagle" was the name given to MacArthur at the time he became an honorary chief.

Over there lies danger
Wise Eagle (General MacArthur), you are still there
Brace yourself and take courage
That is what the Lakota boys say[30]

Two more Lakota victory songs celebrate bravery against the Axis. The second one even taunts non-Native society, urging them on in the first line.

I took the German land and I won
I took the Japanese land and I made peace
All over the world soldiers are saying this

United States, do your duty
Mr. Roosevelt said remember Pearl Harbor
The Indian boys went over there and now the Japanese are crying[31]

The Navajo version of "The Marine Corps Hymn" mentioned at the beginning of the chapter, written by Jimmy King, and sung before the Battle of Okinawa follows. The melody is the same as the English version. This is clearly the most acculturated song presented in this chapter. Essentially the first two verses attempt to translate the original song into a Navajo-language version and still keep the meaning as close as possible to the earlier song. However, the third verse is distinctly unlike the first two. It is sung a cappella, far closer to a chant. The wishes expressed for peace and eternal harmony in the third verse/prayer are completely unlike the Anglo-American song. The assertion of individual fearlessness is also very much in line with the traditional ideal of being a warrior.

We have conquered our enemies
All over the world
On land and sea,
Everywhere we fight
True and loyal to our duty
We are known by that
United States Marine
To be one is a great thing

Our flag waves
From dawn to setting sun
We have fought every place
Where we could take a gun
From northern lands
To southern tropic scenes
We are known to be tireless
United States Marines

(Last verse like a prayer)
May we live in peace hereafter
We have conquered all our foes
No force in the world we cannot conquer
We know of no fears
If the Army and the Navy
Ever look on heaven's scenes
United States Marines will be there
Living in peace[32]

The "Ho Chunk Flag Song" that follows refers exclusively to the Ho Chunk national flag, the feathered eagle staff, and not the American flag. This song is similar to a flag song of the Menominee of Wisconsin recorded by Frances Densmore at the close of World War I. It provides a good example of intertribal syncretism.

Our beloved flag went across the ocean and came back
Are you really glad to see it back again?[33]

The Ho Chunks composed songs for each branch of the service in World War II. The "Ho Chunk Marine Song" mentions a famous battle by name.

127

Japanese
The Ho Chunk soldiers took care of you
And took Okinawa away from you

The "Ho Chunk Air Force Song" also mentions a famous place of battle. The middle two lines are a description of battle in the air. The first and last lines stress the willingness to sacrifice oneself in combat.

I have said that he came willingly
My friend, I came from the other side of the clouds
I made Iwo Jima into a puff of smoke
I have said he came willingly[34]

The "Ojibwe Air Force Song" is a wish for a safe return from fighting, perhaps even medicine, for a Red Lake Ojibwe whose son was a pilot overseas, written after it came to him in a dream.

While I am flying around in the sky
I know that I will come to land safely on Earth[35]

Bud Friday, a Canadian soldier, wrote another Ojibwe Veterans Song. Friday became one of many soldiers who stormed the beaches at Dunkirk. After two unsuccessful attempts, Friday recalled, "That's when I had a vision in my dreams. An old man said, 'I'm going to give you something that will help you win this war.'" Friday believed the old man to be the Great Spirit. In the 1990s, the vision came to him again, telling him it was time to sing the song with a healing purpose.

I am overseas
I am overseas
Do not feel sad
Don't feel sad
Do not feel sad
I'll be coming home soon
I'll be coming home soon
Do not feel sad mama
I am coming home
I am coming home[36]

The sheer volume of Native songs about World War II, the fact that they remain popular today, and the fact that new ones paying tribute are still being written all the time underscore how much of a watershed event the war became in Native lives. No other war brought such cultural and social change in such a short time. The large number of Native songs written by adapting old styles to newer needs and traditions says a great deal about Native cultures' strength and ability to adjust. Only a few decades before Native peoples had faced the potentially self-fulfilling accusation of "vanishing," doomed to fall before advancing "civilization" by their alleged inability to deal with "progress." The great Native revival of cultural forms in World War II proved that notion completely false.

Warrior and Women's Societies

It is impossible to properly tell the story of Native cultural contributions and syncretism in the military without paying tribute to the role of Native women. Native women's societies sometimes preceded and prepared the way for warrior societies to emerge after the war. The War Mother Societies stood out more than any other. These groups originally began as an Anglo-American institution, one that women of the Kiowa, Comanche, Cheyenne, Otoe-Missouri, and Pawnee nations took, adapted to their own needs, and combined with practices from earlier women's societies.[37]

Speaking very broadly, traditionally women's societies properly prepared warriors prior to warfare, invoked sacred powers of protection for absent warriors, and welcomed and honored the warriors on their return. All three functions were, in a sense, also a part of Anglo-American War Mother Societies. Yet the important differences were of degree, intensity of preparation, and elaborateness of ceremonies. Anglo functions are far more casual. The invocation of sacred protection is also far less sustained and not nearly as omnipresent as in Native ways.

The Kiowa War Mothers began near Carnegie, Oklahoma. The Purple Heart Club began in Stecker, Oklahoma. Both revived preservation societies but with Anglo-American names. Kiowa women's societies invoked *daudau*, supernatural power for warfare, and gave protective medicine to Kiowa servicemen in the form of peyote buttons in buckskin pouches. The return of the servicemen brought the revival of the Kiowa Ohomo Society. Bustle Keeper Charley Whitehorse made a patriotic banner with a star for each member, identical to the stars used by Anglo-Americans in War Mother Societies, with a silver one for a living soldier and a gold one for one killed in battle, a clear example of syncretism. Kiowa women's societies held a summer celebration for Kiowa veterans at the city park in Carnegie, Oklahoma.[38]

The Comanche War Mothers carried out the Na'wapina'r or purification ceremonies before the veterans left. On the veterans' return, the women's society gave the Nah'o'kee'nukha, the Victory Dance or Dance of Joy. In a precursor to the powwow circuit that would grow exponentially after the Korean War, celebrations in Oklahoma were attended by not only Kiowas and Comanches but also by members of the Caddo, Wichita, Pawnee, Ponca, and even Arapaho and Cheyenne tribes further north.[39]

The central role women's societies played in the revival and growth of martial traditions is a direct challenge to the old stereotypes of submissive Native women. Going into warfare in World War II was treated by Native peoples as traditionally as possible as a state that required extensive coping rituals on both a societal and individual level. The revival and growth of these cultural forms were a sure sign that the newer tradition of the veteran as a warrior was something permanent and highly valued by Native peoples.

Propaganda Images: Ira Hayes, Code Talkers, and a "Declaration of War"

The image of the flag raising at Iwo Jima became one of the most enduring icons of the war. When the public heard that an American Indian was one of the flag raisers, many took this as a hopeful sign of American society's inclusiveness. In less than a week's time Hayes went from being another grunt in combat to a celebrity constantly mobbed on tour. In the aftermath of the war, all it took was the first time Hayes was arrested for public intoxication to quickly erase the new inclusive image and replace it with far older ones, the drunken Indian and the helpless primitive unable to cope with "civilization."

Hayes's friends in the service gave a very different picture from the passive, easily intimidated, shy loner portrayed by journalists and a terrible Hollywood movie starring Tony Curtis. Fellow platoon member Arthur Stanton described Hayes as outgoing, friendly, and eager to talk about his pride in being Pima. Hayes described in detail how important the Pima struggle for self-determination and self-sufficiency was to him and his people. Not surprisingly for a man from a subsistence farming economy, he was particularly concerned about Native water use rights.[40]

Another member of his platoon, Keith Rasmussen, recalled that the epithet *chief* was a sure way to get Hayes angry, though Hayes, mindful of military discipline, never showed any sign of letting it turn into a physical confrontation. "He would just glower at them something terrible," said Rasmussen. "I didn't feel it was right to denigrate anyone. I would prefer to call him 'brave.' He liked that. He was not the loner portrayed. He carried himself with confidence." Hayes was close to his buddies in the platoon like most men in wartime, but still not nearly as close as he became to Navajo Code Talker Teddy Draper. The two were constantly together, trading stories, until Draper received transfer orders.[41]

His fame from the flag-raising began Hayes's troubles in earnest. This much seems accurately portrayed: Hayes clearly had as much trouble dealing with the trauma of combat and postwar adjustment as most men. He also had the misfortune of having to deal with sudden fame. Many turn to drink to deal with any one of these, much less all three at once. Yet Hayes was apparently such an *inexperienced* drinker that he easily passed out from a few beers or less than a bottle of wine. He drank sporadically, when he was under the greatest stress, and never daily or even weekly.[42]

Ironically, Hayes's death was a fluke and was not from the hopeless alcoholism portrayed by the press and Hollywood. Hayes actually had sworn off drinking entirely during his last few months. His family described him as being hopeful about the future and optimistic. Hayes died from exposure with less than half a bottle of wine in him. But absent this lapse or ten degrees of difference in the temperature outdoors, Hayes might have lived to an old age.[43]

Hayes is definitely not remembered for his sporadic encounters with alcohol by the Pimas or by Natives in general. The issue of his death is treated like the accident it was, and Hayes's memory is not sullied by the manner of his demise any more than if he had died in a car accident. To Natives he remains solely a war hero honored for winning the Silver Star and for bringing attention to Native soldiers with the flag raising. The Navajo Code Talkers depict him on their medals issued by the Navajo Nation, both dressed as a traditional Pima warrior on horseback and in the flag raising. This is in spite of the fact that Hayes was neither Navajo nor a Code Talker. In Urshel Taylor's painting of the flag raising, Hayes is also dressed as a traditional Pima warrior alongside the white Marines dressed in modern military uniform. To Natives Hayes is simply among the most brave (and certainly the most famous) Native servicemen of the war, and thus worthy of honoring for those reasons alone.[44]

The Navajo Code Talkers are the best-known group of Native veterans of the war. Because the Code Talkers are so highly regarded by both Natives and the military, their story is treated with great reverence and Natives, not whites, successfully guide how their story has been told. Code Talkers are revered precisely because their achievements are a great *intellectual* feat alongside their acts of enormous physical courage in battle. After Phillip Johnston, the son of a missionary to the Navajos, convinced Major General Clayton Vogel to recruit Navajos, the Code Talkers devised their own unbreakable and unwritten code on their own, one that was never breached by the Japanese nor transmitted inaccurately, an amazing feat of mental dexterity never equaled by any other codes of the war.[45]

The irony remains that Native languages the American government failed to suppress played an important role in the American military victory in the Pacific war. What has usually been obscured to non-Natives is that there were many different tribal groups of Code Talkers utilized in both world wars, the Korean War, and the Vietnam War. What is also often misportrayed is that this was a complex code they invented, not simply ordinary conversations in Navajo. Captured Navajo POWs, for example, could not fathom the code and so the Japanese tortured them to no purpose.

The Navajos used this feat of military bravery and military intelligence to promote an enormously positive image of themselves and gain a prestige and recognition that sadly eludes most other Native veterans. The number of books, articles, and films dedicated to the Code Talkers easily outnumbers all other media about Native veterans combined. In 1999, the toy makers at Mattel even began making GI Joe Code Talker action figures that are sold throughout most of Arizona and New Mexico.[46]

One other clever Native use of white media came from the Iroquois' "Declaration of War." The Six Nations historically are the strongest proponents of complete sovereignty for tribal nations. They were among the first Native groups to somewhat successfully defend their ways of life using the American legal system and appeals to white popular opinion. World War II proved to be no different. When faced with a draft they regarded as a violation of treaties and an infringement upon their sovereignty, the Iroquois took their case to court. After that failed, draft-eligible Iroquois took to volunteering before they could be drafted, but only as foreign nationals.

Even that measure brought a great deal of resistance from the authorities, who took preliminary steps to prosecute Iroquois as draft evaders. Some Iroquois then suggested a staged repeat of their entry into World War I, when they declared war several years prior to the United States because of the abusive treatment some Iroquois suffered in Germany. Wearing Plains Indian warbonnets to make an obvious appeal to the popular Hollywood misconceptions of Indians, several Iroquois posing as Six Nations spokesmen issued a "Declaration of War" from the steps of the Capitol in Washington DC, with massive media coverage but no authentic backing from actual Iroquois leadership. The stunt worked as intended. Federal officials dropped all prosecutions for draft evasion and allowed Iroquois enlistees to join as foreign nationals.[47]

Much of the same type of propaganda use of Native images from World War I took place during World War II. "Lo, the Indian Takes the Warpath" from *Reader's Digest* or "Braves on the Warpath" from the *American Legion* were fairly typical. As historian Jere Franco points out, most white media of the time preferred to give their audience what it perceived to be "colorful" anecdotes rather than substantive or even neutral nonracist pieces. The use of stereotypes and epithets by the media remained extremely common. While motion pictures changed to reflect a push for recognizing the value of other cultures by some in the government, news media had none of the newer acceptance.[48]

Conclusion

World War II was a turning point for Native peoples. It brought an end to the de facto segregation and isolation imposed upon Native peoples by the reservation system. Most Native peoples went from a reliance on subsistence farming and hunting to a cash wage economy in an incredibly short time. What has not received much notice is that one of the main ways that Natives coped with the new realities came from the creative adaptation of new cultural forms. Native veterans and communities created a newer *permanent* and far more widespread tradition during World War II, one that allowed veterans to make military service meaningful to them according to traditional dictates. Even when faced with white stereotypes, Natives used such notions for their own ends. A widespread cultural revival aided Native adaptation to dramatically changing conditions and confirmed Native cultures as the greatest strength of American Indians, not the liabilities many whites believed. This war became the closest thing to an unambiguously "good war" as seen by Native peoples, and the high enthusiasm reflects that. For every war since, both Native participation and the wars themselves became harder for many Native people to justify. Native participation dropped sharply, even while respect for individual Native servicemen remained.

7

The Half-Hidden Spirit Guide Totemic Mark

Korea

DONALD LALONDE FROM THE Sault Ste. Marie Reservation joined the air force during the Korean War. The elder Lalonde had a spirit guide totemic mark on his right forearm just like the one his son Harold got three decades later in the navy. Depending on the uniform, the marks could be either hidden or in plain view of their fellow servicemen. These marks speak as an apt metaphor for Native traditions in the military, at different times hidden or in plain view to outsiders, but both permanent and consciously chosen. The Lalondes carry on a family tradition, both in choosing military service and in practicing traditional spiritual ways while in the service. Two of Donald's brothers served during World War II, another in the army in Korea, and Donald's son Harold is still on active duty in the navy today. The Lalondes regarded "the world as an empty place without [such] guides" and saw in the military a way to maintain traditions and use them as a source of strength and a way of adapting to the pressures of the larger society.[1]

World War II saw the sporadic beginnings of an atomizing assault on Native communities, a diaspora that assimilationists tried to impose upon reservations couched in the bureaucratic yet still ominous label of Termination. Yet the war was as much a boon for individual members who left as it was a disaster for those who stayed on the reservation homelands. This pattern continued during the Korean War and intensified afterward. Native experiences during the Korean War and after became, ultimately, both catalyst and overture to the Red Power struggles of the 1960s and 1970s. Some of its most famous leaders were Korean War veterans, who were far less willing to be as passive as they perceived the World War II generation to be.

Native veterans of the Korean War are an unstudied group in one of the least-studied wars in U.S. history. The Korean War suffers from being in the shadow of World War II. Many of the servicemen took part in both wars, and some went on to serve in the Vietnam War. But the Korean War was dramatically different in ways both subtle and obvious. Trying to understand this war by using the one before it is as frustrating to us now as it was to both the public and its leaders back then. The leaders of the United States and the participants in the Korean War tried to impose, unsuccessfully, the same patterns that worked in World War II. The experience of the Lalonde family stands as an example of what Native people gained from the Korean War. This war stood as a way to continue traditions both tribal-wide and specific to particular families such as the Lalondes, yet syncretic in approach and well adapted to facing modernity and changes.

The Social Backdrop of Native Communities

Reservation systems since John Collier's reign in the BIA often functioned as walls, acting both as defense to outside intrusion and as barriers confining the actions of those within. Reservation governments, until relatively recently, have in many cases also been de facto forms of internal colonialism, using "cooperative" Natives to control those thought of as less than manageable. At the same time they provided cheap access to natural resources for outside commercial interests.[2] Termination, the drive to end reservations once and for all, had its beginnings at the end of World War II as a result of conflicts over the status of reservations and the question of assimilation. Most whites with assimilationist notions managed to misinterpret both questions to suit their worldview. They misinterpreted Native mobility driven by economic need as desire to merge with Anglo society and abandon traditional identity. Reservation governments, until fairly recently, often functioned largely as bureaucratic institutions that mostly benefited white commercial interests and a small number of self-selected Native elites. But the anti-Communist postwar hysteria falsely labeled reservations as "Communist or socialist." The great majority of Native people became caught in the middle, forced to defend reservation systems most had little liking for because to lose them meant losing their remaining homelands, lands with immense spiritual significance. The struggle over Termination and its slightly less onerous successor, Relocation, stretched from the sporadic clashes at the end of World War II to a full-blown, extended, constant struggle that became cultural life and death in Native eyes, dragging on all the way into the early 1970s. The Red Power movement became the unintended and unwanted child of Termination. Its conception extends as far back as the Korean War, where many of its leaders first engaged the outside world.

In Canada the situation of Native people had been historically better than that of Natives in the United States. Ironically, however, the circumstances of Native communities slowly worsened with each twentieth-century war. No comparable attempt to Termination, or trying to abolish Native landholdings (reserves), came until much later, in the late 1960s. Native veterans' numerous attempts to organize politically always met attempts at suppression by the Royal Canadian Mounted Police (RCMP). The public ignored these attempts due to the widespread Anglo-Canadian belief that Native assimilation was positive. The lack of a Termination effort by the government and a lack of rank-and-file veteran members that the Vietnam War provided in the United States led to a less vibrant Red Power movement. (Canada did not send troops to Vietnam.) RCMP suppression, coupled with FBI disruption of ties between American and Canadian Native activists, also made contact between the two groups initially difficult. In the place of Red Power came a long, painful effort to form Pan-Indian groups that had to be extremely moderate in their methods because of political crackdowns by the RCMP. The National Indian Council was the leading group, with mostly Korean War veterans.

Native Response to the War

Both American Indians and the larger American society did not see winning or losing the Korean War as the same sort of all-out struggle as World War II. North Korea was not nearly as obvious and ominous a grave threat as the Axis to either Native peoples' existence as nonwhites or the future of the United States. Thus the complete mobilization that World War II had brought did not happen during the Korean War, either among Native people or Americans in general. Mobilization came as a smaller-scale renewal of that seen in World War II, mostly along the West Coast. About 29,700 American Indians served in the Korean War.[3] In Canada the practice of not counting off-reserve Native people as "officially" Native gave a severe undercount of those involved. Officially only "several dozen" served, but the government admitted the true number to be "in the high hundreds," a high percentage since only around 26,000 Canadians served in the Korean War altogether.[4]

The military never formally segregated American Indians outside of the Indian Scouts. But just as in the world wars, some units had large numbers of Native servicemen. Units with a high percentage of Natives in the Korean War included the 164th Infantry, the 231st Engineer, and the 188th Field Artillery Battalions of the North Dakota National Guard. Few people are aware that the famous Navajo Code Talkers continued into the Korean and Vietnam wars. Only in 1968 did they finally disband and get public recognition.

The experiences of the two most famous Native servicemen of the war give two different views of the state of Native people at this time. Recall Corporal Mitchell Red Cloud from the Ho Chunk (Winnebago) tribal nation. Too badly wounded to stand up on his own, he ordered his troops to tie his torso upright to a tree and kept firing until his death. This allowed his comrades to escape unharmed. Red Cloud subsequently received the Medal of Honor posthumously, as well as a ship named for him in 1999, the USNS *Red Cloud*.[5] In contrast, after the death of Sergeant John Rice in the battle for the Pusan perimeter, officials barred him, also of the Ho Chunk nation, a burial plot in the ironically named town of Sioux City, Iowa. The funeral actually stopped in mid-service after the funeral director realized Rice was not white. This treatment provoked nationwide outrage. Cemetery officials defended barring Rice's remains and claimed to not be racist, saying, "People, like animals, prefer to be with their own kind." President Truman himself intervened and offered the family a plot in Arlington National Cemetery. Senators Marion Butler from Iowa and Guy Gillette from Nebraska, Secretary of the Interior Julius Krug, and a colonel as a representative from the Joint Chiefs of Staff all attended Rice's second funeral.[6]

Rice's case had further ironies beyond the fact that he was buried at Arlington; black, Latino, and Asian soldiers were denied burial plots there. William Oliver, the president of the United Auto Workers Fair Practices and Anti-Discrimination Department and Solidarity House, used Rice's case in testimony before Congress on January 4, 1952. Oliver simultaneously decried racism of any sort and proudly noted the longtime presence of American Indians in the UAW. Yet Oliver called for the assimilation of Native people in a manner that very much resembled Termination, in openly assimilationist terms. Congress, he said, must "finally emancipate the Indian people" by *allowing the sale of their land*.[7]

Vine Deloria Jr. and D. L. "Pappy" Hicks also illustrate the changes war brought to Native communities. Both veterans, they took different yet parallel paths after the war. Both chose active engagement in the outside world, but in ways that kept them intimately involved in the struggles of tribal peoples. Deloria occupied a position comparable to that once held by W. E. B. Du Bois in the black community, a highly visible symbol of ethnic militancy combined with scholarship. He became best known for his books and as president of the National Congress of American Indians in the mid-1960s.

Hicks is little known outside of the military and his own people, the Cherokee. From 1959 to 1980, Hicks directed covert operations in Southeast Asia for the CIA, recruiting and leading more than 40,000 Hmong and other hill tribe members against the Vietnamese Communists. On the surface, Hicks stands at the opposite political end of the spectrum from Deloria. Yet the Hmong's history of conflict with the Vietnamese is in many ways comparable to that of Hicks's own people. Both are indigenous groups with a long history of struggle against relative newcomers. Hicks also led the effort to rescue and resettle Hmong people in the United States in the long aftermath of American withdrawal from the region. Since leaving the CIA, Hicks has been the head chief of the Texas Cherokee Nation and, like Deloria, a steadfast defender of Native sovereignty.[8] That two men on opposite ends of the political spectrum came to nearly identical positions on the issue of resisting assimilation demonstrates that the common experience of being alienated by the state's actions upon one's homeland and people can overcome ideology.

Ceremonies and Personal Medicine

Tribal ceremonies at the start of World War II had been intended as much to mobilize the energies and involvement of an entire tribe as to provide traditional protective medicine for individual servicemen. But with the lesser mobilization for the Korean War in general, tribal ceremonies were not as widely used to call Native communities together in support of the war.

Besides the Lalondes, other veterans used personal medicine or felt a traditional spirit guide protected them. Seneca veteran Charles McLaughlin joined the Army Air Corps (which soon became the air force) during the Korean War. He often spoke to his wife in later years of the feeling of being protected by his guide, but as often happens, he felt the matter too personal to discuss easily with others. Pressure from his Anglo in-laws to hide his Native heritage from his own children added to his difficulties.[9]

Warm Springs veteran Reginald Winishut also spoke of how he used traditional ways to adapt to the war: "In Korea I relied on old Indian ways . . . my spiritual teachings from home . . . to lead my comrades in clearing mines."[10]

Warrior Societies

A dramatic growth in warrior societies seems to be the greatest single change in Native cultures with the advent of the Korean War. As a direct response to Termination, some tribal nations revived their warrior societies out of fear that traditions would be lost.[11] Two Kiowa warrior societies, the Kiowa Gourd Clan and the Kiowa Black Leggings Society, revived in 1955 and 1958, respectively, at the height of conflict over Termination. Kiowas considered the Gourd Clan more assimilated, with more Christian members, followers of the "Jesus Road" as opposed to the Red Road. Unlike the Black Leggings, they allowed both non-veteran and non-Native members. Yet despite being considered more assimilated, the Gourd Clan was only revived several years earlier, by Fred Tsoodle. The Gourd Clan also was absent for a far shorter period of time; it had been suppressed in the early 1930s after forty years of continued government efforts to do so. In preservation days a Kiowa could not be a member of both groups. Now it is quite common.[12]

Regalia worn by the Gourd Clan's members is a mix of an earlier women's society revived during World War II, the Jaifegau, as well as Native American Church and Pan-Indian dress. Members wear the traditional red blankets or capes and bandoliers to symbolize blood spilled by warriors. Each veteran carries a straight lance covered with service decorations and with service insignia on his red cape. The group's tipi is another syncretic mix of the old and new traditions. The left side has traditional yellow and black war trails painted onto it. The right has depictions of modern battles, tanks, and paratroopers. The divisional crests and military insignia of all Kiowa veterans are also on the tipi, as well as the names of all Kiowa veterans killed in action.[13]

Gourd Clans similar to the Kiowas' spread to the Alabama-Coushattas, the Otoes, the Osages, and the Omahas, introduced by non-Kiowas who were close friends or related by marriage to the Kiowas. Gourd Clan ceremonies spread to intertribal events in Oklahoma, Texas, and California, in a form of Pan-Indianism similar to the spread of the Native American Church by the Comanche. Prescient of present conflict between Native people and the New Age movement, Anglo hobbyists in the Boy Scouts stole the Gourd Dance ceremony and did "their own" versions of it in the 1970s. The Boy Scouts even stole the name of the Gourd Clan, enormously angering Kiowas over casual, haphazard, and imperfectly imitated (and thus sacrilegious) versions of the dances.[14]

The Black Leggings place greater emphasis on martial tradition and veteran status. Members wear leggings in place of the traditional black paint worn in prereservation days. The ceremonies begin with a consecration, then War Memorial songs with the naming of all Kiowa veterans killed in action, and traditional Scalp and Victory dances (done with actual scalps from enemy soldiers) by the women to celebrate the safe return of veterans and honor the war dead on both sides. Feathers on the lances and guns represent battles; shorter feathers signify slain Kiowas. The Empty Saddle ceremony is then conducted, with a riderless horse representing those killed in action, at times followed by the induction of new members with the citing of their military records. The emotional high point of the ceremonies is the Reverse Dance, where the members fire their guns and howl with building intensity, not halting until a combat veteran stops the drum by placing his lance upon it. Then he must recite a deed done in battle.[15]

The Naishan Apaches, more commonly known as the Kiowa Apaches, are one of the smallest tribal groups, numbering only in the hundreds. Most of their rituals ceased being practiced in the 1920s. Their small numbers forced them to rely on other tribal groups for a model for their societies, as well as ethnographic information. Apache Ben, his wife, Rose Chalepah Chaletson, and their son, Alfred Chalepah, began the Manatidie (Blackfoot) Society in 1959. They based their "Apache Flag Song" on the "Kiowa Flag Song." Simultaneously the Apache Service Club revived, modeled on other War Mother Societies of the Plains. Exactly like Kiowa War Mother Societies, the members wore a red blanket with the name and rank of a relative sewn on it.[16]

Termination split these societies much as it did whole tribes facing the loss of their status and land. In 1963, the Blackfoot split into the Chalepah Apache Blackfoot and the Redbone Apache Blackfoot over whether to accept the end of tribal government. Some considered the Chalepahs assimilationist or progressive while others regarded the Redbones as more traditional. Part of the Redbones split off yet again to form the Apache Veterans Association. Over time and as faction leaders died off, the splits between the groups ended.[17]

Comanches first honored their Comanche Code Talkers and other veterans at the Comanche Homecoming in 1952 at Walters, Oklahoma. Comanches frequently joined warrior societies in other tribes, especially the Kiowas, at least as far back as 1957. But in their case, conflict over Termination split the tribe so disastrously that, in spite of the wishes of most of the veterans of Korea and World War II, no warrior society could be formed. When President Richard Nixon finally dropped Termination as an official policy, the Comanches formed five warrior societies in only six years.[18]

Dennis Banks, a Korean War air force veteran, founded the American Indian Movement (AIM), a group modeling itself on warrior societies but with a far more explicitly political focus. Other notable AIM leaders included such Korean War veterans as Bill Means and Claude Bellecourt. With that exception, other warrior societies remained distinctly tribal rather than Pan-Indian. The American Indian Veterans Association briefly attempted to become an intertribal group between World War II and the Korean War. It split into tribal groups before ever meeting, and not out of any kind of animosity.[19] It is important to note that Pan-Indianism is relatively recent. It is one of my arguments that Pan-Indianism is as much a result of the Anglo creation of the idea of "the Indian" as it is a coalescing of common Native interests. Pan-Indian identity began, after all, as a creation of the most assimilated Natives educated in white institutions. While Pan-Indian alliances have a long history dating to pre-Columbian times, Pan-Indian identity could make little headway as long as Native people remained the most segregated ethnic group in the country. Only with the permanent end of that isolation brought by World War II did a majority of Natives first confront an Anglo public that often regarded them as homogenous and monolithic. While Natives are forced to deal with such a view, and have often used it to their advantage, Pan-Indianism remains distasteful at best to many Natives because of its assimilationist potential and origin and its stereotypical promotion and implications.

War Songs and Flag Songs

Many of the songs about the Korean War come from Kiowa songwriters, famed from that time until the present as the most popular on the powwow circuit. The Kiowa "Black Legs Honor Song" for their veterans is reproduced below. The "they" in the song refers to other Kiowas and to a lesser extent other Indians, not the larger dominant society. The approval of Anglos is not sought and in any case could hardly be received in a ceremony practiced at a reservation remote from most whites.

> Black Legs members arise, get up and
> Let us dance
> And they shall look upon us
> They are outstanding young men[20]

Another Black Legs song is the "War Dead" or "Funeral Song."

> Kiowa young men, they are warriors that have been to battle
> You hear he-man stories about them
> They are warriors and that is the way they really die[21]

Their flag song is sung when raising and lowering the flag. At first glance it might appear to be a more formal Nativized version of an Anglo-American flag song. Yet the meaning changes dramatically if one knows that the Native association of the flag with the actual body of the deceased is far more important than any association with a political nation-state.

> Be raising the flag carefully with respect
> It has been involved in wars all over the world
> Because it is respected all over the world
> Even on the moon it is standing at attention like a soldier[22]

The "Korean Veterans Song" for the Lakota reproduced below is by Lakota Thunder. The meaning of the second line has no real equivalent anywhere in Anglo-American culture or Christianity. The sacred pipe is a traditional source of spiritual medicine for the collective Lakota people. Perhaps the closest thing comparable in Western civilization would be the Ark of the Covenant. Yet the comparison breaks down, for the Korean War certainly did not become a holy war for Native peoples in the same way as war was for the Israelites against the Canaanites. What is being culturally and spiritually sanctioned by the song and ceremony is the veteran's sacrifice and actions in wartime, not the war itself or its aims.

> You have gone to shoot in Korea
> With the blessings of the sacred pipe
> You have gone to shoot[23]

Another Lakota flag song is specific to the Korean War.

> Lakota hoksila, do your duty
> Stick by the United States flag
> Look at it (the flag)
> The Koreans are charging[24]

In the 1950s Ellis Chips, an Oglala from Wamblee, South Dakota, composed the Sioux National Anthem during the 1950s.

> The flag of the United States will stand forever
> Beneath it the people will live on
> That is why I do this (honor the flag)[25]

Probably the most famous Native dance of all time, the Ghost Dance, appears to have been revived during the Korean War. But this is difficult to say since ghost dancers today often keep their ceremonies extremely well hidden. The "Ghost Dance Korea Song" is a pointed reminder of ritual preparation for war.

> You boys in Korea
> You should have taken your pipes
> And prayed to Wakan Tanka
> That you would come out alive[26]

Winslow White Eagle sang a Ho Chunk (Winnebago) Victory Dance song at Wisconsin Dells, Wisconsin, on March 1, 1956. A Kiowa Methodist minister named Linn Paughty recorded it. I could not find a translation of it, unfortunately. Particularly in the aftermath of the Korean War the powwow circuit began to grow exponentially, possibly as a response to the threat of Termination but certainly as a result of the end of isolation. Pan-tribal and pan-religious contact became the norm. Paughty himself is a good example of syncretism as both an ordained Christian minister and the holder of one of the most sacred traditional roles, the hereditary keeper of the medicine bags of the Buffalo Medicine Society.[27]

Nativizing the Military

During the Korean War the U.S. military continued its long-held practices of adopting American Indian tactics and names and symbols for military units and weapons. In 1951, General Lawton Chiles ordered Ranger training extended to all U.S. infantry. At least one officer in every company and one NCO in every platoon is required to be trained in tactics learned in the eighteenth century from Native people.[28]

The best-known use of Indian imagery for propaganda purposes came from the highest-ranking Native in the military. Vice Admiral Joseph "Jocko" Clark, the first Native to graduate from the Naval Academy and commander of the 7th Fleet, led his self-proclaimed "Cherokee Strikes," surprise raids and bombings of supplies behind enemy lines to boost morale. Clark never shied away from acknowledging his heritage, but he also seemed willing to appeal to Anglo stereotypes. One of the best-known photos of him shows him wearing a Plains Indian–style warbonnet while onstage with Bob Hope. Naval historian Samuel Eliot Morrison has described Clark as "part Cherokee, part Southern Methodist, but all fighter." The image of the Indian as natural fighter continued. At least one Native veteran believed it himself. Ute Marine Corps veteran Darrel Gardner, a runner for reconnaissance during the war, believed Indians have a sixth sense "like an animal."[29]

Conclusion

It has become a near cliché, while being no less true, that the Korean War is "the forgotten war." What the phrase fails to convey is that this war was a sharp break with the two previous "good wars" and both a harbinger of much that would happen in the Vietnam War and a bridge to an allegedly less morally certain era. Despite the sentimental claims of some, the "simpler times" of the 1950s were every bit as socially uncertain as the times to follow. Those who realized that fact most strongly included American Indians, especially Native veterans, and above all Native veterans who became tribal leaders and activists.

Native veterans had a clear and unambiguous understanding of these facts when faced with the hypocrisy of a dominant culture that could speak of "liberating" Native people by forcing the sale of sacred homelands. Native people, led by veterans of the Korean War such as Joseph Gary, the president of the National Congress of American Indians at the height of Termination, drew on Pan-Indian alliances while rejecting Pan-Indian identity or any other form of assimilation from the dominant culture. At the same time they fell back on tribal identities precisely because these stood as the cultural traits and social groupings most under assault. Both in the service and after, cultural and spiritual ways gave Native veterans strength, a sense of renewal and continuity, and spiritual sanction for their struggles on the battlefield and off.

8

An American Ka in Indian Country

Vietnam

RAY LEANNA FROM THE Crow Creek Reservation joined the army in 1945. He went to China, where his unit worked with both the Nationalists and the Communists in rounding up the remnants of Japan's Imperial Army. Leanna had a low opinion of both sides in China's civil war. Nevertheless, he felt an obligation to do his duty. In 1961 he went to Laos as part of the Special Forces to train guerilla fighters for the Royal Army. The recruits came from the local Hill Tribes. Though he came from the other side of the world, the people Leanna met thought of him as much like themselves in appearance, tribal culture, and even experience in fighting off relative newcomers. The local Ka tribesmen thought so highly of Leanna they called him an "American Ka," even offering him a bride. Leanna felt flattered by the show of respect but declined the offer.[1]

Leanna's attitude and experience resembled that of other Native veterans in several ways: he disliked both sides in the cold war struggles the United States involved itself in; he had a deep sense of obligation; and he was respected by indigenous communities both near and far away. If Leanna had served in the conventional forces as a foot soldier, he would have walked point and been called "chief" while his officers and NCOs casually referred to territory held by the National Liberation Front (NLF) as "Indian Country" and the local bases as "Fort Apache." Coming home, he and the other Native veterans faced a fundamentally different experience than did their non-Native buddies. The war was every bit as unpopular among Natives as non-Natives, but unlike some Anglos, both pro-and antiwar, Native communities did not expect the

Native veteran to shoulder the blame for the war. Native communities instead made a great effort to shoulder the veteran's pain. Widespread acceptance by a veteran's Native community likely became the most positive thing in his life. The war reinforced, or even created, mutual bonds between veterans and their communities, as well as between indigenous communities in other nations.[2]

The war also further alienated Natives from "mainstream" American society in a profound way, and not just because the military compared the conflict to the old Indian Wars. Atrocities against Vietnamese by American soldiers sickened many Native servicemen, who often identified with the Vietnamese more than Anglo-Americans. The rising civil rights and Red Power movements played a huge part in Natives' alienation and identification with the Vietnamese. Some Native veterans frequently got into fistfights over racist treatment by non-Natives in the service. Cherokee soldier Dwight Birdwell even attended a Black Power meeting in Vietnam.[3] This generation of Natives was the most alienated Natives had ever been from whites, precisely because it had the greatest amount of contact with whites. This generation finally and completely rejected any and all notions of assimilation, a sea change that may be permanent. That alienation expressed itself in two ways: a building upon ties with the most traditional parts of Native communities, and an often explosive contempt for all the wrongs done to Native peoples.

The Social Backdrop of Native Communities

This generation of Native veterans became both the Termination generation and the Red Power generation.[4] The political battles over Termination still loomed overhead during almost all of the Vietnam War. Termination began to lose favor in the late 1950s as a result of strenuous Native efforts to defeat it and local and state governments not wanting to take on federal obligations. The federal government then refocused its efforts on Relocation (which actually preceded Termination as official policy), where the government enticed or coerced Natives on reservations to leave for the cities. Only in 1972 did President Nixon formally abandon Termination as a stated policy. Fear of Termination remained very real and ominous for Native communities. Internal tribal conflicts over how to respond to Termination sharply divided some communities such as the Comanches into the early 1970s.

Native communities by the 1960s had greatly urbanized; a lower proportion of people lived on the reservations due to the government's policy of Relocation and Native flight into the urban and migrant labor workforces. After World War II most Natives left the reservation at some point, for work, school, the military, or a combination of the three. This process could be either gradual or sudden. Relocated Natives often just received a bus ticket, left to their own devices. Those who moved voluntarily often did so in stages, first to nearby small towns, then to mid-sized cities, then to the big cities. Often they relied on relatives or friends who prepared the way for them with a place to live or work. By the time the United States became heavily involved in Vietnam, enough Natives had been off-reservation long enough for large numbers to grow up having never seen their traditional homelands. In some cities, such as Minneapolis, Natives formed or were forced into "red ghettos." In other cities, such as Los Angeles, there were no predominantly Native neighborhoods, but there was still a Native community at large.

Native communities reacted to the Vietnam War in a fundamentally different way than did Anglo-America as a whole. Most either opposed the war from the outset of heavy U.S. involvement or supported it based on Native historical experience. (In "mainstream" America, opposition took several years to build.) "This time they were the cavalry, and it was kind of like what the cavalry did to us and they had to reconcile that when they were there and when they came back," said Harold Barse, a Kiowa who counseled many Native Vietnam War veterans. Cherokee soldier Dwight Birdwell began his tour as an idealist but later turned sharply against the war when he saw parallels to his people's own experience: "I still wanted to believe in the war—these so-called gooks were the people we were fighting for!—and blended in with all of that was the thought of the cruelties inflicted upon the American Indian at the hands of the U.S. Army. Being of Cherokee heritage, I didn't want to turn around three or four generations later and perpetuate the same sort of abuse myself, especially with people who were poor farmers just like my people were poor farmers, and in some cases looked almost exactly like Indians I knew back in Oklahoma."[5]

Yet antiwar protest remained relatively unheard of in Indian communities. Most Natives regarded draft dodging with disdain, as something unthinkable. It is ironic to note that while the two "good wars" had a lot of Native draft resistance (including tribal-wide campaigns of defiance), Native draft resistance became rarer during the Vietnam War, especially compared to the rest of America. The chance to take part in now well-established veteran traditions going back to at least World War II overrode political objections. In at least one case, an Aleut veteran who grew up in the forced detention camps for Aleut Indians during World War II volunteered for duty in the Vietnam War. Richard Chagin defends his choice today ambivalently, saying, "You know, I'm not really patriotic or anything like that. . . . It's not that much, but by God it's all we got."[6]

Canada presented a very different situation. Canada did not send troops to Vietnam, so one might think discussing Canada's Native peoples would be out of place in this chapter. But many Canadians joined the U.S. military, including an undetermined number of Canada's Native people. Many of Canada's Natives are part of tribal nations divided by the U.S.-Canada border, with large numbers on both sides who frequently cross, often "illegally" from the governments' points of view. The border is a deeply resented intrusion upon traditional beliefs about sovereignty. The border also financed warrior society activities through "smuggling" untaxed cigarettes and gasoline. Some of the warrior societies in and near Canada formed in the aftermath of Vietnam asserted that smuggling was not illegal, reasoning that the border intrudes on Native sovereignty and to recognize it limits that assertion of independence. Canadian authorities and some tribal governments in turn labeled warrior societies as criminal syndicates or gangs, even trying to criminalize membership. Some tribal governments also saw these warrior societies as threats to tribal sovereignty since their actions jeopardized the treaty relationships from the councils' point of view. Canada has witnessed violent confrontations between Native ex-veteran militants and the governments lasting from the early 1970s all the way into the present. In the United States such confrontations peaked in the early and mid-1970s, especially at the Red Power movement's version of the Alamo, Wounded Knee II.

Warrior Societies

Many warrior societies in existence today formed after the Korean War as a direct response to the fear of Termination and the loss of tribal traditions. Native veterans of Vietnam often expanded the warrior society role to an explicitly political one. Ironically, this most often happened in Canada, especially among tribal nations split by the border such as the Mohawks and Ojibwas.

The Ohoma Lodge or Hethuska split off from the Kiowa Tia Pah of Oklahoma in the early 1970s. Its members honor veterans on the Fourth of July with a Scalp Dance, charging dances, and battle stories. Some of the groups splitting off, such as the Tai Piah of Carnegie, Oklahoma, and the Gulf Coast Tai Piah, formed from Anglo hobbyists rather than Native veterans. But mostly Natives made up the newer Gourd Dance societies that split off in the 1970s. These included the Omaha Tai Piah, Cherokee, Osage, Cheyenne, and Arapaho societies. A number of Gourd Dance societies based on lineage also formed among the Comanches, such as the Chief Satanta and Quanah Parker Descendants.[7]

Forrest Kassanovoid, Melvin Kerchee, and Bernard Kahranah revived the Comanche War Dance Society in 1970 with the help of other Comanches in Cache and Indianoma, Oklahoma. Its members include Anglos; the Comanches liken their inclusion to the practice of adopting captives in the past. Their songs are mostly Ponca and have Ponca lyrics, though some Comanche songs with all vocables are also sung.[8]

The Tehda Puku Nu or Comanche Little Ponies revived in 1972 with World War II veterans as their elders and Peyotists influenced by the Gourd Dance societies. Often they sponsor and cohost events with Gourd Dance groups. Its members' regalia includes a circular insignia of four horses, which is worn on blankets and bandoliers. Knights from chess games are attached to the tops of their ceremonial rattles.[9]

The Tuh Wi or Black Crow Lodge revived in 1976. Its founders, Joe Attocknie and Brownie Sorvo, received funding for presenting traditional dances at the Bicentennial Festival in Washington DC. In 1989 they honored the Comanche and Choctaw Code Talkers in a ceremony in Oklahoma City. In 1991, they honored returning Desert Storm veterans.[10]

The Wild Horse Butte Tokalas, a Lakota warrior society, began in 1982 with a predominantly Vietnam-era membership but included both older and more recent veterans. Its membership also includes Anglo members who are longtime friends of veterans. Its main function is to serve as an honor guard or flag bearers at powwows, funerals, and other events.[11]

Ponca veteran Gordon Roy joined the Ponca Heyoshas after leaving the air force in 1977 after twenty years of service. At age fifty-one Roy finally got his Indian name, Black Bull Buffalo, which was given to him by the Heyoshas. Roy felt honored to carry on the name of a relative greatly respected in his community, his great-uncle. In Ponca traditional naming one cannot adopt the name of a relative while he is still alive, and one must always conduct oneself in a manner that honors the memory of that relative. Failure to do so means the loss of one's Indian name.[12]

The first of the much more overtly political warrior societies, the American Indian Movement (AIM), formed in 1968. AIM became the first of a number of warrior societies willing to take part in semi-military confrontations with the authorities that were calculated to draw attention to their causes while staying just this side of insurrection.[13] As will be shown in the next chapter on Wounded Knee II, often they responded to government use of military tactics against civil disobedience.

The Rotiskenrakete (literally, "men who carry the burden of peace") or the Mohawk Warrior Society formed on the reservations in New York State and in reserves in Quebec in 1974, seizing an island between Canada and the United States and declaring an independent nation named Ganankieh. Throughout the mid and late 1970s and into the 1980s, its members became the most vocal and active pro-gambling Mohawks in a series of armed confrontations with those opposed to bringing gaming in, including the tribal councils. In 1991, both sides set aside confrontations over gambling after a company sought to turn a Mohawk burial ground into part of a golf course. The Mohawk Warrior Society and others opposed to the desecration of the burial ground fought with local police, townspeople, and finally one-fourth of the entire Canadian Army, over 3,500 troops, in the Oka standoff.[14]

Other Iroquois warrior societies formed during these times included the Oneida Warrior Society. This group organized to oppose Oneida tribal chairman Jim Thompson and succeeded in forcing him from office. The Tuscarora Warrior Society also began in 1987 as another pro-gambling group. All three warrior societies have been in continuous conflict since 1993 with both the state of New York and tribal councils over the issue of smoke shops and state taxes on them, which is seen as yet another threat to Native sovereignty.[15]

Across Canada a number of both tribal and intertribal warrior societies emerged in the aftermath of the Vietnam War as veterans returned from the war and AIM's influence increased despite the efforts of both the FBI and the Royal Canadian Mounted Police (RCMP) to disrupt such ties. The Anishinabe Okiidija or Ojibwe Warrior Society began in 1975 after the Cache Creek blockade, a takeover of a highway to protest poverty on the reserves, and before the Native Caravan, a march on Ottawa. AIM leaders such as Clyde Bellecourt heavily influenced the Okiidija and the Regina Warriors Society as well, and they, in turn, influenced other societies in Canada.[16]

The Manitoba Warrior Society is the largest warrior society in Canada. In 1995 members occupied Ts'Peten or Lake Gustafsen, a sacred Sun Dance site barred to Natives. The Canadian government responded with a siege nearly as violent as the Wounded Knee II standoff, with over 77,000 rounds fired by the RCMP, followed by the longest trial in Canada's history.[17]

The spread of warrior societies shows some of the clearest cases of intertribal syncretism. Much of the *intra*tribal conflicts, especially those among the Mohawks, erupted over competing definitions of the role of a warrior and the correct way to maintain traditional ideals of sovereignty. Iroquois warrior societies maintained that all Iroquois males are called upon to be warriors and should not worry about outsiders' opinions on the matter. Tribal councils placed far more emphasis on unity and deference to public and elected figures, insisting that the warrior societies' interpretation of *warrior* in the oral traditions is a mistranslation of *young men*.[18]

In 1982 the least politicized Iroquois veterans' group, the North American Iroquois Veterans Association (NAIVA), formed. Its main emphases are putting on an annual veterans' honor powwow and raising money for local schools, scholarships, and an educational exhibit on Native veterans. NAIVA's membership is both intertribal and interethnic. It is their practice to have an Anglo cochairman and to admit Anglo veterans related by marriage to Iroquois.[19]

Why would Canada be the setting for so many more violent confrontations many years after such incidents declined in the United States? In part, the U.S. Red Power movement became somewhat crippled by being forced to deal with heavy-handed prosecutions and disruptions of activist groups. Canada went through a long series of constitutional crises that at times threatened to break apart the country. Anglo-Canadians and Quebecois struggled with the issue of the status of Quebec within Canada. These three-sided conflicts became very much a matter of conflicting attempts at nationhood. With not enough numbers to effect change at the polls, some of Canada's First Nations people fell back on disruption and confrontation. Canadian authorities increasingly relied on tactics of military control of Native populations that had been perfected in the United States during the Red Power heyday. Unlike in the United States, it is perfectly legal and a common practice in Canada for the authorities to use the military for policing in standoffs.[20]

Ceremonies and Personal Medicine

Cherokee scholar Tom Holm has found that large numbers of Native veterans of Vietnam went through ceremonies for honoring and protection before leaving for the service, carried personal medicine while in combat, and took part in ceremonies for healing and honoring upon their return. An outreach program for Native veterans, however, found that only 40 percent of Native veterans went through healing ceremonies. Holm derived his figures from a survey he did for the Veterans Administration, one in which the responders' self-selecting might have biased the result. The outreach program dealt with those most likely to still be going through trauma from their wartime experience.[21] The real figures are likely somewhere in between those of the two studies. What is more pertinent may be a comparison to non-Native veterans and their practices. Compare how many Christians carry or wear a cross, for example; either number is quite high.

One Kiowa veteran recalled that while he was on patrol he saw an image in a jungle stream of an old Kiowa man dressed traditionally, wearing one eagle feather. The old Kiowa told him, "Take heart, be strong, this is what you must do." After that his fear of combat went away. Another Native veteran told of praying and having an eagle appear before him. "The eagle told me he would be my eyes in battle. After that I knew everything that was going on. That helped me survive."[22]

Another Native veteran recalled hearing the voice of his deceased grandmother warning him against stepping on a landmine. "I was going to take a step when . . . something flew in my face. I heard, 'Don't step there, grandchild, the danger is very near.' They laid an ambush and I just about tripped a booby trap. I know that it was my grandmother's voice . . . she warned me."[23]

Lumbee veteran Delano Cummings remembers he visited the graves of his family by the river to seek their counsel each time before leaving for Vietnam. During three tours of intense combat duty he often called on the spirits of his ancestors for strength. He took the code name of his unit, Moon Dash, as a sign that he had followed the right way of being a Lumbee warrior. At the end of his third tour of duty in Vietnam, the voices of his grandfathers told him that he had done his duty and warned him it was time to leave; to stay would endanger his life and his state of mind should he survive. Cummings followed their advice and did not sign up for a fourth tour.[24]

Choctaw veteran Charles Ray Battiest carried his medicine pouch, a cross, and a Bible with him at all times. A devout man who prayed daily in Vietnam, he relied on his spirit guide to protect him from harm. After the Vietnam War, that same prayer to his Creator and advice from his guide helped him recover from the trauma of war. He still relied on these deeply held beliefs several decades later. Such a mix of traditional and Christian beliefs was common. Seminole army veteran

Stephen Bowers, like most of his people, grew up as a Baptist. But he also went through traditional healing rites after Vietnam.[25]

Ponca air force veteran Gordon Roy made it a point to perform the traditional dances on U.S. military bases and in Germany and Vietnam. Overseas, he found that the Hollywood image of Indians had preceded him, which he believed worked in his favor because it had created curiosity and respect in advance: "They [Vietnamese] think a lot of us. When I first went over to Vietnam, they came up to me and said, 'You Chinese?' 'No, Indian.' 'Oh, Indians don't lie. They tell the truth.' Well, not all Indians [I thought]. I said, 'Where'd you hear that?' 'Oh, we watch movies.'"[26]

Cherokee air force veteran Steve Russell regretted not being able to perform the Cherokee purification ritual called Going to the Waters while in the service. But since the rite requires several days, other Cherokees, and the right structures to make steam, he had little choice. He also regretted not being able to keep the traditional hair length, long and uncut on the back and cut short on the sides and top. Like nearly all of even the most traditional Cherokees, he never followed the old tradition of wearing long hair under a turban. He reluctantly decided against petitioning his superiors to keep his traditional hair length after seeing the harassment a Jewish airman went through for seeking to wear a yarmulke. Russell carried his medicine pouch with him at all times in the service but kept it hidden.[27]

Navajo healer Sam Begay performed the Blackening Way ceremony for Paul Keams, who had become troubled by ghosts of his enemies, to restore his *hozho* (balance, harmony, or peace) after his time in Vietnam. The Blackening Way is a shorter version of Enemy Way, a ritual describing the killing of Yei Tsoh, a monster from Navajo oral tradition who sometimes consumed Navajos. Keams symbolically took on the identity of Monster Slayer, a Navajo culture hero who blackened his skin so as to become invisible. Keams attributes never being harmed in Vietnam to a protection prayer said by his father. Keams related that while in Vietnam, "I told my commanders there are things I can't do because of my religion. Digging graves is one of them."[28]

Cheyenne veteran Langburn "War Dog" Fisher became an artist some years after the war, doing traditional art that had sacred Native meaning but was considered unusual by Anglo standards. After getting permission from authorities, he made a traditional necklace of human finger bones with ten knuckles and hair. Fisher believed his artwork helped him cope with his internal scars from the war and preserve Cheyenne heritage. At an art show at the Black Kettle Museum, Cheyenne priest Frank "Toby" Starr blessed Fisher, his necklace, and the museum. Later, in commemoration of the massacre at Sand Creek, Fisher built a warrior's burial scaffold.[29]

Apache veteran Ernie Dogwolf Lovato saw similarities between Vietnamese and Native beliefs.

> I related more to the Vietnamese people than to the Americans. . . . I sat in the opium dens and when I started hallucinating the people around me were actually my Indian people. The den was very much like it was with my people because of how similar their ways were to some of our religions, especially in the Native American Church. . . . I used that den to find my inner self. I would say their medicine people taught their elders the same. . . . On the spiritual side I taught the Vietnamese how close they were to our religion. . . . It was a form of meditation to them. It was like a powwow, or after the sweats.

Lovato was not the only Athapascan soldier to see similarities between Vietnamese and Natives. Bruce Heaton, an Ahtna Athapascan from Chitna, Alaska, saw women giving birth in the center of the house gripping a rope that hung from the ceiling, exactly how Native women gave birth back home.[30]

Comanche/Lakota veteran Ed Humming Eagle Ramon also coped with the war through his beliefs and viewed it through his own culture's perspective.

> You come to that stage in combat helicopter assault . . . you begin to subscribe to those principles of the *ta sunkeska olewan*, which is the Whitehorse Society's hymn or song. It is *kola ta ho . . . yelo*, which is a pledge to brotherhood that goes beyond friendship. It asserts that you do not fear death and that you would love your friend forever, your combat companion, and that you would never leave them lying on the battlefield. . . . I know that I survived in combat

because of some sort of a self-image bias, or some sort of a com-
mitment that I was a warrior. . . . Probably the thing that allowed
me to function would have been some very deeply imprinted, very
rote ideas about warfare, and about what a warrior should do to
maintain his honor. . . . In the recovery process, or in retrospect.
. . . We have found over the years the beauty and value of *oon hey*,
being honored by the people, and the *wicasa iyotanyapi*, forever
am I to be a respected individual. . . . I don't look upon myself as a
seer or dreamer. . . . I am not truly *wanagi yuha*, but I own a spirit,
but in a way I am.

Ramon then described being saved by visions of his deceased grandmother: "My grandmother, *nakio hani*, came to visit me. My Lakota
was very weak and not fluent, but I understood every word that she
said. . . . My grandmother told me, 'You are a good boy, and you
are going to be okay.' And then she left me. . . . This was such a real
experience to me. . . . I felt blessed that I was able to see her in three
dimensions. . . . It was something holy for me."[31]

Songs

Like the three previous wars, the Vietnam War produced opportunities
for Native composers to honor their peoples' veterans. Kiowa elder Jack
Anquoe composed this honor song for Vietnam veterans in 1983.

> *Tain nah zeddle bey nah Vietnam toyah*
> They had strong hearts in Vietnam[32]

The Alliance West and the Intertribal Veterans sing the "Comanche
POW Song." The song consists entirely of vocables, the "hey ya heys"
and "heyas" that are roughly the Native equivalent of scat singing in
jazz. The song is unusual for a veteran's honor song or war song in
that it has sound effects in addition to vocals and drums, namely the
sounds of mortar and artillery fire. The song is dedicated to Samuel
"Doc" Pewewardy (Comanche), the father of Alliance West's leader,
Professor Cornel Pewewardy (Comanche/Kiowa).[33]

The "Vietnam Song" is sung by the Black Lodge Singers, a Blackfoot
group except for one member who is Yakima and Ute. Unfortunately,
a translation could not be found for it in time for this study. The

"Vietnam-Desert Storm Song" that follows is another song by the Black Lodge Singers. It is sung in English except for the vocables. The song is one of thanksgiving for the return of veterans, as well as a song of pride.

> Korea, feels so good
> Vietnam, Desert Storm
> Feels so good, feels so good
> Weyo hoheyah

A folk-rock song is the most famous song composed about the Vietnam experience for Native veterans, not one written for pow-wows. Robbie Robertson, a Mohawk musician who became famous as part of The Band, wrote "Hell's Half Acre" for his debut solo album in 1987.

> It's a way up in the Black Hills where we come from
> There's a girl and she warned me don't pick up that gun
> By the law of the land, by the promise that might is right
> She would hold me and cry, don't you go off and fight
>
> Somebody knocking at my door
> I been called to war
> Say goodbye to Tobacco Road
> Wear my colors, call my brothers
> And for my country I'll go[34]

The most striking thing about the first verse is how Robertson makes the same assumption most Anglos do about Native veterans. Notice that Robertson is writing of a Lakota veteran (the Black Hills are their most sacred site) and not his own people, the Mohawks. Robertson is following the habit of many Anglos of regarding the Lakotas as stand-ins for all Natives. The Tobacco Road reference is clearly Robertson's belief that poverty played a big part in Native veterans' choice to enlist. "Somebody knocking" seems to refer to a draft notice. The percentage of Natives who were drafted is small; over 80 percent volunteered. The reference to "my country" suggests Robertson believes Natives think in conventionally patriotic terms instead of having the dual loyalties most feel toward both the United States and their tribal nation.

> Back in the land where the buffalo roam
> Oh this is my home
> She said you've changed, you're not the same
> Clouds of napalm and the opium
> The damage was already done

In this last verse, Robertson does not seem to know about traditional ceremonies for healing. He assumes Native veterans abused drugs as much as Anglo veterans, when actually such abuse was much rarer. Robertson was beginning a personal journey back to his Native heritage when he wrote this. Since then, he has become well respected for his mix of traditional styles and themes with rock and folk.

Nativizing the Military

In most nineteenth-century wars involving the United States, the military depended heavily on Native allies and their skills. In Vietnam these practices became commonplace again. Forty thousand Hmong, ten thousand Montagnards, and Ka and other hill tribesmen fought against the North Vietnamese and National Liberation Front (NLF), groups they regarded as the latest set of intruders on their homelands.

Without indigenous allies in Vietnam, "there'd be 10,000 more names on [the Vietnam Memorial] wall," according to the head of recruitment for the CIA in Southeast Asia, Cherokee officer Captain D. L. "Pappy" Hicks. Many American Indians took part in U.S. military recruiting and fighting alongside the Hill Tribes of Southeast Asia against the North Vietnamese and NLF. One Cherokee veteran, George "Sonny" Hoffman, described "getting in tight with the Yards as getting in touch with my tribal roots." Special Forces in Southeast Asia learned the tribal customs, mixed Hill Tribes' garb with their own uniforms, and took part in the local tribal rituals. The Kohos initiated Hoffman into their tribe, placing a brass bracelet on his right wrist with tribal marking signifying he was a member of the Cai Cai band, and gave him the Koho name of Y Sonny Eban. Ironically, many Montagnards identified more with figures from American western movies, such as

John Wayne, incorporating cavalry scarves and cowboy hats into their dress. Wayne even received a Rhade tribal bracelet, signifying the tribe accepted him, after filming *The Green Berets*.[35]

The Long Range Recon Patrols (LRRPS) also show the influence of indigenous ways. The units called themselves "Hatchet Teams" because they decapitated their enemies in imitation of Rogers' Rangers. Their hatchets had the nickname of "totems." Even the North Vietnamese showed signs of having learned American Indian tactics. They referred to the practice of troops traveling single file, silently, and evenly spaced on the way to a raid as "Indian file."[36]

The war's end brought a mass exodus of Southeast Asia's indigenous peoples to the United States. After South Vietnam collapsed, Hicks and other Native veterans lobbied heavily for the evacuation of America's Hill Tribe allies. Around 150,000 Hmong and 3,000 Montagnards emigrated to the United States, settling mostly in Minnesota, North Carolina, and Texas, often not far from the Native soldiers they had fought alongside, such as the Eastern Band and Texas Cherokees. The Hmong honored Hicks in their traditional way by having his name and image included on the pictographic scarves that the Hmong use to tell their oral histories.[37]

The Vietnam War saw the first widespread use of intentionally negative images of Natives by the military since the old Indian Wars of the nineteenth century. NLF-held territory became "Indian Country" and U.S. firebases "Fort Apaches." Military planners and conservative politicians used Indian war imagery repeatedly to justify the Vietnam War. General Maxwell Taylor in testimony before the Senate Foreign Relations Committee justified the forced relocation of Vietnamese civilians by saying, "It's very hard to plant the corn around the stockade when the Indians are still around. We have to get the Indians farther away." John Wayne's *The Green Berets* featured North Vietnamese that "talked and whooped like marauding Indians." The U.S. Army showed Western movies to South Vietnamese troops, who knowingly yelled "VC!" whenever Hollywood "Indians" appeared onscreen. Many reviewers also commented on the consciously "Indian-like" appearance of Sylvester Stallone in the Rambo movies.[38]

The U.S. military also referred to defectors from the North Vietnamese and NLF who fought on the U.S. side as Kit Carson Scouts. One source claimed the Kit Carson Scouts received their name from Lieutenant General Herman Nickerson, supposedly because he was "part Indian and a western history buff." I have not been able to find any evidence of Nickerson's alleged Native heritage or of his identifying with Native people. His name does turn up on a number of Scottish Mason and genealogy sites. That a military historian for the Marine Corps argued as such fits into the pattern of using images of Indians and the Wild West to justify the war.[39]

Conclusion

The story of Native veterans of the Vietnam War has many ironies. This war affected Native communities even more deeply than it affected Anglo America. Yet Native communities also proved to be more resilient than Anglo America, recovering more quickly from the war's trauma. Though the war deeply divided "mainstream" America, it proved, ultimately, an enormously unifying experience for Native communities. Urban Indians struggled to reconnect and unite with tribal communities. The latter discovered they had new allies among people the federal government hoped would forget they were ever Indian. Intertribal ties were created and strengthened in an unprecedented way, even encompassing tribal peoples on the other side of the world. The Vietnam experience also created a new direction for warrior societies and Native ideals on the right way to be a warrior, as we shall see in the next chapter. This was not an easy or instant process; a great deal of pain and struggle was part of it. But it is a tribute to Native cultural resilience that the outcomes resolved themselves as they did.

9

Bringing the War Home

The American Indian Movement, Wounded Knee II, Counterinsurgency, and a New Direction for Warrior Societies

ONE OF THE GREAT IRONIES of the Vietnam War is that American military planners and conservative politicians treated Communists like Indians and Indians like Communists. Both sets of enemies became "Reds" in both meanings of the slur. Often *both* American Indian activists and the government agents who dealt with them came straight out of combat in Vietnam and brought that experience of fighting a guerilla war to American soil. Protests or civil disorder sometimes escalated into heavily armed semi-military confrontations.

In 1973 in the middle of the unfolding Watergate scandal, America woke up to potentially face what seemed to be something straight out of the last century: another Indian war. The second violent conflict at Wounded Knee probably fascinated more people than any other event in American Indian history in the twentieth century precisely because it combined all the elements of both an old Western and modern political drama. This confrontation lent itself to simple "good guys versus bad guys" explanations. AIM depicted itself as the beleaguered good guys with a role-reversal twist, as a tiny, brave, but poorly armed and outnumbered band of Indians out to right longstanding wrongs after being pushed to the edge of human endurance by injustice. The government and its apologists used counterimages of a band of radical Communist outside agitators, thugs, thieves, and white wannabes creating a phony event, facing disinterested and restrained federal peacemakers trying to mediate an internal tribal dispute. Both sides at Wounded Knee II became far more confrontational in an openly forceful and military way and far more willing to use media and the law as military and political weapons than either fully admitted.

One of the many ironic outcomes of the Vietnam War was that some of its Native veterans took up arms against the very system they had seemingly defended in war, often only a few months earlier. American Indian veterans of Vietnam and other wars led the defense (or occupation, depending on your point of view) of Wounded Knee. Warrior society ideals heavily influenced AIM's leaders and members. But AIM chose to apply the warrior society concept in a way quite different from tradition, ironically influenced by the *anti*war movement. AIM influenced other Native activist groups/warrior societies for decades, leading to a change that may be permanent and every bit as purposeful as Native veteran traditions. Government officials also chose to take a political and legal conflict and turn it into a military one and resolve it using a set of military tactics disguised as legal ones. This set of tactics is the very essence and definition of counterinsurgency.

Counterinsurgency at Wounded Knee II

Counterinsurgency (COIN), or low-intensity conflict (LIC), has its origins in the theories of Brigadier Frank Kitson, a British colonial military officer who served in Malaysia and took part in putting down a Communist insurrection. In 1971 he wrote *Low Intensity Conflict*, a handbook to teach military officers his techniques. Colonel Vic Jackson taught Kitson's methods at the Civil Disorder Management School at Ellsworth AFB. Jackson provided military reconnaissance for the government at Wounded Knee II. Colonel Volney Warner of the 82nd Airborne Division also trained in COIN at the school. Warner became the military advisor and liaison for federal law officers at Wounded Knee. He in turn reported directly to General Alexander Haig, one of Nixon's few advisors not removed by the Watergate scandal.[1]

Kitson designed his techniques to make the military ready to deal with "subversion." He defined subversion broadly as "making those governing do what they don't want to do" by means such as protest, political pressure, or (most appropriately for AIM's tactics) small-scale violence. Kitson particularly concerned himself with Che Guevara's writings emphasizing that acts of subversion or insurrection themselves could create the conditions for a revolution, rather than dissidents having to wait for an economic or social crisis. To counter this, Kitson called for a militarization of the police and legal system through building a series of intimate ties. Law under COIN becomes one more weapon for the military to use, a "propaganda cover for the disposal of unwanted members of the public." The target of these weapons is as much the population a government wishes to control as it is the rebel group. If the military or police are unable to attack the dissident group directly, it becomes necessary to "damage" or "poison" the population itself to destroy the rebels' support and "regain population control." The destruction of the insurgent group by the military and the law must be complete under Kitson's doctrine, and it must be done in full view of the local population to discourage the public and to discredit the insurgents and their goals permanently.[2]

In 1973 AIM occupied the hamlet of Wounded Knee to protest the corrupt and brutal tribal government on Pine Ridge Reservation after the banning of protests. Many FBI agents and the Special Operations Group (SOG) of the U.S. marshals (USM) arrived within two hours of the takeover on direct presidential orders. SOG was specially trained in riot control, sniping, and combating civil disorder or "subversion." Almost all SOG members were military combat veterans, including some former Green Berets. Colonel Volney Warner and Colonel Jack Potter of the 6th Army arrived as military advisors. Colonel Joe Baker from Ft. Bragg, North Carolina, also provided intelligence. Warner became the de facto commander since federal lawmen admitted they were not trained to deal with military situations. (See table 2 in the appendix for a breakdown of the numbers and equipment used by both sides.)

Government law officers came heavily armed with M-16s, M-1s, and armored personnel carriers (APCs) with .30 caliber machine guns, as well as the more typical shotguns and handguns used by police. The U.S. military advised, armed, dressed, and transported federal law officers, who became de facto government troops. They carried out largely *military*, not law enforcement, duties, including patrolling perimeters, performing sentry duty, manning bunkers, cutting off supplies to insurgents (the term government agents and spokesmen

themselves used), and responding to an armed feint and pincer movement from AIM and the recently self-proclaimed Independent Oglala
Nation (ION).[3]

Oglala tribal leader Dick Wilson and federal law enforcement officials paid, trained, armed, and supplied with ammunition local Native
vigilantes called the Guardians of the Oglala Nation (GOON) using
federal funds. The all-white Ranchers' Association (RA) also received
federal ammunition and took part in the shootouts and blockades
alongside government forces. The FBI also used psychological operations, or psyops, in the form of the COINTELPRO program, as extensively documented in *Agents of Repression*. This included the use of
rumors, disinformation, agent provocateurs, and possibly as many as
forty-two informants inside Wounded Knee.[4]

Law enforcement made an enormous mistake, one that the officers
themselves later admitted, in choosing to confront the occupiers with
such massive force. Wounded Knee II is the only known modern case
in America of an armed takeover where the public overwhelmingly
favored the armed group over their own government officials, and by a
margin of two and a half to one. Public sympathy and fear of a public
outcry similar to what happened after the deaths at Kent State became
part of the reason government troops could not end the standoff by
a simple all-out assault like the Attica Prison takeover that had occurred shortly before this. On one occasion when government forces
did lift the blockade, both ION supporters and vigilantes flooded into
Wounded Knee. The vigilantes set fire to the trading post and began
a firefight with ION. Members of ION successfully put out the fire and
drove off the vigilantes.[5]

AIM Learns Lessons from the Vietnam War

Carter Camp (Ponca) and Stan Holder (Wichita), both Vietnam combat
veterans, led the military defense/occupation of Wounded Knee. The
physical dimensions alone were impressive. Nine bunkers guarded
the approaches to Wounded Knee and near the buildings, situated in
two concentric rings and providing overlapping support fire. The dry
creek bed and trees along the banks provided cover when moving from
bunker to bunker. Burned-out cars blocked the roads themselves but

could be moved for visits from negotiators. The bunkers stood chest high, dug four feet deep using the equipment from a barely started public housing project nearby, with lateral trenches at ninety-degree angles. The housing project also provided materials for the bunkers and trenches. ION members built both with dirt or sand packed between boards above ground. Cinder blocks turned on their sides provided gun ports. Boards overhead supported blankets or tarps for both concealment from the surveillance planes and helicopters and protection from the rain. Cement bags, or trash bags and pillowcases filled with dirt or sand, provided further protection. Sand and dirt piled high on the sides of the clinic, communal kitchen, and buildings used for sleeping by noncombatants provided protection and kept warmth inside. The well-built bunkers even drew the admiration of government agents, who proclaimed them far better made than government or vigilante bunkers.[6]

Camp and Holder took great pride in the degree to which they mixed their tactics of older indigenous ways of fighting with what they had experienced in Vietnam. AIM began the defense using forty-five males in four squads. As more people slipped in that number grew. Up to 150 males became involved in the fighting. Since there are no indications AIM had more than ninety-six weapons, most had to share. A Vietnam veteran with at least two tours of combat duty led each squad. The largest squad, also referred to as the assault squad, was highly mobile and not intended to be centered on the defense or manning of any of the bunkers. Bunker squads served twelve-to eighteen-hour shifts. The members ate and slept near or in their bunkers. Roving foot patrols kept out infiltrators and aided backpackers who smuggled in much of the settlement's supplies. Citizen band radios kept patrols in touch and tracked the government force's movements and intentions.[7]

For support, ION set up committees with various responsibility including food supply, housing, medical needs, information, immigration, and internal security. Lorelie DeCora, the leader of the Iowa chapter of AIM, ran the clinic. The medical teams came in for one week at a time, negotiated by the National Council of Churches. Most of the medics had experience from the Vietnam War. One team came from members of the Chicano militant group Venceremos. Some turned out to be government informers, such as those claiming to be from the nonexistent Red Star Collective. Traditional medicine also healed the wounded and sick. AIM's medicine man, Leonard Crow Dog, a Lakota from Rosebud Reservation, slipped past the government perimeter into Wounded Knee. For supplies ION relied on a mix of donations, smuggling, and raiding. At first the government allowed supplies into Wounded Knee. Later the government became far more strict, even rationing the number of sanitary napkins allowed in out of fear they would be used as wicks for Molotov cocktails. At the same time, hundreds of backpackers smuggled in supplies on foot over what became nicknamed the "Ho Chi Minh Trail." ION also resorted to theft, "living off the land" in military terms. One rancher complained of losing sixty-three cattle and fifty chickens to ION cattle rustling and chicken stealing, using nine horses rustled from one of his neighbors. (The most interesting part of this story is that ION members could herd cattle and carry chickens past several hundred lawmen and vigilantes, at night no less.) Holder insisted ION tried to keep the "European style" out of their ways of fighting. There was no disciplinary or corporal punishment, no real chain of command. In place of military hierarchy, ION used traditional Native ways of informal leadership based on earning followers' trust by continued success.[8]

AIM and ION members also used traditional protective spiritual medicine at Wounded Knee II. Crow Dog provided not just healing but also traditional warrior purification rituals prior to battle or death. On the eve of the first government deadline to surrender, all AIM and ION members who intended to fight underwent ceremonies. After a sweat lodge, Crow Dog painted a red stripe or circle on each of their faces while chanting a blessing in Lakota. The members then each entered a white tipi and made a sign over a buffalo skull. The ceremony signified a willingness to die in the coming battle. Magpie feathers were given for coups and to celebrate the deeds of ION members. Most AIM members also used protective personal medicine in the form of medicine pouches. Nearly all the Vietnam veterans had carried the same pouches overseas. Federal agents noticed during the arrests in the aftermath that most veterans accepted being arrested calmly, until agents opened, searched, or damaged their medicine pouches.

Searching a medicine pouch angered Native veterans, as this was akin to desecrating sacred items.[9]

ION's tactics and structural defenses made up for their being overwhelmingly outmatched in weaponry and supplies of ammunition. AIM claimed they had no more than 250 rounds of ammunition in the entire camp. The FBI claimed to have found 2,770 rounds in the aftermath. Assuming the second figure is true and that ION used an equal amount during the siege, that still is only roughly 1 percent of the half-million rounds fired by the government and vigilante groups. By all accounts ION members carried their ammunition in small pouches or in their pockets and used it sparingly, saving it for the anticipated government assault. As for weapons, many were old or inoperative. Photos of the siege show some weapons held together by tape, many with pieces of string for gun slings. ION had only three military weapons (including an inoperative Thompson submachine gun) versus the hundreds of government ones, plus mostly old and small caliber hunting rifles. To compensate, ION relied on improvisation, bluff, and public pressure. ION members carved wooden replicas of a .30 and a .50 caliber machine gun mounted on tripods and allowed members of the media and other visitors to see them, but not too closely. Some members carried toy plastic M-16s or "guns" made of pieces of pipe with wooden stocks attached. AIM prominently displayed the single (and very famous) AK-47 during every visit with negotiators. News photos of the weapon led to wild rumors about the number of automatic weapons AIM possessed and equally bizarre assertions that this "proved" AIM was Communist. For perhaps the only time in their lives, many white conservatives across the country angrily demanded to know from their congressmen why the government did not do a better job of gun control.[10] The FBI initially believed AIM had nearly 1,000 people at Wounded Knee, with up to 300 armed with automatic weapons, grenades, anti-aircraft weapons, bazookas, mortars, and explosives; it was even thought that AIM had two aircraft. Though such incredible exaggeration quickly ended with the reports of the first informants, the government's assumption that AIM was far better armed than it was played a part in its reluctance to order an assault. Federal officials estimated they would lose 10 percent or nearly thirty of their agents in an assault.

These worries limited the government's response to an extremely permeable blockade and confused firefights. The shootouts used enormous quantities of ammunition in a largely ineffectual way against well-fortified ION bunkers and a highly mobile defense that often could not be pinned down. For more than two months a lightly armed and outnumbered group of Natives used a mix of traditional and modern military ways and counterculture protest to hold off a heavily armed and technologically sophisticated force of lawmen and vigilantes who worked for the most powerful nation on the planet. The government did not successfully arrest most of ION until after the standoff. Only 129 people (including thirty-three pre-occupation residents) remained at Wounded Knee when the government came in after the negotiated surrender. Two to three times that number slipped away in the night.

AIM as a Warrior Society

AIM's own contention has always been that its members see themselves as a warrior society. In one of its own leaders' words, "[It is] what we idealistically try to be." The most accurate way to describe AIM in the 1970s is that it was an outlet for Natives who wanted to be a part of the warrior tradition but could not in the newly "conventional" way of becoming a veteran. AIM's leaders always claimed to have modeled AIM on the civil rights movement. A better case could be made for Vietnam Veterans Against the War (VVAW). Many VVAW were medics at Wounded Knee II. Like VVAW, AIM proved successful at using small-scale violence to draw attention to itself and its causes and intimidate authorities, staying just this side of full-blown insurrection. ION members included veterans of COIN training themselves, of Long Range Patrols in Vietnam, of combat control for the air force behind enemy lines, and of the Phoenix Program of covert assassination for the CIA. Many ION members spoke of learning very well the lessons from the National Liberation Front they fought in Vietnam, especially that mobility and determination of a people fighting for their homeland could defeat an enemy weighed down with technology and with lesser motivation or staying power.[11] Wounded Knee II became the Red Power movement's version of the Alamo, a defeat that has been turned into a heroic story of facing down overwhelming odds.

That mythic stature was created at Wounded Knee II by AIM's use of tactics learned in the military.

Wounded Knee II as an event marked a sharp break with warrior societies' tactics, both in the United States and Canada. In the United States nearly all takeovers had been peaceful prior to Wounded Knee II. Afterward AIM became stigmatized as irredeemably violent, even though it had usually not used force prior to this and did not commit most of the violence during Wounded Knee II. Largely crippled for the next decade as it tried to survive many punitive legal trials, AIM did not recover until the mid-1980s. Its newer membership is made up of younger activists, usually neither veterans nor ex-convicts. Other U.S. Native warrior societies, except for most Iroquois ones, were notably less politically active and more like cultural pride groups and veterans' groups. But in Canada, confrontation as a form of political activism for warrior societies became more the rule than the exception. For three decades Canada experienced deep turmoil over the constitution and the status of different groups under it. In negotiations over their constitution, Natives were not numerous enough to exert political influence at the polls and had little choice but to rely on more dramatic and forceful tactics.

Conclusion

Much like how many Anglos turned the Battle of the Alamo from a devastating loss into a symbolic last stand victory, admirers of AIM similarly turned Wounded Knee II into a rallying cry for their side. But its importance lies elsewhere. Wounded Knee II marked a change in the meanings many Natives attach to warrior societies and how to be a warrior. Tom Holm has argued that Native activists of this period syncretized their activism to create newer warrior traditions. To expand upon that one step further, the nature of the often-violent government response as well as that of AIM drew both directly and immediately upon the Vietnam experience. Most of the newer type of warrior societies discussed in chapter 8 also either drew upon similar experiences or became influenced by the example of AIM, such as the Ojibwe Warrior Society, the Manitoba Warrior Society, and the Iroquois warrior societies.

Many Native people in the United States and Canada still valorize some of the activists involved in Wounded Knee II. Two in particular, Leonard Peltier and Anna Mae Aquash, have achieved such stature that many Native people refer to them by first name only, "Leonard" or "Anna Mae." Of greater importance than such symbolism is the question that AIM, its supporters, and ideological/cultural descendants in other warrior societies raise about the right way to be a warrior. Many Vietnam War veterans who were also members of AIM or other warrior societies either saw no contradiction in fighting first for the military and then against the government, or more often rejected the nation-state system they had earlier been agents of. Partly they emulated their ancestors' warrior traditions of a century or more ago, even while they learned how far they could push the system without the disastrous consequences of the past. The current place of these two sets of warrior traditions in Native cultures is something we shall return to again in the conclusion.

10

"Fighting Terrorism since 1492"

The Gulf War, the War in Afghanistan, and the Second Iraq War

LESS THAN A MONTH AFTER September 11, 2001, at the annual powwow in Mesa, Arizona, instead of a Native color guard of military veterans, two Anglos—a firefighter and a policeman—led the grand entry procession of Native dancers and posted the colors. This was a truly remarkable statement of public sympathy, especially given the often-troubled history of how law enforcement treats Native people. It seems to me there were two very strong messages. The first was very obvious, one that seemed to be taken to heart by Anglos in the crowd. To cops and firefighters: you are on front lines, too, in many ways as dangerous as combat. But there was also a subtle message that, I feel sure, some Anglos missed and most Natives got: this "war on terror" is work better suited to law enforcement, not soldiers.

To anyone Native or anyone familiar with Native history or cultures, this change came as truly remarkable. (For non-Native readers, imagine seeing a burial at Arlington National Cemetery with firefighters instead of a military color guard.) To my knowledge, there has only been one other instance at a powwow where Native veterans did not act as the color guard during the posting of the flags. In 1991, following the Oka standoff between members of the Mohawk Warrior Society and the Canadian federal government, Mohawks at the Oka powwow refused to post the Canadian flag. Instead they posted the flag of the Mohawk Warrior Society. Many Native people in Canada were stunned by the extreme response of the national government, which had sent in one quarter of its entire army to defend the right of a company to build a golf course on Mohawk sacred burial grounds.

What these two powwows shared was the shock of a similarly traumatic act of great violence, one that made many question the very stability of their surroundings and thus accept such a central change to powwow tradition.

For September 11, the trauma for Indian Country involved both the shock of witnessing the deaths of three thousand people *and* a certain shock of recognition. As I explained to my classes, "Take September 11, and recall all the shock and anger and outrage you felt. Now imagine it happening every week for four hundred years, week after week with no let up, and you get some idea of what Native people went through since Columbus." But part of that shock of recognition was also sympathy for the people (as distinct from the enemy governments or terrorists) of the nations the United States went to war against. For these wars in the Middle East, much of Indian Country saw explicit parallels with their peoples' histories.

Native servicemen often took part in wars that rightly should be called imperialistic. Only occasionally can we find cases where the motives set forth by war planners helped or tried to help tribal peoples, such as the Montagnards during the Vietnam War. U.S. aid to the Moskitos in their uprising against the Sandinistas in Nicaragua is a second example. A third effort came in the aftermath of the U.S. invasion of Panama to overthrow Manuel Noriega. Sergeant Julius Tulley and thirty other Navajos went to Panama as part of "Nuevo Horizontes" (New Horizons). Six thousand guardsmen from eighteen states built schools, clinics, and bridges and provided medical care. Tulley and the other Navajos "felt comfortable" with the local Panamanians. Panamanian Indians and mestizos quickly accepted them, invited them to visit another island away from the construction sites, and asked about their religions and whether the images on television about American Indians were true.[1]

But finding any case of U.S. intervention that Native consciences could support became increasingly difficult post-Vietnam. Most Native servicemen and other Natives increasingly had to disconnect the U.S. nation-state's wars and invasions from Native reasons for time in the service. The very nature of these interventions made such acts as using Native ceremony to build community support difficult, impractical, or impossible. Frequently the interventions happened too suddenly and government leaders did not even consult with the U.S. public as a whole until after the fact. Thus Natives' opinions about these invasions usually did not even matter to those in power.

For example, I could not find any information on Native servicemen who took part in the U.S. intervention in the Dominican Republic in the mid-1960s, though it is likely that several hundred Natives took part. There is also little evidence specifically on Native servicemen who took part in interventions in Grenada or Lebanon. Lakotas at the local American Legion Post from Parmalee, Mission, Rosebud, and St. Francis did hold a ceremony to honor those who died in Grenada and Beirut.[2] But this is more an act of remembering and solidarity with the families of deceased veterans than support for the interventions themselves, or even remembering the Native part in it. Even Native-oriented media paid little attention.

But during the wars in Afghanistan and the Second Iraq War, Indian Country had some of the earliest and most vocal, penetrating, and sustained criticism, with few equals from any other sector of the larger American society. Historical experience drove Native opposition; Native peoples see what the United States does in the Middle East as part of Manifest Destiny. One of the most popular T-shirts in Indian Country after September 11 had a bold, three-to six-inch-high phrase proclaiming, "Homeland Security: Fighting Terrorism since 1492." Either above or below the phrase are photos of famous Native warriors and chiefs, often holding guns. I have seen these T-shirts with photos of Geronimo, Chief Joseph, Sitting Bull, Quanah Parker, Satanta, and Manuelito with other Navajo leaders. Sometimes the photos have Native leaders in the crosshairs of a gun sight. Narragansetts have their own version of the shirt in support of their struggle with the state of Rhode Island over taxes, as do some Western Shoshone in their struggle with the Bureau of Land Management.[3]

I have seen the phrase used on Web sites, homemade posters, and banners and heard it in everyday conversation. I saw a huge display featuring the phrase at the memorial for Lori Piestewa at Arizona State University. When I wore the T-shirt to my classes on the days I taught about Columbus, I received almost all positive reactions, as I did once when I forgetfully wore it underneath a jacket in an airport, and then removed the jacket. At the ASU powwow, a member of the American Indian Veterans Memorial Organization broke into a broad grin when he saw my shirt and told me, "You know, that is so true! Ain't it?" Then he stepped in closer and more emphatically insisted, "*Ain't it!?!*" Never before have there been U.S. wars where opposition to them rang more true for Native people, precisely because of Native historical experience with colonialism done for economic gain and control of resources.

"Iraq's Indians" and Indian Country during the Gulf War: Sympathy, Ambivalence, and Opposition

Reports of Native support for the war itself for the reasons the first President Bush stated were rare, or at least hard to find. Support for the troops is an entirely separate matter. What one finds looking at Native media of the time are examples of great ambivalence as the closest thing to support for the war's aims, with two major exceptions. Saddam Hussein's possession of biological weapons and using chemical weapons against the Kurds provided the most compelling reasons for many Native people to support the war, based on Natives' own experience with disease used as a weapon of genocide. Many also sympathized with the plight of the Kurds as a minority group facing violence from the state. Armstrong Wiggins, a Moskito Indian from Nicaragua studying in the United States, described having a Kurdish classmate and finding much in common with them. Wiggins proclaimed, "In my heart, I am a Kurd." Seneca historian John Mohawk likewise described Kurds as "Iraq's Indians." Many Natives, like many Americans, argued that once committed to war the U.S. military should go into Iraq and overthrow Saddam and not stop at simply expelling him from Kuwait.[4]

In 1991 a group of Ojibwe activists, the Minnesota Peace Drum, led a protest for peace in Washington across the street from the White House. A spokeswoman for the group, Bea Swanson, insisted, "We're there for totally immoral reasons. . . . The American way of Life and the flag . . . I am not always one who feels those are things worthy of protecting."[5]

Almost immediately after the start of the ground war in Kuwait, Brigadier General Richard Neal referred to Iraqi-held enemy territory as "Indian Country" in a briefing to the media, a term commonly used during the Vietnam War. This time the use of the phrase brought a torrent of Native protest. National Congress of American Indians president Wayne Ducheneaux exploded, "By God you still get this kind of . . . from the leaders." (The reporter more than likely censored profanity.) Ducheneaux argued that President Bush himself should apologize. Margaret Cooper, an activist with a veterans memorial group from the Lac Court Oreilles Band of Chippewas, also said her veterans group wanted an apology from Bush. The Cheyenne River Sioux Tribe expressed a similar wish. Santa Clara Pueblo governor Walter Dasheno, Tony Martinez of the Eight Northern Pueblos Council, and Arizona state senator James Henderson Jr. (Navajo) all called the comment offensive or racist. Mohegan veteran Sam Brushel commented to a reporter, "If I was over there and serving, I would have thrown my rifle down and walked away." Lieutenant Colonel John Tull, speaking for the U.S. military central command in Saudi Arabia, said Neal was unavailable for comment. Pentagon spokeswoman Michelle Rabayda tried to distance the Pentagon from the use of the phrase, saying "Indian Country" had no official definition in military manuals.[6]

Lakota soldier Eric Bentzlin or Wicahpi Etan (Came from the Stars) became the first of four Native servicemen to die in Iraq. Friendly fire killed Bentzlin. In accordance with Lakota tradition, his family put all reminders of him away. His mother, Barbara Anderson, complained the military had no understanding of Native traditions. She wanted a lock of her son's hair but could not get one because of the condition of the remains, and she turned to a medicine man to deal with her grief. Bentzlin's parents were not a couple at the time of their son's death. Thus her son's stepmother notified her of her son's death rather than the military. Anderson spent over a year lobbying for a change in the rules of military notification, without success.[7]

Kevin Shore, an Ojibwa from the White Earth Reservation, became the most famous Native veteran of the war. Confined to a wheelchair from Gulf War Syndrome, Shore wheeled across the country to raise awareness of the illness and protested the lack of government attention to the problem. Joyce Riley von Kleist, a spokesperson for the American Gulf War Veterans Association, said, "There's a Kevin Shore in every city we visit. He's an inspiration to thousands of other Gulf veterans fighting the same fight." Shore turned to traditional healing to cope with his illness, describing "this disease [as] a blessing of sorts, opening my eyes to a spirituality I would otherwise never have discovered."[8]

Navajo singer Delphine Tsinajinnie wrote "A Soldier's Birthday Song" at the request of a mother whose son had just left for Desert Storm. The mother asked that the message, "My dear baby boy, my world is happy on your birthday," be passed on in the song, and said this to Tsinajinnie in "her native Hebrew."[9] This is the first traditionalist song I know of written for a non-Native serviceman since an honor song was written for General MacArthur in World War II.

In 1992 Flathead veterans of the Gulf War formed the Veterans Warrior Society. Their expressed goals were "to promote renewed fellowship . . . [and] provide an accurate history . . . research and understanding and healing." Thirteen veterans of the war were recognized for their service in their 1996 powwow held at the community center in Elmo, Montana.[10]

Middle America may have celebrated the Gulf War as supposedly ending U.S. reluctance to invade other nations (overcoming "Vietnam syndrome"). But I could not find even a single instance of anyone Native ever saying anything like that in the wake of the war. In fact Anishnaabe author/columnist Jim Northrup reported that one Native Vietnam War veteran mockingly suggested Americans take down all their yellow ribbons and send them to the Kurds to wrap their feet while wading through the cold mud in the mountains. Northrup added in his commentary, "Enough already with those yellow ribbons." Most of Indian Country felt something closer to relief that more Americans did not die in the war and mourned the failed outcome of many of the war's aims, a view Anglo-America grew to share. In fact, some Native veterans came out of the Gulf War more cynical than ever about using American military power. One organization based in San Diego called Native American Gulf War Veterans endorsed a call in 1999 for an end to bombing Serbia. The one short-term benefit of the war to Native people was the release of surplus military rations from Desert Storm that were distributed to tribes, urban Indian organizations, Indian schools, shelters, senior citizen centers, and halfway houses.[11]

"This Happened to Us, Too": Indian Country Reacts to September 11

In some ways the attacks on September 11 ignited a hostile atmosphere much like the anti-Japanese hysteria that gripped the West Coast following the attack on Pearl Harbor. One of the biggest fears of many Natives became being mistaken for Middle Eastern. Locally, the president of the American Indian Graduate Students Association, Richie Meyers, advised everyone to avoid traveling alone at night and to avoid groups of whites that had been drinking or seemed angry. He advised men to shave off any facial hair they had. Angela Cavender Wilson, a Dakota professor, talked the next day about the need for introspection and understanding why so much of that part of the world hates the United States. A conservative student group on campus responded by attacking her as "un-American" and named her their "Socialist Professor of the Month."[12] I also personally saw the moderators of at least one online Native listserv call for the mass murder of Arabs and Muslims and attacked anyone who disagreed with them as "pro-terrorist," expelling a number of members.

Still, the reaction of most Native people to the attacks combined sympathy for the victims and something unusual elsewhere in the United States following the attacks: thoughtful reflection and soul-searching. Harriet Gumbs, a Shinnecock elder, wrote, "I would tell President Bush for one not to be talking out of a forked tongue. . . . We can gather our strength from knowing our president is interested in the least of us, the poor and the rich and the Indian in between." Elgean Joshevama, vice chairperson of the Hopi nation, said to a reporter, "You have to ask, 'Why did this happen?' The U.S. has not respected people in other countries. . . . The U.S. has pushed people around, and bullied, and people can only take so much." Lakota journalist Frank King III called for forgiveness and a turning away from violent solutions: "If there is any lesson that I could teach my children it is that violence resolves nothing and hate destroys us all."[13]

King and other Natives joined in this call for forgiveness. Lakota activist/actor Russell Means wrote, "George W. Bush has the opportunity to become the greatest president this country has ever produced. All he has to do is turn the other cheek and reach out to every country and all the peoples of the world." Means then sketched out the alternative, "the perfect, never-ending war, a war against the unknown . . . worse than the drug war." Professor of Native American Studies Henrietta Mann likewise called for forgiveness and pointed to Native peoples as a model: "If we, as the First Nations, can forgive our history since 1492, everyone else has the ability to forgive. . . . This is my hope for you and for the America that we all love."[14]

Others also saw similarities between their own people's experience and people in the Middle East. Lakota/Cheyenne activist Jodi Gillette insisted, "A lot of non-Indians here probably don't understand . . . that this happened to us too." Cheyenne author Suzan Harjo agreed: "Supposedly we as a people are now thirsting for revenge. . . . Revenge is not justice. . . . Revenge may cause us to become evil-doers ourselves. . . . Are we to be terrorists to others?" Activist professor Ward Churchill speculated, "It may not only have been the ghosts of Iraqi children that made their appearance. . . . Maybe those Native people claimed for scalp bounty in all forty-eight of the continental states? Or the Raritans whose severed heads were kicked for sport along the . . . very site where the World Trade Center once stood?" Famed Lakota scholar/activist Vine Deloria Jr. gave perhaps the most succinct reaction: "It was predictable. I'm surprised it didn't happen sooner. We treat them like dirt."[15]

Noted Powhattan historian Jack Forbes held nothing back in his criticism, drawing direct comparisons between Osama Bin Laden's followers and those of President Bush. According to Forbes, the attacks were "carried out by right wing fanatics. . . . [Al Qaeda] bears too close a resemblance to some fundamentalist and reactionary movements within the Christian and Jewish (Israeli) worlds . . . not different from the violence and terrorism favored by U.S. Christian Right groups who supported terrorism against Native people in Central America under Reagan and Bush. . . . [The attacks were a] victory of conservative and militarist agendas . . . pulling the strings."[16]

Alfred Taiaiake, a Mohawk writer and professor who teaches about indigenous governance, not only drew comparisons between Bin Laden and Bush but also argued the attacks made sense to anyone possessing the mind-set of either man.

> It would be too simple to say that the U.S. had it coming. The fact that the U.S. as a country is getting back what it puts out . . . is so obvious as to be meaningless. . . . 9-11 was not an attack on us. . . . It was not even an attack on the U.S. It was an attack on the U.S. military's occupation of the Arab homeland and massive payback for the U.S. government's crimes against Muslims in Arabia. . . . The attack on the World Trade Center was not unprovoked or unreasoned. . . . It was entirely logical . . . if you subscribe to a philosophy in which war is an extension of politics and terror is another tactic. . . . Only a naïve fool would accept the propaganda proclaiming American innocence spewing forth in sickening doses from the U.S. television networks. . . . Instead of asking why does half the world hate us the citizens of the U.S. are told to sit in their churches, to pray for their victimization, and then open up their prayer books and sing the hymns of war.

Taiaiake then described George W. Bush singing the "Battle Hymn of the Republic" in his church, compared it to Muslim fundamentalism, and called for Natives to stay out of what he saw as an unjust war carried out for profit as well as religious hatred.

> To tell the truth, there's no difference between George Bush singing these words to Americans and Osama Bin Laden preaching a fatwah to his similarly deluded followers. . . . These enemies are very much alike. . . . This is mass hypocrisy on a scale to drive anyone crazy! . . . Yet there are many of our people who identify so strongly with our oppressor that they begin to feel and think just like him. . . . This is not a noble struggle. . . . This is not a just war. . . . This is not even a necessary cold war. . . . The war . . . is a longstanding fight to guarantee American access to cheap oil and make the world safe for the rich to profit off the poor. . . . We Onkwehonwe, the real people, must keep in mind that this is not our war. . . . Let us resist,

and refuse to join in the chorus as all the good Christians march off to murder Muslims singing their national anthems and the "Battle Hymn of the Hypocrites."[17]

Lakota activist James Starkey appealed to his people to remember their spiritual traditions and turn away from being caught up in the wave of patriotism: "Brace yourselves for the deluge. . . . It will be difficult to separate the saber rattling from the sorrowful. . . . Brothers and Sisters, do not be fooled by the wiles of the trickster. This entire argument is a family fight between the Three Cousins—Judaism, Islam, and Christianity. . . . Truly they are Eya, the great consumer. Grandmother Earth will not continue to allow the Three Cousins to run amuck." Paul Joseph Monk, a Lakota human rights activist, gave perhaps the harshest criticism: "When I see the flag flying and the media patter of 'God Bless America,' I feel like puking. . . . My country is not America. I know her as Unci Maka (Grandmother Earth). . . . I, for one, am not proud of the 'America' everyone is jumping on the bandwagon to rally behind. . . . There will come a time when my heart will tell me 'It's time to go,' and then I can give up this life of 'dual citizenship' with my oppressor."[18]

One of the few public figures in Indian Country to share in the war hysteria and public displays of anger was David Yeagley, an alleged Comanche working for a leading reactionary, David Horowitz. Yeagley did not hesitate to invoke stereotypical images of both Comanches and Natives in general. He also linked the war to his favorite issue, support *for* "Indian" mascots in sports, and ended his call for war by justifying and even sympathizing with the invaders who brutalized Natives.

> It's simple. This is what American people want to hear. Well, let them hear it from a Comanche Indian. I declare war. Are there any warriors left in Washington? If so, let them show themselves now. If not, let those in power be forever remembered as people without moral character, without resolve, and without respect. I call upon all Indians everywhere to put our hearts on the warpath. Don't try to remove all Indian warrior mascots from schools and universities. We need warriors!

Yeagley also did not hesitate to use blatant racism against Palestinians and Middle Eastern people. His arguments against sympathy for Arabs are strikingly similar to the Manifest Destiny beliefs used by white racists against Natives.

> Many people see a similarity between American Indians and today's Palestinians. I'm Comanche Indian. I see no similarity whatsoever. Comanches were once "Lords of the South Plains." Arabs living in Palestine have never dominated anything but goats. . . . Palestinian Arabs are not indigenous to Palestine. They are leftover Arabs, residual of another age. . . . Arabs intermarried, enslaved, and otherwise lorded over every culture they encountered. . . . Palestine was little more than a wilderness of nomads, loosely associated groups of provincial subdivisions with frequently changing administrations. The people were a "pan-Arab" mix of gypsy-like leftovers. . . . The ancient, indigenous inhabitants of Palestine are long perished from the earth. . . . A stronger people, modern Jews . . . came in and conquered (without annihilating) the Palestinian Arabs. . . . As a Comanche Indian, I'm sensitive to this history. I believe the conqueror has a right to what he has conquered. No one owns the land. Only he who is strong enough to possess it will control it and the people living on it. That's the law of war.[19]

But Yeagley was very atypical of Native reactions to the war and has a tiny following at best. How much he sincerely thinks of himself as a "warrior" is open to question, since he never joined the military and speaks openly of hating his alleged heritage and wanting to assimilate. Most Natives had a scathing reaction to his words. "Comanche Patriot?" wrote Efiza Jackson to him. "The Comanches are a Sovereign Nation. Where is Dr. Yeagley's loyalty? He should teach a course on Comanche Treason." Cheyenne activist Suzan Harjo wrote a widely read critique of Yeagley as a "small and unworthy man." In July 2005 it became clear that at least part of why Yeagley's views were so atypical was simple: Yeagley likely was not, in fact, Comanche as he falsely claimed. His stepmother was, however, and thus he is enrolled with the tribe, perhaps fraudulently.[20] Yeagley's case is striking for the contrast it provides with Ward Churchill and the "little Eichmanns" episode, which will be discussed in greater detail in the next section.

Most Natives dealt with September 11 with compassion, not anger. Indian Country overflowed with sympathy and a desire to honor the memory of the victims and help or heal the survivors and victims' families. Members of the Lummi nation in Washington State built two honoring totem poles. The first one weighed one ton and went to Sterling Forest in New York for the victims of the September 11 attacks. The second pole stood fourteen feet high and honored veterans and those on United Flight 93. The Lummis sent it to Shanksville, Pennsylvania, accompanied by ten of their members and a Native color guard. The House of Tears Carvers designed both poles.[21]

Other Indian nations also offered aid and tribute. Children from the Crow Creek Sioux River nation in Monique Hauq's fifth grade class wrote to Lori Falzone's fourth grade class in Brooklyn to try and help them cope. Mohawk steelworkers, many of whom helped build the World Trade Center and also personally witnessed the destruction of the towers, helped in rescue efforts and were honored in the memorial ceremony to commemorate the victims and thank the rescue workers. Seminole elders and healers gathered with their community in Brighton, using cleansing smoke with traditional herbs for the protection of the souls who died in the September 11 attacks. Other efforts included donations for families of victims from the Prairie Band of Pottawatomi and the Morongo and Pechanga bands in California. The Eastern Shoshones, the Pequots, and the Tunica-Biloxis all contributed funds, vehicles, or blood from drives.[22]

The FBI found Al Qaeda plans for an attack on the Grand Coulee Dam near the Colville Reservation. The new Homeland Security Act ignored tribal governments' role. Fifteen tribal nations are on the Canadian or Mexican borders, with thirteen more near the borders. Six more reservations host or are near nuclear missile silos. The new act classified them as local governments under state jurisdiction, meaning they would have to go through state governments to get federal funding against terrorism, abridge their own sovereignty, and solicit from institutions historically more hostile than the federal government. Senator Daniel Inouye of Hawaii, a longtime ally of American Indians, filed legislation that hurriedly changed the act. The situation became potentially even worse after the Supreme Court's *Oliphant* decision, which limited tribal rights to arrest or charge outsiders. Conceivably, tribal police might have to call in the FBI to arrest possible terrorists, either making it easier for potential terrorists to slip away or giving any criminal charges grounds for dismissal.[23]

The attacks ironically did lead to somewhat better relations between New York State and reservation governments. New York governor George Pataki, who had been elected on an anti-gaming platform, reversed himself after September 11, making Indian gaming the centerpiece of economic recovery for the state after the loss of nine billion dollars in state revenue following the attacks. His new pact with Mohawks and Oneidas on gaming ignored the wishes of both local whites opposed to gaming as well as many Iroquois, most notably Oren Lyons, Onondaga historian and faithkeeper for the Six Nations.[24]

Some anti-Indian and anti-sovereignty groups crassly saw the fear inspired by terrorism as a chance to gain support for their hate mongering. After President Bush signed Executive Order 13388, Citizens for Personal Responsibility (CPR) argued in a press release that Natives were inherently less trustworthy than whites and thus Indian tribes should not be allowed access to information involving national security. CPR further argued that Indian tribes would only use such information for sinister purposes against whites: "[Indians] . . . made a conscious choice not to assimilate. . . . Radical activists within Indian Country now have unchecked power to take advantage . . . based upon motives that are more related to securing a homeland and resources for themselves." In reality the executive order had little to do with Indian nations, only asking for "the highest priority to . . . the interchange of terrorism information among agencies." Yet this did not stop CPR from nothing less than calling for the federal government to "eliminate tribal leadership as a Homeland Security jurisdiction."[25] Were CPR's suggestions actually to be carried out, the country as a whole would be less secure, not more. Tribal governments are not "given" information by this order; they are only urged to give more priority to passing along information on terrorism that they already possess.

Fortunately there is no indication that anyone in a position of power even noticed CPR's paranoid arguments. Indian Country faced much the same anthrax scares following the initial attacks as the rest of the

United States. Cheyenne River Sioux tribal member Tracey Angie opened a letter on October 30, 2001, containing white powder. Tribal police gave the letter to the FBI, who reported it tested negative. The BIA office in Albuquerque received letters that were cross-contaminated after going through the Washington DC, mail facility. Two employees were tested and the regional office was closed temporarily.[26]

Two painters specializing in Native American–themed art utilized Native imagery in patriotic works following the attacks and sought to summon the moral authority and romantic notions many associate with Native cultures. Painters Jerry Bean and John Guthrie both drew connections between Operation Noble Eagle, the official name for military operations in the United States against terrorism, and American Indian warrior traditions. Bean painted a U.S. Air Force fighter with Indian warriors on horseback flying alongside it titled *On the War Path*. His Web site sold prints of the painting with the pitch, "The Chiefs were called upon to defend America's skies. . . . The Chiefs flew over 500 combat sorties. . . . *On the War Path* . . . recognizes accomplishments of past, present, and future Chiefs." Guthrie, himself Cherokee, chose a more subtle approach. His painting *Noble Eagle* had an eagle in front of an American flag with an eagle feather below wrapped in beads "in remembrance of those who perished."[27]

Although so far we have only anecdotal evidence on how September 11 affected whether Natives joined the military, recruiters in and around the Navajo nation did report an increase in inquiries. But only a normal amount signed up. A few did specify they joined precisely because of September 11. Marine Corps Staff Sergeant Larry Long reported, "I had one guy say, 'This is the reason I'm here. They did this to my country and I want to support my country.'"[28] For all the parallels many tried to draw between September 11 and Pearl Harbor, at least in this case that analogy rings false. A surge in Native enlistment does *not* seem to have happened. Especially when compared to World War II, many Native people said this was not their war even while sympathizing with the victims of the attacks and supporting Native servicemen.

"Little Eichmanns" and a "Small and Unworthy Man"

The two names most Americans will likely recall in connection with the War on Terrorism/Long War and American Indians will be Lori

Piestewa and, sadly, Ward Churchill. I include this discussion of the outcry over Ward Churchill's activities very reluctantly, in part because of the blind partisanship of both his supporters and critics. I fully expect both sides to be angry that I did not wholeheartedly endorse either point of view. But above all I fear the attention paid to him plays into one of the very things that many (myself included) most dislike about Churchill: his penchant for making himself the issue rather than far more important concerns in Indian Country. Sadly, this media event has likely garnered more attention than anything having to do with Natives since Wounded Knee II.[29]

On September 12, 2001, longtime AIM activist Ward Churchill published "Some People Push Back: On the Justice of Roosting Chickens." Later he developed his essay into a book, *On the Justice of Roosting Chickens*, published in November 2003. One paragraph in the essay and book became infamous but hardly received any notice at the time.

> Let's get a grip here, shall we? True enough, they were civilians of a sort. But innocent? Gimme a break. They formed a technocratic corps at the very heart of America's global financial empire—the "mighty engine of profit" to which the military dimension of U.S. policy has always been enslaved—and they did so both willingly and knowingly. Recourse to "ignorance"—a derivative, after all, of the word *ignore*—counts as less than an excuse among this relatively well-educated elite. To the extent that any of them were unaware of the costs and consequences to others of what they were involved in—and in many cases excelling at—it was because of their absolute refusal to see. More likely, it was because they were too busy braying, incessantly and self-importantly, into their cell phones, arranging power lunches and stock transactions, each of which translated, conveniently out of sight, mind and smelling distance, into the starved and rotting flesh of infants. If there was a better, more effective, or in fact any other way of visiting some penalty befitting their participation upon the little Eichmanns inhabiting the sterile sanctuary of the twin towers, I'd really be interested in hearing about it.[30]

Churchill's argument in this paragraph is twofold: Technocrats in the World Trade Center taking part in U.S. government actions overseas and in multinational corporations serve the same purpose as Eichmann did, to provide bureaucracy that makes genocide possible, but under U.S. military/geopolitical doctrine, the other victims were "collateral damage," unintentional but acceptable losses. The second part of his argument is undeniably historically accurate. Anyone doubting that could read, for example, of President Clinton's secretary of state Madeline Albright justifying the deaths of half a million Iraqis, mostly children, as "worth it" to punish and weaken Saddam Hussein. Pointing that out does not mean someone agrees with such an amoral doctrine. Just the opposite: Churchill pointed to such sickness in high places in order to condemn it.

The first part of Churchill's argument can very validly be criticized not only as wildly inaccurate but also as an argument that worsens the situation rather than improving it. Federal bureaucrats and executives in multinational corporations are not sending people to death camps. Enforcing policies that make it more likely people starve is despicable in any moral code worthy of the name. It is contemptible opportunism and predatory capitalism, not genocide. His argument widens the definition of genocide to include moral callousness, and by doing so he makes it harder for people to take both actual genocide and the deliberate impoverishment of the Third World seriously. Essentially Churchill failed to see that Marie Antoinette–like attitudes and policies are not the same as Nazi mass murder. To use a Nazi analogy for a city where the attacks took place that has a large Jewish population is also reckless. Finally, to see the deaths of state and corporate bureaucrats as just punishment for their greed or indifference is against every traditionalist Native value I know of and shows Churchill to be completely out of touch with Native communities' opinions.

But none of these were points that Churchill's newest critics (distinct from his longstanding critics in Indian Country) chose to make when they singled out this passage. Subtlety and debate were never their aim. Instead they largely came after him for saying something he never, in fact, actually said, that *all* victims of September 11 were supposedly Nazis or Nazi-like. Churchill is partly to blame for his own clumsy writing, like most of his work designed for shock value. But most of the blame should fall on his new set of critics for persistently accusing him of saying things he never actually said. It quickly became clear that many of his newest critics were not concerned much with the truth, being eager instead to brand opposition to the war as pro-terrorist, with Churchill's statement as alleged proof. Instead his newest set of critics chose to focus on a sound bite, a grand total of two words, "little Eichmanns."

Not until January 2005, more than three years later, immediately before a scheduled talk at Hamilton University, did his comments bring any great reaction. The outcry from some segments of the conservative movement was intense, cynical, and calculated. Fox Network television commentator Bill O'Reilly led the charge. O'Reilly had just been through a lengthy bruising scandal of his own; he had been sued for $60 million over his alleged sexual harassment of producer Andrea Mackris over a period of several years. O'Reilly made Churchill the subject of over two dozen segments on *The O'Reilly Factor*. The hysteria led directly to most of Churchill's speeches at universities being cancelled due to bomb threats, death threats, and weapons brandished on campuses where he was scheduled to speak. Some on the right went so far as to call for his execution for treason. Racist talk radio host "Gunny" Bob Newman quoted Churchill's statement, "I want the state gone," as alleged proof. By that bizarre standard, many conservatives are traitors for their similar hostility toward the federal government. Newman's poor reasoning did not stop other conservatives such as MSNBC's Joe Scarborough from joining his call.[31]

Churchill refused to back down, arguing he had nothing to apologize for. He did give a very qualified statement regretting that anyone had misconstrued what he said as an attack on the majority of the victims of September 11 but laid the blame for that misinterpretation on his critics for lying about what he actually said. Under incredible pressure, threats of being fired, and many threats to his life, Churchill resigned as head of the Ethnic Studies Department at the University of Colorado, writing, "It is my considered view that the present political climate has rendered me a liability in terms of representing either my department, the college, or the university in this or any other administrative capacity."[32] Churchill and his supporters gave no explanation as to why the same excuse would not also be true of his job as professor and ducked the whole question of whether he gave encouragement to the ones out to get him and other activist professors. It was very hard not to see Churchill's resignation as lacking the courage of his convictions and throwing his attackers a bone, hoping they would go away.

In Colorado some Natives, some in academia, and many on the political left rallied around him. More often, those on the left condemned the statements while defending Churchill's right to free speech. Some, such as his successor at Ethnic Studies, Emma Perez, saw the attacks on him as part of an orchestrated attempt to set a precedent for the suppression of any leftist views in academia, any criticism of the war, and ultimately any attempt to teach critical thinking or criticize any aspect of American society within a classroom setting. John Mohawk was one of the few Natives outside Colorado to express any sympathy for Churchill's circumstances: "A lot of people in America . . . wanted Americans to personify their heroes, to be Rambo. . . . Academia is in many ways the antithesis to that spirit. . . . Academia is traditionally rightfully skeptical of the Rambo approach which is part of the reason why ultra-nationalists are suspicious of academics who they feel are . . . insufficiently cheerful about unfounded military adventures." Mohawk went on to urge Churchill to apologize, saying, "The people who went to work in the World Trade Center that morning, with negligible exceptions, were not plotting American hegemony. They were pursuing careers. . . . The connection to Eichmann is far too much of a stretch for any but the most theoretically-minded."[33]

What most Americans outside of Indian Country viewing the controversy did not know, and what made Churchill particularly vulnerable, was that he was already one of the most loathed persons in Indian Country long before this episode. The roots of this intense dislike go back to the heyday of the American Indian Movement. By the late 1970s AIM increasingly faced heavy-handed federal government disruption and harassment, including tactics designed to create distrust within AIM. To a great extent federal agents succeeded. Most of the AIM leadership split into two factions, each accusing the other of being federal informants. On one side stood Autonomous AIM, led by Churchill and Russell Means. On the other side stood National AIM, led by Dennis Banks and Claude and Vernon Bellecourt. In spite of their titles, Autonomous AIM is largely made up of the Colorado AIM chapter, while National AIM is largely the Minneapolis AIM chapter. What was once a national movement is now mostly local AIM chapters working on their own, while doing their best to avoid being caught up in the longstanding feud within the original AIM leadership.[34]

Churchill and his supporters claim he was singled out for his beliefs. This is simply not true. Many Native professors and activists have beliefs equally or more radical. Churchill's current problems stem from his lack of (fellow?) Natives willing to defend him caused by, over the years, his alienating virtually every Native leader and activist by continually putting leftist revolutionary ideology before Native needs. At their worst, both Churchill and his following insist Natives subordinate their own needs to the leadership of white would-be revolutionaries, making the automatic false assumption that Natives are natural allies of revolutionary leftists.[35] Churchill has a history of repeatedly attacking tribal governments and leaders as collaborators, an indiscriminate condemnation that denounces, along with the corrupt, the very people who have done the most to preserve Native homelands, many of them justly highly revered with a lifetime of service to their people. Churchill also confuses being abrasive and obnoxious with being anti-establishment or taking a strong stance. His behavior attracts headlines but usually distracts from the issues, discredits people of even slightly similar views, and degenerates into a debate about his lack of personal ethics.

The controversy also revived questions of Churchill's claim to be Cherokee or Muscogee. At its ugliest, the focus by his newest critics on his descent (or lack of) is the reassertion of nakedly racist desires by some whites to claim power to decide who is or is not Native. Most (but not all) of Churchill's writing does not hinge on whether he is Native, since in either case it reflects the views of a white leftist. More important is that Churchill is not Native, Cherokee, or Muscogee by culture. His beliefs and worldview are not American Indian, nor are they shared by virtually any Natives. His following is overwhelmingly white with scant Native support. I saw Churchill at ASU as the keynote speaker at the Local to Global Justice conference. On a campus of over 40,000 students, perhaps 15 percent of whom are Native, I doubt there were more than ten Natives in the audience of over 500. (Most of the Natives I saw there came out of curiosity and did not applaud him.)[36] Yet speakers such as N. Scott Momaday and Linda Tuwahi-Smith at the same campus drew standing-room-only crowds of Native students.

Because the hard right targeted Churchill, most Native leaders refused to join in the criticism no matter how little regard they had for Churchill, with a few exceptions. The leaders of National AIM, the Bellecourt brothers and Dennis Banks, saw an opportunity to silence a rival and seemingly did not care that they aided some of the most anti-Indian and reactionary forces in the country. One of the worst, Ann Coulter, wrote "The Little Injun That Could." Coulter included vicious racist jokes about genocide: "Time to pack up the teepee and hit the Trail of Tears."[37] In doing so she exposed yet again the double standard that the media and many white Americans practice. Similar comments directed at blacks or Jews would have ended her career.

Most of the public remained wary about ousting professors for their views. Churchill's newer critics turned to reviving longstanding charges of plagiarism and other academic misconduct, some of which were cases several decades old. The University of Colorado committee focused on seven charges. Churchill decried the results as "predetermined" and "quibbling over footnotes." He argued that the lack of inclusion of historians with expertise in Native history made the committee's findings worthless.[38]

As a historian specializing in Native history, let me give my assessment of the charges. For at least some of them, Churchill is correct in saying the charges have little or no substance. The charges that are true mostly show sloppiness or poor scholarship, not malice.[39] The most widely known of the charges against Churchill was the most troubling from the standpoint of Native ethics and historical concerns and needs. Some critics claim Churchill manufactured evidence of the U.S. Army using biological warfare against Natives. Sociologist Thomas Brown wrote a hysterical and almost unhinged article titled "The Genocide That Wasn't: Churchill's Research Fraud." At the start of the controversy over the "little Eichmanns" comment, Brown posted it on his Lamar University homepage. He withdrew it under withering criticism. For one thing, Brown came perilously close to arguing there was never *any* genocide against Natives. As Brown himself admitted, his anger throughout his article clouded the issue. A later and calmer article still maintained Churchill "fabricated" evidence about the 1837 epidemic among the Mandans. Churchill used the work of Cherokee demographer Russell Thornton as his source. Yet Thornton himself only called what Churchill did "embellishment," not fabrication nor fraud.[40] Fabrication, after all, means manufacturing what did not exist before. Fraud means deliberate deception, often for money. What Churchill actually did was argue an interpretation without bothering to notice that the evidence did not back him up, which, after all, is much like what Brown himself did.

Churchill cited for support the oral traditions of the Mandans themselves, which do say the epidemic was deliberately spread, but by white traders not the army. Mandan/Hidatsa journalist Jodi Rave argued this was an abuse of oral traditions. Churchill seemed to be grasping at Mandan oral traditions as a last straw to cover up his sloppy misreading of Thornton's work. Rave and others are right to be angry about such crassness on his part. Worse is that Churchill added claims not present in Mandan tradition, such as the spreading of the disease by blankets.[41]

Just as important, by his carelessness on this matter Churchill did enormous damage to any scholar trying to argue, as most specialists in American Indian history now do, that Native peoples suffered outright genocide, not simply "tragic but inevitable loss" as apologists for genocide often claim. On this as on many issues, Churchill seems incapable of thinking ahead to how his recklessness damages causes he claims to favor. He seems deaf to the adage common to most Native cultures that one should weigh one's words carefully before speaking since they can never be taken back once uttered, and they can take on a life of their own beyond one's control.

Not long after the start of the "little Eichmanns" episode, a similar controversy arose about an alleged Native, this time on the political far right. Kiowa activist Cinda Hughes raised questions about David Yeagley's claims of being Comanche. This was not the first time his heritage was questioned. Comanche educator and artist Juanita Padapony also challenged his alleged Comanche ancestry and pointed out that he did not represent Comanche views. Yeagley himself admits there have long been "rumors" about his lack of ancestry and often comes close to admitting his impersonation.[42]

As best as I have been able to find out, no Comanches outside of his alleged mother and brothers ever heard of Yeagley before he asked far right activist David Horowitz to rescue him from obscurity and promote him. Most Comanches and other Natives, when they are not deeply offended by his anti-traditional and racist ideas, regard him as an eccentric or a joke. He has even been widely accused of getting plastic surgery and using tanning makeup and eyeliner to appear "more Indian" but only succeeded in getting nicknamed "Michael Jackson."[43] With or without his alleged Comanche blood, Yeagley is yet another case of an image of "the Indian" used to promote white wishful thinking. In this he follows in the tradition of not only wartime propaganda discussed in previous chapters but also other bizarre eccentrics on the political right claiming to be Indian, such as John Huffer ("Chief AJ") and Rita Ann Suntz ("Pale Moon Princess").[44]

Unlike Ward Churchill's writings, Yeagley's writings are utterly dependent on his claim of Native identity. With virtually every sentence he writes, Yeagley is trying to convince you he is The Great Comanche Warrior And Leader. Yeagley's insecurity about his identity is very revealing. In essence he continually begs the reader, "Trust me, I really am Comanche." To Native readers his writing style is racist parody much like the most stereotypical Tontospeak of New Age imposters, such as "Mary Summer Rain." Most of Yeagley's writing is bigoted rants against Indians and promotes the superiority of whites. His claims about himself have numerous obvious falsehoods.[45]

Yeagley responded to Hughes's charges by claiming there was a vast left-wing conspiracy out to get him and abuse his family. In fact Hughes did little more than ask extensively within the Comanche nation and report what she found. Only two Native papers and one Democratic Web site noted the controversy, in part because Yeagley sent lawyers to suppress the story by threatening Hughes and the *Native American Times*.

Bizarrely, Yeagley claimed Hughes's charges proved "Indian and

Black trash" were out to get him. Racist paranoia is part of virtually everything he writes. Part of his Web site is dedicated to support for the anti-immigrant and white supremacist Minute Men. Yeagley has also been praised by the neo-Nazi groups Stormfront and the National Alliance, as well as a pro-eugenics magazine, *American Renaissance.* He eagerly embraces white racists and had a Stormfront neo-Nazi as moderator for a section of his forum on Jews. Yeagley spoke at the anti-Indian and anti-sovereignty One Nation, where he praised the "white blood flowing . . . the purest I've seen" and called for a moratorium on mixed-race marriages. Yeagley later coauthored several articles with Barbara Lindsay. (Lindsay, who claims distant Cherokee ancestry, was expelled from a Cherokee group for her membership in One Nation.) Yeagley praises the brutal dictatorship of the shah of Iran and calls for Iranians to ally with whites and Jews against the Arabs he despises. His forum, Badeagle.com, has few Natives. Some that claim to be are clumsy white imposters. Actual Natives tend to get kicked out of the forum and censored, as Suzan Harjo did when she criticized him a second time. Most striking, Natives on his forum are *kept segregated from whites.*[46]

Even if Yeagley had not tried to suppress the story, his dubious claims attracted far less attention than Churchill had garnered because Yeagley's assertion to represent Native opinion or even be Native was always laughable. Indeed the reaction of most Natives has been to regard him as a joke. It is precisely because of the reasonable fear of Native activists that Churchill is mistakenly seen as representative of Native views that more attention has been given by Native activists to try to shun him. What both Churchill and Yeagley represent are the insistence by both the political left and right on finding professional tokens. Most Native activists refuse to get drawn into the left versus right false dichotomy, instead defining themselves by how traditional they are. Natives are by historical circumstance far more radical than anyone holding beliefs like those of either Churchill or Yeagley. Left versus right is a construct of Western society that does not mean much within Indian Country; it is simply one more thing from white society to avoid.

As of this writing, the controversy made Churchill a martyr in the eyes of some on the left and a symbol of everything wrong with academia to those on the right, and confirmed the belief of many in Indian Country that academia is out of touch with Native peoples. The committee looking into the allegations of Churchill's research fraud recommended by a vote of six to three that Churchill be fired. Yet clearly they reacted far more to the staged outcry of conservatives than to the substance of the charges. I would recommend suspension as the three dissenting members did and demand Churchill publicly apologize and compensate the parties wronged.

Churchill is now in more demand as a speaker than ever before. Firing him will not silence him, nor should it. I would rather he were seen as the white leftist that, culturally at least, he is. Those on the political left need to understand he represents their wishful thinking, not Native people or Native needs. Firing him will also do nothing to restrain his excesses; if anything it will worsen them. Worse than that, firing him sets a dangerous precedent, one we should expect will cheer those who see Joe McCarthy as a role model. But it was Churchill's own recklessness that almost provided an opportunity for O'Reilly, Horowitz, and others to silence activist professors. Only the increasing failures and unpopularity of the war kept many more activist professors from being purged from universities.

The War in Afghanistan

Much like during the Vietnam War and both wars in Iraq, some top federal officials continued to use Indian war analogies during the War in Afghanistan. An unnamed "senior U.S. official" compared Al Qaeda to Natives. Describing how Al Qaeda members might be using stealth to fool the U.S. military and intelligence agencies, the official said, "We don't see any of his Indians doing anything on his behalf." This comment brought an angry response from Jimmie Oyler, the Principal Chief of the United Tribe of the Shawnee, who demanded an apology from the president: "Dear Mr. President: If a 'senior U.S. official' made the . . . reported statement, please inform your senior officials the American Indians are not Osama bin Laden's 'Indians.'"[47]

In spite of the short attention given to the war by most of the public, some Natives did raise their voices against it. A group of Native and non-Native veterans led a protest in Washington DC, at the entrance to the Veterans Administration, protesting both the lack of attention to veterans' needs and the war in Afghanistan. Apache veteran Steve Mungie called the war "Mr. Bush's silly little game out in the desert." Lakota elder Elaine Quiver held a prayer vigil calling for peace at Bear Lodge, a Lakota sacred site commonly known to outsiders as Devil's Tower: "So many people called me up and said we needed to do something. . . . I think this [war] should never have happened." Lakota elder Leonard Little Finger compared the feelings of the U.S. public about September 11 to Lakotas' feelings on Wounded Knee: "Recrimination, retribution. Oftentimes it's hard not to seek these things. But we Lakota believe that it's better to pursue what we call the wholeness of well being."[48]

Umatilla soldier Lucas Eastwood went through a Longhouse ceremony before leaving for Afghanistan. He received as a gift a beaded feather from the Sam family that had been with another warrior in another land. Eastwood described patrolling in Afghanistan: "I believe in God and I love Indian war dancing and all, but I'm all about getting home safely!"[49]

White Mountain Apache nation member A. A. Guenther described for the tribal paper the motives of PFC Charles Kitcheyan in Afghanistan: he was "there out of love for their homeland and a desire to bring to justice those who would rob us of our freedom and our way of life." Ironically, however, Guenther then went into great detail to depict Kitcheyan as Americanized. Baptized at the Whiteriver Lutheran Church, Kitcheyan joined the Lutheran Pioneers. Guenther called Kitcheyan a "proud Apache and proud American." Guenther quoted the famous "valley of the shadow of death" passage from the Bible and ended by writing, "You honor your tribe, your country, and your church Charlie."[50]

The Blackfoot nation held a memorial for one of its members, William Carlson, who was killed in Afghanistan. Carlson was an ex–Green Beret turned civilian contractor working as part of an elite special operations force assigned to the CIA Directorate of Operations. Officially he was in Afghanistan to track terrorists and according to in initial reports he was listed as a member of the State Department. After the State Department denied having anyone over there, the CIA finally admitted he worked for them. His uncle Patrick Carlson described him as very traditional and always going through ceremonies.[51] Only the *Native American Times* mentioned his heritage. Not even other Native-oriented media picked up on that aspect of the story. The lack of support for the war likely played a part in this, in addition to his working for the CIA and agency secretiveness. If Carlson had died while still a soldier rather than a civilian CIA contract worker, I believe his death would have received more notice and his memory greater acclaim. Carlson became the second Native to die in combat in the War on Terrorism/Long War, after Lori Piestewa. The lonely reception his death received compared to Piestewa's was quite striking.

"The Same Forces That Went against Us as a People": The Second Iraq War

American Indians are not the only ones to see parallels between U.S. domination of the Middle East and the Indian Wars. John Brown, a former member of the Foreign Service who resigned over the Second Iraq War, points out many leading supporters of the war reveled in seeing the current war as like the Indian Wars. Robert Kaplan and Max Boot wrote in a *Wall Street Journal* article, "the American military is back to the days of fighting the Indians." Kaplan also wrote *Imperial Grunts*, which President Bush reportedly read during one of his many holidays. Among the passages in this book: "Welcome to Injun Country was the refrain I heard from Colombia to the Philippines, including Afghanistan and Iraq. . . . The War on Terrorism was really about taming the frontier. . . . We have a lot more savage wars ahead."[52]

Brown pointed out numerous parallels in the thinking of advocates of both sets of wars. I elaborate on most of these points below.

1) The paradigm of Americans as "the attacked" versus the enemy as "the attackers" even when most or all aggression came from the United States.

2) The belief in preventive strikes or preventive war, often justified by assumptions the enemy is relentless and violent by nature.

3) Believing a demonized and supposedly more primitive culture can be made "just like us," civilized or remade into the image

of Western man. In the case of American Indians, the cure was supposedly capitalism and Christianity. For Muslims and Arabs, the cure is alleged to be Western-style democracy, though the religions of both groups are assumed to be the root cause of their "primitivism." But built into this assumption is that the enemy's adaptation of white American culture is an inherent good or sign of success.

4) Unilateral action in a war that is also domestic, as the enemies of the United States in the War on Terrorism/Long War are assumed to be within as well, sometimes including critics of the war or of the Bush administration.

5) A biblically driven narrative justifying the wars. Many European and Anglo-American colonists saw America as the Promised Land, the "City on the Hill." Many current war proponents see the Second Iraq War as the fulfillment of biblical prophecies. Israel also plays a strong role as a proxy fighter for U.S. aggression versus Arab states, with the explicit understanding that U.S. Christian conservatives give Israel unquestioned support for its own belligerence in the region.

6) The use of Indian reservations as a model for Iraq and Afghanistan, with American trustees controlling Iraqi oil.

7) Similar fighting methods, using overwhelming force against the "primitives'" insurgency tactics. Both sets of wars saw the use of "the enemy of my enemy." In the current war, that means using Shiites and Kurds to fight Sunnis.

8) The possibility that perceptions of the enemy could change. Arabs in the future might be romanticized by whites as the Noble Savage, much like Indians.

In winning acceptance for the continuation of old tactics under new labels, Hollywood likely played a huge role. Communications professor Jack Shaheen points out the common threads in old westerns' demonizing of Indians with anti-Arab films. Both peoples are shown as inhuman savages who do not think like an unnamed "us" that is presumed to be white Christian American. Both groups are shown as thriving on violence and disorder and using stealth. Shaheen also could have added that both are often shown as filthy, stupid, or lusting after white (especially blond) women. Hollywood had begun redoing old western movies at their most racist, with Arabs taking the place of Indians, as far back as the 1970s. Filmmakers often were quite blunt about their intent. *Iron Eagle* producer Ron Samuels described the appeal of doing his film: "It reminded me of the old John Wayne westerns." In a critique of one of the most anti-Arab films ever made, *True Lies*, Don Bustancy and Salam al Marayat pointed out if the film's star, Arnold Schwarzenegger, "had killed Redskins wearing feathers instead of brown skins wearing beards and kuffiyehs we'd have a classic racist cowboys and Indians movie."[53]

The Israeli film company Golan-Globus (later Cannon Films) also had been basically remaking old westerns with the "Arab as Indian" theme, often starring leading Hollywood conservatives, such as Chuck Norris. (Worth pointing out is that Norris claims to be part Cherokee.) Anti-Arab filmmakers often tried to deflect criticism of the racism of their films by blatant tokenism, hiring black actors such as Louis Gossett and Denzel Washington. In some respects Gossett and Washington became black versions of Tonto, not in the sense of being stereotypical but in being servants to white racist needs. They were cast in these movies largely to assure white audiences the films' stereotypes were somehow not racist and to encourage non-Arab minorities to join in hating Arabs.

The Second Iraq War marks the fifth war in U.S. history where war supporters have invoked the image of the enemy as "Indians" and have used Wild West imagery. Christian Broadcasting Network reporter Paul Strand described combat with the enemy while traveling with Third Infantry using racist epithets: "I'd say there are Injuns ahead of us, Injuns behind us, and Injuns on both sides too." Fox News military analyst and retired Marine Corps colonel Bill Cowan called for a revival of the Kit Carson Scout program once used in Vietnam to be used in Iraq. He argued, "It's Kit Carsonized-Iraqis who should be leading the way into Fallujah," the scene of some of the heaviest U.S. losses of the war. Cowan reasoned, "Iraqis will accept brutality from other Iraqis, but not from foreigners."[54]

The political left also employed the same kinds of pejorative images. In *Common Dreams*, a leading journal for self-described progressives, Jim Lobe wrote an article titled "Bush Circles Wagons, But Cavalry Has Joined the Indians." In the wake of the scandal over the torture, abuse, and possible murders of Iraqi POWs, Lobe described Democrats and other critics of Bush as "Indians" attacking the Bush administration: "In Washington over the last few days it seems that the Cavalry has joined the Indians. U.S. President George W. Bush, backed by his vice president and national security adviser, ha[s] been circling the wagons around Defense Secretary Donald Rumsfeld since the White House told reporters that the president had given him a mild rebuke over the prisoner abuse scandal in Iraq."[55]

Opposition to the war came from perhaps the most famous Native spiritual leader, Arvol Looking Horse. Looking Horse went as part of a peace delegation to pray in Baghdad. He told reporters, "An elder told me that if I did not go to that land, a great black cloud would come all around the earth." The elder described sickness you could smell in the air. Looking Horse traveled with five other Native elders and two Anglo reporters. The delegation prayed with what Looking Horse called an Iraqi "spiritual elder," likely an imam or ayatollah. Saddam Hussein tried to speak with the delegation, but they refused to meet with him, claiming time constraints prevented them. (More likely they realized how such a meeting could be misconstrued as support for Hussein.) Looking Horse argued, like so many others, that the war was about control of resources: "This country chooses places to help if it can give us some oil, gold, or drugs. What's going on today is about money and power. But being of a spiritual people we still have to think about the future of our children."[56]

Perhaps the most famous Native author in the United States, Sherman Alexie (Spokane/Coeur d'Alene), chose to criticize the impending war using irony and humor: "We will only win the metaphorical and clichéd war on terror when George W. Bush proclaims a metaphorical and clichéd victory over terror, and that proclamation will only be uttered if the Democratic presidential nominee creeps within three percentage points [of winning]." Alexie then wryly noted, "I find it ironic that the U.S. wants to go to war with Iraq because it keeps breaking treaties."[57]

Criticism of the war remains intense and wide-ranging. Tex Hall of the National Congress of American Indians questioned Bush's spending $87 billion for Afghanistan and Iraq, arguing it could be better used at home. Ojibwe journalist Larry Adams wrote a blistering editorial in which he called Bush "America's first illegally elected president . . . Bush ALLOWED Afghanistan's attack on the former World Trade Center to be justified by spending billions of dollars on an unnecessary war to get one man in Iraq. . . . [He leads] Republican megalomaniacs out to destroy a world." Seminole Vietnam veteran Dean Chavers angrily stated in the *Seminole Tribune,* "The hoopla over this pissant war with Iraq seems out of place. Everybody argues about Vietnam. . . . Somebody ought to start arguing about this one."[58]

Still more Native figures joined in the criticism. Navajo journalist Brenda Norrell tied the war to Navajo concerns about Big Mountain, pointing to Bush's ties to Peabody Coal. Cheyenne activist Rene Still Day called the United States "the aggressor, the bully, the warmonger." She described the United States as becoming a police state and grew angry over talk of prosecuting human shields as traitors. Still Day defended them as Medal of Honor winners and nuns. She critiqued Bush's plan for Iraq's oil: "The oil of Iraq will be placed in trust for the people of Iraq. . . . Anyone already living in Indian Country knows how that will work—It won't!" Victor Redstar, a Nez Perce and descendant of Chief Joseph, believed, "The forces that started this war are the same forces that went against us as a people."[59]

Elders of one of the larger Native nations, the Tetuwan Oyates or the Teton Sioux Nation Treaty Council, issued a strong statement from Tony Blackfeather against the war, calling for UN intervention to stop the United States.

> If America, or the world for that matter, wants to understand the mindset behind the war, it's simple. Ask an Indian. The current invasion . . . is the latest chapter in the American colonial process. . . . We see the same history unfolding that our people have [experienced] and continue to experience. . . . Our genetic memories recall the massacres in our own country. . . . This is the same history. . . . It is a mass murder for oil and resources—the same thing they did to us—the same people are in Iraq that killed my Lakota people and

stole our Lakota land. . . . We are not involved in this so-called war. . . . We cannot condone the use of what are our resources . . . to support the invasion of Iraq. . . . The United States is trying to put the Iraqi people under the same reservation and trust system they have used against our people. . . . The appointment of 23 American "ministers" . . . sounds very similar to the Indian agents installed on reservations. . . . The Lakota Nation stands with UN member states . . . condemning the invasion of Iraq, calling for a ceasefire and a withdrawal of U.S. and British armed forces. . . . The Teton Sioux Nation agrees with British Middle East expert Patrick Seale . . . [that] the Americans and British have lost the war politically and morally. . . . When will Americans realize that the people who died on September 11 died for nothing if America refuses to examine its own role in the tragedy? When will Americans learn their way is not the only way? . . . We are hopeful that our world of nations will stand together against the abuser, the schoolyard bully, and the violator or international law. . . . The people of the Lakota Nation pray for the peoples and nations . . . experiencing the weight of American imperialism.[60]

Persistent and unambivalent criticism like this did not prevent non-Native media from seeing what they wished to see and using the moral prestige of Natives to rally support for the war. Mark Shaffer of the *Arizona Republic* argued, "Reservation patriotism [was] at a high level." He depicted support for the war as nearly universal in the Navajo nation, although each Navajo he interviewed in his article spoke ambivalently about the war or opposed it. Robert Holliday, a jewelry stand operator in Monument Valley, believed Navajos joined up "to get a job and dollars for school later on. But if a war breaks out, that turns out to be a bad decision." He thought the war was just but admitted to being worried it could go badly. Mike Gray of the Oljato Trading Post simultaneously argued that the war was already out of control but that the United States should "shoot them all if need be." Rose Hulligan, a schoolteacher at Kayenta Middle School, accused the United States of "trying to make a bogeyman" and having a "divide and conquer mentality." Navajo president Joe Shirley Jr. joined in the criticism of the war as "a waste," decrying the dead lost to Native families and the diversion of federal resources to the war and away from reservation needs. But like the overwhelming majority of Natives, he voiced his support for the troops themselves.[61]

There is an enormous outpouring of Native support for the troops of the Second Iraq War but not for the war itself. Even in the few cases in which Natives took part in supposedly pro-war rallies, the events' intent blended with comfort of servicemen's families or support of troops as the overriding sentiment. At a rally of 150 people at Window Rock in the Navajo nation, Kathy Anderson described her son, Miguel Cortez, as in Iraq "trying to do the right thing." But virtually everyone else interviewed by the *Navajo Times* at the rally listed support for the troops as their sole motive for coming out. At Haskell Indian College, Native veterans held a ceremony to support the troops. One Native veteran of Vietnam and the Gulf War lamented, "It's really a shame we have protests going on." But every other veteran interviewed at the ceremony by *Native Voice* spoke of support for the troops as often as they indicated support for the war. A few argued for supporting the war because of Native experience with biological war; they also supported Kurds as oppressed indigenous minorities. At least one veteran also pressed for prosecution of any companies and governments that provided weapons of mass destruction to Iraq, including members of the U.S. government or U.S. corporations.[62]

Some returning Native veterans and their families led criticism of the war. Specialist Gerald Dupris of the Cheyenne River Reservation and Staff Sergeant Julius Tulley of the Navajo nation held a news conference to argue that poverty in Indian Country was worse than it was in Iraq. Both soldiers, along with the chairman of the National American Indian Housing Council, argued that conditions had worsened as a direct result of the war. The Bush administration had cut the federal budget for Native housing from $647 million to $582 million. A spokesman for the Bush administration admitted funding was "tight" but claimed private funding would make up for it. One well-known peace activist in Indian Country, Tlingit poet and playwright Diane Benson, saw the conflict forever alter her own family. The army kept her son Latseen Benson in Iraq after his enlistment ended, over his strong objections, using the highly controversial Stop

Loss program. Diane Benson accused Stop Loss of being an unofficial draft. Latseen Benson lost both his legs and part of his arm to a roadside bomb. He never wanted to go to Iraq, hoping instead to go to Afghanistan, where he believed his service would actually help end terrorism.[63]

No matter their position on the war, Native communities still worked to honor or build support for servicemen through ceremonies. The Northern Cheyennes performed a Victory Dance for one of its members, Lance Corporal Lamar Wandering Medicine, organized by his parents, Mark and Ilo. Wandering Medicine counted coup on flags he took from Saddam Hussein's presidential palace. He also received a new name, Powerful Wolf, at a ceremony performed by Charles Littleoldman. A dozen other veterans came to the ceremony. His father, Mark, described it as proper and something he did not receive on returning from Vietnam. Lamar retold the story of running his tank over the first of four Iraqis he killed in combat.[64]

Twenty-nine members of the Tohono O'odham nation called up for the military were honored with traditional prayer songs and a warrior prayer chanted by Christine Johnson and the Nolic Singers. Journalist Gabriela Rico described the singing of the "national anthem in the O'odham language" but neglected to say whether it was the U.S. national anthem or the O'odham National Anthem. Likely the question did not even occur to her, but given what I have seen at powwows I feel certain it was the O'odham National Anthem. Traditional counselor Joseph Enos described how other O'odham would help them cope once they returned: "They will have a four-day cleansing, because they will have done stuff that is unnatural." Using ceremony to cope with war could extend even to non-Natives. A group of Green Berets stationed in Kuwait requested a blessing from a Native pipe ceremony. A group of Nez Perce veterans held the ceremony for Company A of the First Battalion of 19th Special Forces Airborne in Lapwai, Kuwait.[65]

Criticism of the war could mix with ceremonies held to honor veterans who died in combat. At the funeral for Sheldon Ray Hawk Eagle, a Lakota killed in a helicopter crash in Iraq, the procession featured a spirit horse, a riderless horse draped with a blanket made of a modified American flag and an eagle feather. Hawk Eagle's family and friends held an overnight vigil with Christian and Lakota prayers, honor songs, and color guards from all five Sioux reservations. In remembering Hawk Eagle, many noted his descent from Crazy Horse. Barbara Blue Coat, his aunt, said to a reporter, "There's nothing around here on the reservation. No jobs, so we encourage our boys to go to the military for education. But now, war broke out and it's a different story." Winona Washburn, a high school classmate of Hawk Eagle's, wrote an honor song for him and sang it at his funeral.

> Our Eagle soars with wings today
> If you listen closely you will hear the angels pray
> He'll be watching from above
> Still sharing of his love
> Today our Eagle soars with wings[66]

Conclusion

The messages coming from Indian Country during the wars in the Middle East point toward a new pattern for Native communities. Sympathy and support for Kurds, September 11 victims and families, and veterans and their families stood side by side with strong protests of unjust and unwise wars. Honoring veterans remains as widespread as ever in Indian Country, but opposition to the wars has also never been stronger. From the beginning there was little sign of enthusiasm among Native people for these wars, and the lackluster recruiting and enlistment reflects that. Most Natives saw clear parallels between what happened in their Native nations and what is happening in the Middle East. None of this diminishes the respect Natives have for veterans, even while some non-Natives choose to ignore or have misunderstood Native points of view. We shall see the same pattern in the next chapter as we discuss the meaning of the life story of Lori Piestewa. How her life is depicted shows that anyone thinking participation in the military will win Natives acceptance from non-Natives is in for a brutal shock.

11

"A Woman Warrior, Just Like Lozen"

The Meaning of the Life of Lori Piestewa to Natives and Non-Natives

The Meaning of Lori Piestewa's Life to Different Audiences

THIS CHAPTER WILL BE THE most emotional and the most brutal one in this book, so much so that I feel I must warn the reader, especially anyone related to Lori Piestewa. For Native readers, this chapter will seem equal parts tribute and mourning that others did not share in taking part in paying respect to Lori Piestewa's life. No doubt the antiracist or nonracist non-Native will share many of the same sentiments. I say this not only to caution the reader but to point to one of my purposes in including this chapter. I write this not simply because she became such a public figure, or because I lived in Phoenix during the time of most of the events described and participated in a few of them. Lori Piestewa's life vividly illustrates just how little has changed in more than a century of Native veteran traditions. It also reflects how the gulf in understanding between Native and non-Native can easily widen into an outright canyon.

Lori Piestewa first came to the public's attention as a member of the U.S. Army's 507th Maintenance Company in Iraq. Her unit was ambushed after making a wrong turn near Nasiriyah, Iraq. Ten of its members were killed or captured, the most famous of whom was Lori's friend Jessica Lynch. When U.S. commandos rescued Lynch from an Iraqi hospital, they also recovered nine bodies, including Lori's.[1]

The local Native community marked the one-year memorial of the death of Lori Piestewa at dusk in Pioneer Park in downtown Phoenix. Mary Kim Titla from the San Carlos Apache nation spoke of the high regard Native people had for Lori. Titla ended her speech by giving Lori one of the highest compliments an Apache woman can give, calling her, "a woman warrior, just like Lozen, not thinking of herself as different or better than others, as strong as a man, but braver than most."

Lozen was an Apache woman who fought alongside Victorio. Titla's words were far from the only tribute to Lori at this memorial. Color guards from the Sylvester Henry ROTC (the high school in Tuba City, her hometown), the Hopi nation, the American Indian Veterans Memorial Organization, the Fort McDowell nation, the Ira Hayes American Legion Post from Sacaton, the Pima nation, and, ironically, from Cesar Chavez High School all marched in memory of her at the close of the ceremony after several hours of dances and speeches in her honor.

The speakers included an aide from the office of Congressman Trent Franks, a Republican from the 2nd District. Her voice rising in anger, she vowed that "no tyrant" would take Saddam Hussein's place and that Lori's sacrifice would not be in vain. These remarks stunned much of the crowd. Most Natives had looks on their faces as though they had been punched in the gut; they showed shock and disbelief, horror, and anger. Once the comments set in, forced and almost dutiful applause broke out perhaps half a minute later. Some scattered cheers, whistles, and roars of "Yeah!" also came (mostly from Anglos who attended), which was very out of character for this solemn memorial. I do not mean to single out this young aide for what seemed to many to be a blatant attempt to capitalize on a soldier's death for votes. No doubt both she and Franks sincerely believed that many appreciated a message that Lori's death served a purpose, to supposedly bring freedom to Iraq. I bring this up merely to stress a central theme of this chapter, which appropriately closes this book: the use of Native veteran service by some outsiders to mean what they would like it to mean, compared to what Natives themselves say that service means.

The Beginnings of Native Women's Veteran Traditions: From Women Warriors and Healers to Soldiers and Nurses

In Native cultures women warriors generally could find acceptance, but they were not the norm. My mentor in my master's program, Donna Akers, described to me how her Choctaw people once viewed women warriors. Choctaw male warriors accepted the occasional woman warrior, as long as she did her part. A few Choctaw women warriors even had wives of their own.[2] Akers's explanation for warrior roles in Native societies is that young male aggression needs an outlet so that violence is not turned on other members of the culture or community. We do know that in a few Native tribes, women served in the Indian Scouts. The Crows, for example, had many women who served, the most famous of whom was Emma Rides the Bear. Interestingly, no Crow women served as nurses.[3]

Finding specialties in indigenous medicine that correspond exactly to the role of a nurse is difficult as well. Many Native cultures did and still do have women healers. These could often be extremely specialized, ranging from diagnosticians to hand tremblers to bone setters.[4] The Congregation of American Sisters were the first American Indian women veterans we know of outside of Indian Scouts; they were Lakota Catholic nuns from Ft. Berthold Reservation. Father Francis Craft founded and led the order. Craft was a Mohawk mixed-blood (with a one-eighth blood quantum) whose ancestors sided with the rebels during the American Revolution. Craft himself briefly enlisted in the Union army at the incredibly young age of ten as a messenger; he was given permission to do so by both his father, a captain in the army, and the governor of New York, Dewitt Clinton. Wounded on the first day of the Battle of Gettysburg, Craft returned home. He went on to fight as a mercenary for France during its war with Prussia in 1870, later leading his own company of mercenaries on the side of Cuban rebels fighting for independence from Spain in the early 1870s.[5]

Throughout his whole life, Craft debated his own identity as either Native or white with a little bit of Native ancestry. By 1874 he had become a Jesuit and determined to "become an Indian to save the Indian." Lakota leader Spotted Eagle adopted Craft as an honorary Lakota. But Craft's writings reveal a persistent bigotry and identification with Western values: "The history of these Indians . . . would be merely a reprint of the history of Jewish perverseness . . . merely changing Hebrew names to Indians, and somewhat intensifying the malice brutality and pigheadedness of the Jews to suit their worthy descendants, who have still further descended from most execrable ancestors." A poem Craft wrote about himself in his journal near the end of his life showed the same mind-set:

He sowed good seed
He watered it with his own blood
For this barbarous nation.[6]

Craft wanted an all-Native order and founded the Congregation of American Sisters right after the massacre of Wounded Knee. In establishing the order he appealed to the image of famed Mohawk convert Catherine Ketari. He publicly pushed an ideal of assimilation: "We ask Americans to permit Americans to labor for the welfare of our own American people." He insisted the first member of the order choose the name Sister Mary Liguori as "more distinctly American." Craft volunteered the services of his nuns for the Spanish-American War after a scandal alleging sexual liaisons between himself and his nuns. Craft's efforts and those of his nuns won only limited acceptance by a few outsiders. The Order of Spanish American Nurses adopted Craft's nuns as members. Reverend Mother Mary Anthony, formerly Susie Bordeaux, the granddaughter of Spotted Tail and grand-niece of Red Cloud, died of disease during the Spanish-American War and was buried in a military cemetery with full honors, a historic first for a sister in the United States.[7]

Thus from the very beginning the history of Native women veterans showed much the same tensions we have seen throughout this study. Many Native women dealt with many of the same issues male Native veterans confronted, especially assimilation versus the continuation of Native traditions. The lack of attention to this issue is one of the most serious omissions in studies of Native veterans. I include my master's thesis among the works that fail to adequately recognize Native women's roles. Retired Lieutenant Colonel Brenda Finnicum is the only author who has given the subject the attention it deserves.

For the Hopis specifically, there is a long tradition of Hopi women taking part in raids and defending villages. Tim Shaner, one of the directors of the ROTC program in Tuba City, says the Hopi warrior tradition extends to the Hopi women in ROTC, who make up 25 out of 65 members. Delfred Leslie, a Hopi nation judge and religious leader, also describes women as being part of Hopi warrior traditions and points to a warrior society, the Kalatakayum or Sword Swallowers, which still exists and has both male and female members.[8]

PFC Piestewa Becomes "Lori"

Ask virtually anyone Native to talk about Lori Piestewa and you will almost always hear her called simply "Lori." To her own family she was also Qotsa-hon-mana (White Bear Girl). But Native people she never knew, from all parts of the country and worldwide, speak of her as a friend or sister. Natives a bit older speak of her like a daughter, and Native children speak of her like an older sister or a mother. It is rare for Natives to call a public figure solely by his or her first name. I know of only two other cases, Leonard (Leonard Peltier) and Anna Mae (Anna Mae Aquash). What these three figures share in common is striking. Two died by violence, and the third has been on death row for most of his life.[9] All three are famous solely for a very brief episode in their lives that permanently changed the course of their future, ending in death or (in Leonard's case) a kind of living death in prison. All three are or are perceived to be victims of federal government actions. All are seen as set upon by actions beyond their control and by what is seen as injustice. Giving Lori the honor of being publicly referred to solely by her first name is, I believe, a way for Native people to subtly or subconsciously recognize that her death in the war was unjust, as the entire war is unjust.

I spoke at a memorial for Lori on April 9, 2003, at Arizona State University, immediately after the news of her death became public. The memorial came together at almost the last moment, perhaps thirty hours between announcements about it and its start. The organizers expected perhaps thirty people. Over five hundred showed up, along with all the local television and news outlets. It was the largest gathering I had ever seen on the campus outside of sports events, easily outnumbering both the pro- and antiwar rallies combined and far outnumbering campus gatherings by Campus Crusade for Christ ministries and even free concerts. Several Navajo Code Talkers attended, and I felt a bit awestruck to be seated next to one. Rodeo Queens, the Order of the Purple Heart, and people from many reservations came in a spontaneous and intensely emotional outpouring of grief, support, and unity.

The memorial opened with prayers, songs, and introductions by the rally's organizers, Carmenlita Chief and Jerome Clark. Clark described how Lori's story touched him: it was "like losing a sister. What really hurt me was thinking about what it must be like to die so far away from your homeland, the sacred lands you grew up in." Lori's aunt spoke next. Her voice choked with emotion and she struggled to hold back tears as she thanked everyone for their kindness. I spoke after her, with some trepidation to be at so important an event. With television camera lights in my eyes, struggling to avoid feedback from the mike, I gave my speech that I could only hope was good enough for the occasion.

> Lori has already become a symbol across this land in ways I doubt she ever would have guessed. I would say she has probably become the best-known Native vet since Ira Hayes. And like Ira, the loss of Lori has come to mean many things to people in ways that I hope they would have liked.
>
> In the papers and the television, reporters are always linking her name with Jessica Lynch. They were close friends in the army. People look at their friendship much like they looked at the friendships that Ira Hayes had with the white GIS in his platoon. They see those friendships as symbols of hope, signs that maybe in young people we can find ones who will not make the mistakes their parents too often made, of hating people or being afraid of people who are different. . . .
>
> Some people are using Lori's death and the fact of her service to mean what they would like it to mean, that Natives just want to be like everyone else, Americans but no longer American Indians, no longer Hopi and Apache and Dineh and O'odham and hundreds of others. They still don't understand that the flag means something very different for many Native people than it does for most whites, that the words *our country* and *my country* mean different things, this land and nations, and not the nation led from Washington. We can only hope they learn, and we can only do our best to teach them. . . .
>
> Some things that have happened because of Lori's death have brought me hope. When you see Katie Couric talking with the Hopi tribal chairman, telling about how she has learned about the Hopi Code Talkers, that is a positive thing. Many people who never knew

about or understood why the military and our veterans are so important to so many Native people are now learning why this is so.

I am especially pleased and given a great deal of hope by the good
news I heard only last night. Some are pushing to have Squaw Peak
renamed in Lori's honor, as Piestewa Peak. I can think of no better
tribute to Lori and to all our Native women than to remove this ugly
stain and insult of a name, one of the sickest epithets there is, and
replace it with a name that is far more respectful, that honors Lori's
heroism and her sacrifice. I hope anyone who is listening joins me
in wishing this name change happens, and working for that change
in any small way they can.

For far too long, far too few people knew about our Native women
veterans. Lori was probably the most famous Native woman ever
in the military, but she was far from being the only one. . . . Let us
remember and honor all the women in the service, who are in as much
danger as any man, and all the women who sacrifice for their loved
ones, their families, and their nations, all our mothers, grandmothers,
wives, daughters, sisters, aunts, and cousins. Please join me in hoping that some time very soon, we can point with pride to the highest
point in the city and say, "That is Piestewa Peak." Thank you.

To my relief, people cheered throughout my speech, especially when
I spoke about renaming Squaw Peak as Piestewa Peak. I was deeply
gratified by all the people who thanked me, shook my hand, or wanted
to speak with me afterward. I bring all of this up not just to let the
reader know about my very small role in the effort to rename the peak
and honor Lori's memory but also because the memorial illustrated
the incredible depth of feelings her death engendered among Native
peoples.

Tributes to Lori poured in from Natives of all tribal backgrounds
and locations, from as far away as bases in Europe, Japan, Africa,
Australia, and the Middle East. When I first wrote this chapter in 2004,
online tributes alone numbered more than a thousand. Lori's family
traveled across the country as honored guests at powwows, schools,
concerts, and other gatherings, meeting tribal presidents, celebrities,
and thousands of other Natives who all saw in Lori's story something
they deeply identified with.

At least seventeen tribes contributed to her memorial fund. Tohono O'odhams Roy Rios and Jasper Miguel, inmates in the county jail in Tucson, painted an image of Lori on a blanket as a tribute. The blanket depicts her in front of an American flag with a dream catcher and red and pink roses representing her "passing to the next world" as Rios and Miguel describe it. The bottom of the blanket reads, "The strength of our people is within our women." A Navajo-Hopi bike-run event was also organized to honor her memory. The National Native American Games changed its name to the Lori Piestewa National Native American Games, a clear sign they regarded Lori as a universal symbol for Native people.[10] As Jerome Clark said at the ASU memorial, so many Natives viewed losing Lori "like losing a sister."

In Arizona the effort to honor her also focused on renaming a local landmark. The effort to rename Squaw Peak as Piestewa Peak began spontaneously. It seems to have come simultaneously from both Native and non-Native sources. The editors of the leading conservative daily in the state, the *Arizona Republic*, came out early in favor of the name change. Jennifer Dokes, assistant editorial page editor, suggested the paper support the renaming after receiving a number of letters from readers. Most of the board agreed with her. Linda Valdez and E. J. Montini both wrote editorials in favor of renaming. Supportive letters frequently quoted Montini's pointed title for his most famous editorial on the issue, "Who Would Call Warrior a 'Squaw'?" The *Republic* played such a pivotal role that News Watch saluted the paper for its stand.[11]

When the State Board on Geographic and Historic Names met to discuss the name change, Governor Janet Napolitano, Phoenix mayor Skip Rimsza, and the Indian Intertribal Council representing nineteen of the state's Indian nations all came out in favor of the name change, along with hundreds of local residents and a wide range of people from all the state's reservations. After several hours of testimony, virtually all in favor, the board voted 5–1 to change the name. Most who spoke against the name change voiced a desire to honor all veterans instead, without taking anything away from the effort to honor Lori.[12]

The Piestewa Peace Foundation took the call for the name change one step further and began what they refer to as the Piestewa Peace

Process. The foundation called for replacing "squaw" in all site names with "Piestewa," and ending all Indian mascots and team names. Their Web site featured the slogan "Like Custer, Lori Ann Piestewa died for your sins." By implication, Lori thus becomes almost a Christ figure, a sacrifice necessary for a better world. The foundation also sold the same T-shirts I discussed at the start of chapter 10, "Homeland Security: Fighting Terrorism since 1492." As far I know, the only Native to publicly oppose the name change was Don "Four Arrows" Jacob of the Flagstaff chapter of Veterans for Peace. He worried it gave the misleading impression all Natives favored the war.[13]

"Oft-Penetrated Native Woman's Vagina Has a Nice Ring to It": Use and Abuse of Lori's Memory

The local response among non-Natives to Lori's death could not have been more disparate or divided, ranging from equally respectful to fascinated to puzzled, at times ignorant or openly assimilationist, and sometimes even brazenly contemptuous and racist. On the issue of the name change, the public as a whole in Arizona sharply divided, with 32 percent favoring and 28 percent opposing the plan; 40 percent had no opinion. After the name change bill passed, many Arizonans changed their mind and favored renaming the peak, but they rather bizarrely remained opposed to changing the name of the freeway by the peak.[14]

One of the earliest and most frequent reactions to the news of Lori's death is something we have already seen so many times before: dependency theory or seeing Natives in the military as a sign of wanting to assimilate to Anglo value systems and become plain, unhyphenated "Americans." Heidi Williams of Reno, Nevada, wrote a letter to the *Navajo Times* that illustrates this. "Navajo and Hopi AMERICANS," she began, and continued to use "Americans" in all capitals in every reference in her letter. "As a[n] AMERICAN, Lori has instantly become my hero!!!!!" She continued in the same vein, "You just don't hear very often [about] a 'woman' dying for her country. I am so honored." Note that Williams did not say Lori should be honored but that Williams felt honored *by* Lori supposedly dying on her behalf. "May her children grow up proud of her knowing the sacrifices she made for . . . me, my kids . . . AMERICANS, GOD BLESS AMERICA."[15]

Arizona Republican congressman Rick Renzi claimed in a speech to the Navajo Nation Council that he had inside information that Lori "fought to the death . . . Lori charged the enemy." Later evidence showed Lori died without firing a shot. She simply drove, trying to get herself and fellow soldiers away from the fighting. Lori's father, Terry, contrary to what advocates of the war such as Congressmen Renzi and Franks said, could not have been happier to find out her daughter had not killed or fought Iraqis: "We're very satisfied she went the Hopi way. She didn't inflict harm on anybody."[16]

Lori's brother Terry furthered his father's criticism, using public forums to object to the war's backers and their misuse of Lori's memory. Speaking before the National Congress of American Indians (NCAI) at their memorial for Lori, Terry called for all Native soldiers to leave Iraq and come home, more than a year before Cindy Sheehan's famous protests. "It's not right for us Native Americans to be out there doing someone else's job," he told the NCAI. He received a standing ovation from the crowd, made up mostly of Native veterans. Rosanda Suetopka-Thayer, a family friend and liaison, had led the criticism even earlier. On hearing that no weapons of mass destruction could be found in Iraq, she said, "It really is unfortunate that she [Lori] had to sacrifice herself for something that could have totally been unnecessary."[17]

The following month, NBC News aired a previously unseen video showing Lori dying of her wounds in the Iraqi hospital. The Piestewa family called the act "terrorism . . . from our own people looking to make a quick buck." They also launched even more scathing criticism of Bush and the war: "Let us make sure that President Bush, his father and each of his aides and advisors get a copy of Lori dying in agony so that they realize, from the comfort of their homes, that war should be the last option."[18]

Some conservatives tried to use Lori's death to argue that women should not be allowed in combat. Elaine Donnelly, the leader of a group opposed to allowing women in combat called the Center for Military Readiness, spread rumors in her public speeches that Lori might have been raped before being killed in Iraq. Donnelly even hinted at an official cover-up of the alleged fact. Congressman Franks ironically argued that placing women in combat made them unequal: "We . . .

must ask ourselves if we are allowing unnecessary and unequal risks to women, all in the name of so-called equality." Lori's mother, Percy, took issue with those who argued for keeping women out of combat: "If a child decides that's what she wants to, fight for her country, then she should be allowed to do it."[19]

Reactionary activist David Yeagley saw Lori's death as an opportunity for red-baiting and race-baiting. In an essay about her death, Yeagley devoted most of it to attacking all Natives in the media besides him (assuming his claim of being Comanche is actually true) as believing in "liberal, Leftist jargon . . . associat[ing] with anti-American forces . . . dominated by professional, communist-funded activists who make a living by criticizing America and condemning the very heart of America's existence." Yeagley also disparaged "the Black Radical Congress, which bemoans the 'disproportionate' number of Negroes in the military." Yeagley argued, "I've . . . tried to tell Indians that our best future lies in American Patriotism, not in protesting the past, or even lamenting the future. . . . But Lori's done a better job than I. Her message is much louder and clearer."[20] What Yeagley did not know, or more likely chose to ignore, was that Lori joined up to support her children as an unwed mother and that her own friends and family increasingly opposed the war and were pleased that Lori did not harm anyone, "the Hopi way" as her father proudly pointed to.

The spectacle of publicly disparaging and insulting a soldier killed in combat worsened at the start of the call for changing the name of Squaw Peak to Piestewa Peak. These kinds of episodes are not unique. As we saw earlier, Ira Hayes put up with the same kinds of race-baiting, and his memory suffered the further indignity of being disparaged as a drunken Indian ever since. What is unusual is the sheer volume of insult directed at Piestewa's memory and how broadly across the political spectrum the outright contempt for her memory reached.

In Phoenix, the local alternative weekly paper is the *New Times*, which describes itself as being on the left politically but willing to hear all views. *New Times* columnist Robert Nelson led the charge for those opposed to the name change with his column "Squaw Peeved."

"Oft-penetrated Native woman's vagina has a nice ring to it," Nelson began, openly flaunting the racist image of Native women as sluts, whores, and even deserving of gang rape. Then Nelson defended at length the naming of mountains after female breasts, talked about "Native women's honeypots" and "hoo-ha holes," and called for the naming of stalactites and stalagmites as "roof dicks" and "floor dicks." Not content with his extended display of juvenile and racist behavior, Nelson went on to accuse American Indians who wanted the name change of being "pussies who make their living being offended."[21]

If Nelson had simply stopped at doing his best Howard Stern impression, there would be little reason to waste more than a footnote on him in this chapter. What he did next in his column went far beyond that. Nelson went on to attack Lori Piestewa as a bad soldier, an incompetent bumbler, and even a coward and an idiot. "She was not a warrior," wrote Nelson. Lori "lack[ed] the characteristics of courage, intelligence and vision."[22]

The editors of the *New Times* collaborated with Nelson in his racist attacks. They provided a racist cartoon for his column, depicting Governor Janet Napolitano in a Hopi squash blossom hairstyle with a tomahawk, ready to scalp a political opponent. The editors also used their "Letters" page to mock and denigrate antiracist letters written to them after Nelson's article appeared.[23]

The public reacted explosively to Nelson's column; after four weeks the *New Times* declared it would print no more letters on the topic. Local racists gleefully cheered on Nelson: "It has been payback time on all those poor, pitiful, disadvantaged, misunderstood and under appreciated Native Americans for a hundred plus years now, and it will be for centuries to come. . . . Custer died for my sins and I owe them nothing!"; "You have found your calling. I read your piece three times and could not stop laughing"; "Lori Piestewa does not deserve anything named after her. She was a frickin cook who took a wrong turn and got shot"; "The word hero . . . does not represent Lori Piestewa. I would think it rather an embarrassment." Not surprisingly, nearly all the racist letter writers refused to give their names.[24]

Natives and their supporters battled the *New Times* with equally angry words. The media chain that owns the *New Times* worsened the situation by running the column nationwide on all its newsweeklies. Antiracists and veterans took Nelson and the *New Times* to task for their racism, for their contempt for a combat veteran who had just passed on, and for Nelson's joking about the gang rape of Native women in his opening sentence. "You racist assholes!" exploded one California Indian woman. "I find this column offensive beyond words. Robert Nelson claims to be a reporter. I see him as a racist," wrote another. "Robert Nelson . . . all he needs is the robes and the hood of the KKK," wrote a third. The editors responded to these letters, pointing out Nelson's racism with yet more racist jokes that the Native letter writers just needed jobs. Other antiracist letters they labeled as "sermons," "the race card," and, naturally, "reverse racism." The editors' final words on the subject cheered on two letters of support they received, one shouting, "How about you grow the hell up and accept that people . . . don't give a rat's ass about what you care about!"[25]

What is important to note is that Nelson fancies himself one of the leading figures on the political left in the Phoenix area, just as the *New Times* claims to be left of center. In an exchange of letters between Nelson and me he went even further and joined his editors in asserting that anyone who criticized him was a racist that hated whites. (Never mind that just as many letters against him came from people who were angry about his disparaging a recently killed veteran.) He claimed to be the best advocate Native people could have. He also asserted that Native activists and tribal leaders were con artists out for their own financial gain, offering as proof conduct he claims he observed at the University of Arizona but refused to name. He finished his second letter by asking me for contacts on a story about Native prisoners falsely imprisoned on death row. (I obliged because of the importance of the story, but Nelson never wrote anything on the topic.) To his credit, Nelson did offer to apologize to the Piestewa family "if it would do any good"; he never did, however, claiming a colleague's death at the paper left him too grief-stricken to do so. Yet he continued to write his columns, publishing another without a break only a few days after his friend's death. Over a year later, Nelson finally did apologize, admitting he "made a bad mistake . . . mixing tragedy with vulgar flippancy . . . I probably still deserve a good thumping, even now."[26]

The editors of the *New Times* reacted to the whole issue with surprise at such a strong reaction and open derision for those offended.

They not only refused to apologize despite repeated requests from the public for months afterward but openly mocked every letter that objected to Nelson's racist column. As noted before, the persistence of antiracists so overwhelmed the editors that they cut off discussion after four weeks and still continued to refer to Piestewa Peak as Squaw Peak. When a different columnist mocked the name change supporters several months later, members of the public again wrote in, demanding apologies. (This time, one of the letters was published.) The editors never responded.

The *New Times* campaign to stop the name change failed utterly, and the backlash somewhat stymied the paper from reporting on much of anything for a while. (According to Nelson, the issue deeply divided both the staff and management at the *New Times*, despite the derisive front maintained by the editors.) Most of the local non-Native public grew to support the name change to Piestewa Peak but opposed renaming the nearby freeway or local businesses. This left the Phoenix metro area with the surreal situation of more than sixty businesses named after a geographical entity that no longer exists. If you are in the Phoenix area, you can still go to doctors' and dentists' offices, towing companies, realty companies, hotels, and travel agencies with "Squaw Peak" in their names. You can go bowling at Squaw Peak Lanes, ironically located on Indian School Street. You can even order a Squaw Peak steak. The city of Phoenix dragged its feet. There is still a Squaw Peak Water Treatment Plant and the Squaw Peak Police Precinct.[27]

Local businesses, for the most part, refused to change their names and likely will keep them for the immediate future. The expense involved in changing signs and business cards became the most frequently given reason for not changing names, but many also argued "Squaw Peak" had become part of their business identity. A number referred to their names as "tradition" that had, in one case, been in effect for such a "lengthy" amount of time as thirty years. One of the few businesspeople to take a positive view of the changes was Tim Dean, a non-Native owner of an Internet company, who bought up all the possible domain names of Piestewa "to keep them free from being commercialized" and offered them free of charge to the Piestewa family and Hopi tribe.[28]

In the Arizona state legislature, a number of conservative Republicans led by Democrat Albert Hale, former president of the Navajo nation, launched an effort to change the name of Piestewa Peak *back* to Squaw Peak. Another bill by Phil Hanson with thirty-seven Republican cosponsors would have put the board under the control of the state legislature. The Phoenix Oyate Singers drummed and prayed across the street at Wesley Bolin Plaza during the hearings. Former board member Tim Hanson claimed his mail ran ten to one against the manner in which the name change had occurred, though he declined to state how many opposed the actual name change. After months of bitter debate the bills were killed in committee, by only one vote in one case. But the bills' sponsors vowed to try again the following year.[29]

For his part, Hanson expressed surprise that the vote for the bill came on the anniversary of Lori's death. He insisted, "I don't give a damn what the peak is called at this point. All I'm trying to do is return integrity to the process." In his anger, Hanson betrayed thoughts that would have been unthinkable to describe efforts to honor the memory of an *Anglo* veteran.[30] One can easily find Internet sites from unapologetic or thinly veiled racists demanding the name be changed back, or simply from people on the political right utterly convinced that honoring a Native veteran or not using racist epithets as a place-name are "proof" of the threat of political correctness.

Perhaps the most public honor paid by non-Natives to Lori came from one of the least respected media genres, "reality" television. ABC's *Extreme Makeover: Home Edition* and businesses Shea Homes, Cavco, and Breuners worked with the San Manuel Band, the American Indian Council of Governments, and thousands of people of all backgrounds donating time, labor, money, and materials to build the Piestewa family a home, something that had been Lori's dream for many years.[31]

More than a year after Lori's death, another former resident of Arizona, Pat Tillman, was killed in Afghanistan. Tillman was born and raised in California, but the fact that he lived in Tempe and played football for Arizona State University for a few years caused many Arizonans to think of him as one of their own. Immediately after his death in combat in Afghanistan, most of the public called for the renaming of local sites after him. The contrast between how he was honored and how Lori was could not have been more striking.

Within hours of his death, many called for renaming local landmarks. Tillman now has a plaza and a stadium named after him. No angry letters insisted he had not earned it or did not deserve to be singled out for praise among all the war dead or veterans. No one complained about the expense of changing signs, and no one called for waiting periods or resorted to arcane legalistic arguments as excuses for not honoring Tillman. No one publicly smeared his memory, insisted he was to blame for his own death (with one exception), or made racist jokes about him or his heritage. In short, virtually none of what happened after Lori's death, thankfully, happened after Tillman's death. Many of the public actually went one step further and called for the building of a statue and establishing a scholarship fund in his name. This went far beyond the expense involved in changing the markers at Piestewa Peak. To my knowledge, no one except a Latino university student writing for an ASU paper even took any note of the hypocrisy.[32]

Conclusion

Despite the most vicious efforts of some to denigrate the memory of Lori Piestewa or use her life story for their own needs, the deep respect Natives have for her remains undiminished. Native veteran service will not bring respect from outsiders unless respect for Natives is already part of the non-Native mind-set. But it is important for Natives to honor the lives of veterans who are icons representing authentic and deeply felt Native historical experiences. Mandan/Hidatsa journalist Jodi Rave wrote perhaps the best response to Robert Nelson's column.

> Piestewa's death moved a nation. It also moved a mountain. And soon it will bear a fitting name. Piestewa in the Hopi language is said to mean, "the rainwater that collects on the desert floor after a heavy downpour." A downpour of political ugliness surrounded the name change, but from those desert pools of water something good will grow.
>
> Thank you, Lori Piestewa.[33]

Conclusion

Is It Time for Native Veteran Traditions to End?

BY THE TIME GORDON ROY served in Vietnam, his family already had fourteen members who had served in World War II, ten who had served in Korea, and eight others who had served in Vietnam. Four more family members served in the Gulf War and two were stationed in Bosnia.[1] Families like the Roys are not unusual among Native communities, and I hope my work helps explain why military service was so highly valued by Native people for so long. The military provided a means for cultural preservation, revival, and defense in a way that few other Anglo-American institutions have been able to. That cultural renewal clearly shows up in Native warrior societies, ceremonies, and songs. Only the BIA comes close in terms of the scope of the effects a government body had on Native peoples. Certainly the military shows itself to be far more responsive to Native wishes and needs than the BIA.

The effects are clearly two-way. In 2001 the U.S. Army began a recruiting campaign using the slogan "Army of One," a phrase first popularized by AIM's most famous member, Leonard Peltier.[2] An "Army of One" is part of an old tradition in which Anglo-Americans use Native imagery to emulate Native warriors. It is a practice that unwittingly provided a means for American Indians to build distinctively Native veteran traditions. No other ethnic group in North America has anything comparable, not even the Natives of Mexico. Yet the example of Indians in Mexico and Guatemala should also alarm us. Natives serving in the U.S. military could quite easily have been used against other Natives in cases besides the Indian Scouts, and only the comparatively smaller number of Native people in the United States prevented that kind of fratricide. Natives in the military also could be used against other Natives in Canada in the future. In the Oka stand-off on the Canadian border, statistically it is possible there were more Canadian Natives in the Canadian military carrying out the occupation than there were in the warrior society defending Mohawk land.

Cherokee law professor and veteran Steve Russell was the first person I interviewed for this study back when I was still an undergraduate doing research on Native veterans as part of the McNair Program. He was truly patient and supportive with a very nervous beginner. After my speech at the McNair conference at the University of Texas at San Antonio, he said to me, "We need to develop a new tradition, something better. We've just *got to.*" I very naively did not give it much thought at the time and was genuinely puzzled. To me, Native veteran traditions seemed to be a straightforward story of resilience and survival, using the conqueror's institutions for Native needs. Writing their story seemed to be the perfect way for me to resolve the ambiguities I felt about my own time in the service, and that is the approach I used in my master's thesis. I briefly mentioned Native veteran traditions in a paper for a professor, John Larson, at Purdue University. He scrawled a comment, underlined and in big letters, "BUT WHY?!" My first mentor at Purdue, Donald Parman, insisted Natives joining the military was a sure sign of assimilation, and if Indians were not Americanized when they went in, they surely were by the time they left. He and I butted heads on the question a few times (nothing too bruising, because he is a polite man by nature) with him pushing for strictly a policy study. My second mentor, Donna Akers, was happy I took a cultural approach and only sorry I was not able to interview any Choctaw Code Talkers in time before their passing.

When I guest lectured about Native veterans for Dakota history professor Angela Cavender Wilson at Arizona State University, she raised a question to me almost immediately: "What about colonialism? Does this show a colonized mind-set?" Remember that under decolonization theory, veteran traditions are a sign of a colonized mind-set, a warping of tradition and a betrayal of indigenous values. In early May 2004, at a discussion of ASU American Indian students about patriotism and the military, I mentioned her question. A Navajo student and Gulf War veteran shot back, "What does she know about what it's like to rely on someone else for your life?" Backing off his first reaction, he said he respected Wilson's point of view but explained further that once he was in the Gulf and surrounded by hostile enemies, "For the first time, I realized I am an American." What he said, without realizing it, provided evidence that, to some, *would* show a colonized mindset. After looking at hundreds of accounts from Native veterans and interviewing dozens more, I have to conclude that a belief such as his is the exception far more than the rule once you get past the period of the greatest push for assimilation in boarding schools.

I do not think these questions about assimilation or colonized mindsets are nearly as simple as either decolonization theory or what the Gulf War veteran would have you believe. Most Natives never thought of themselves as "simply American" and still do not. Taking part in these wars did not mean you wanted to be an agent of the worst aspects of American imperialism. Yet sadly and clearly, sometimes Native participation did endorse and aid causes that few Natives believed in. More than a few Native veterans had that moment of clarity or revelation where they realized a common bond with the victims of war, the alleged enemy, people who looked like or lived much like them, or whose people had similar historical experiences.

The Crow nation is a good illustration of the changing attitudes about the worth of the wars Natives enlisted to fight in. Thirty Crows served in World War I compared to 246 in World War II, 135 and 131 in Korea and Vietnam, respectively, and only 36 in the Gulf War. Where Tom Holm found an enlistment rate at four times that of Anglos during Vietnam, by at least one count by the Military Family Resource Center, Natives are currently in the military in only slightly higher numbers than Anglos. If anything, adjusted for poverty, Natives may actually now be in the military in *lower* rates than other ethnic groups and are proportionately highest in the branches that offer the most technology training, with the exception of the air force. This is a trend that began before the current war, according to the Department of Defense's own statistics.[3]

While the length of the wars no doubt played a role in how many had the chance to serve, it strains credibility to claim that Natives' belief in the rightness or wrongness of the war itself did not play a part, especially from the later stages of the Vietnam War to the present. This is a complete turnabout from the incredible enthusiasm and participation shown by Natives in World War II, when fighting against the Nazis was something unambiguously righteous for most, to at best reluctant participation filled with self-doubt and criticism of the nation-state in the Second Iraq War.

A final passage from Holm:

> I think that the warrior/savage/mascot/military stereotypes are linked. To many white Americans, Native peoples were the principal opponents of the Euro-American conquest of North America. This conquest has been made into an epic of individual bravery, farsightedness, and self-sacrifice against a savage, militarily adept, merciless, and brave foe. If we Natives had been a bunch of pacifists, the American national saga of conquest would have no great spiritual or symbolic meaning. Expansionism really was a tawdry affair of land swindles, double-dealing, fraud, murder, power plays, greed, and theft. Americans have understandably turned reality into a glorious blood sacrifice in which Indians played a major role.
>
> The stereotypes and the notion that Natives inherently possess a kind of martial expertise only serve to recall and celebrate this American epic. When a lieutenant in Korea sent a Native to walk point on a patrol, he was recalling a stereotype in the American epic that portrayed "the Indian" (a European term) as a stealthy hunter and warrior, steeped in the knowledge of the terrain and attuned to the normal sights, sounds, and smells of the landscape. An Indian would notice anything out of place or unusual. When a crusty Gunnery Sergeant in Vietnam told a new group of boots to the bush that "out there is Indian country and this is Fort Apache," he was reminding them that if stalwart Americans can overcome Indians in the American saga, they could surely vanquish another sneaky, non-white, but ultimately dangerous enemy. . . .
>
> White Americans created the saga and the stereotypes. Because they did so, they literally think they own them and feel as if they can use them in any way they please.[4]

Natives taking part in the military did not, and will not, necessarily win respect from outsiders. It has not, for the most part, changed minds that would have otherwise stayed closed or remained bigoted. Ira Hayes knew that firsthand; many other Natives do, too. What outsiders will respect (and often only temporarily) is the uniform and the institution, not the person inside, and not his or her culture or people. Anyone looking at Hayes's life or at what happened with the story of Lori Piestewa's life would have to conclude the same.

Too many Anglos have a very frustrating series of internal mechanisms and preconceptions built in that let them see whatever it is they wish to see when it comes to Native people. To take the most obvious example, I cannot count the number of times I have heard Anglos assume the Navajo Code Talkers fought to prove themselves to whites, or that their sacrifice somehow "proved" Native loyalty to conventional Anglo-American values. As Vine Deloria and others point out, the greatest barriers to Native equality and sovereignty are all the means outsiders use to render Natives invisible, or to define Natives to their own liking. The political left is often no less immune to this than those on the right. If you shatter their precious fantasy image of Native people, some lash out with bigoted venom, as Robert Nelson did at Lori's memory and at any other Indian who did not fit the images he liked to believe.

What are the consequences of having so many survivors of wartime among Native people? This is a question I have been reluctant to engage. Such a question requires more poetic power than I have, and the best sources I know of on the subject are the works by Silko, Momaday, Erdich, Welch, Red Eagle, and St. Pierre. The question also requires clinical expertise, and so I defer not only to Native novelists but to health care, psychiatric, domestic violence, and alcoholism and drug addiction experts. But even the most cursory look tells us that the price for these traditions is very high, even with traditional ways from Native cultures to help these survivors cope.

Is there a better way? Should Native people look to build better alternative traditions, as Steve Russell told me? Holm argues one of the effects of combat is to mature the young far beyond their years. This in part accounts for the high number of veterans in tribal government and activism. But could other professions do the same and at less of a toll on Native people? Police, fire, rescue, and health care professions all at times offer somewhat similar experiences to a combat zone, and surely the emergency situations in any of these careers mature someone quickly. Natives join the health care and firefighting professions at extremely high rates as well, and perhaps it is time Natives thought of them as deserving honor no less than veterans and pushed would-be soldiers to become paramedics, nurses, firefighters, and so forth. Some tribal nations already have honor ceremonies and powwows for firefighters. Perhaps one day we will (and definitely should, in my view) see Native firefighters, paramedics, and so forth as the honor guards posting the flag at powwows alongside veterans.

Another alternative is to syncretize warrior traditions with activism, as Holm argues has already happened. By this both Holm and I are talking about not simply drawing up a petition or registering people to vote but activism that is so engaged that the potential for danger and sacrifice for one's people at times approaches that of combat, as it did at Wounded Knee II. This indeed is what many young Native men in Canada did at places such as Oka, Gustafsen Lake, and other sites, and are still doing today. Activism gives the members of warrior societies a purpose to their lives much like the most motivated career soldier. It is not my place or purpose to demand or even call for Native traditions to be altered, only to gently suggest and point toward options I believe have greater benefit for Native peoples and cultures. But I am far from alone in this. Most of the Native novelists I discussed earlier argue passionately that serving in wars that Natives do not believe in distorts the meaning of being a warrior in Native traditions.

The military's alleged potential for maturing individuals in peacetime, I argue, is greatly overstated. I matured far more rapidly learning to deal with high crime rates in some of the neighborhoods I lived in than I ever learned at boot camp. Most of the people I knew who came out of the military during peacetime were worse off, and often less mature, than when they went in. In peacetime, frankly, you learn mostly what is "close enough for government work," army slang for how to do as little as possible. The increasing numbers of Native women joining and the increasing numbers of Natives joining branches of the service that offer better training say that perhaps education would be the one remaining reason to still join, except that the services now often turn away the less educated. So is there any reason left for Natives to be a part of the military now, unless the wars are ones Natives believe in? Wars of that type are increasingly rare.

What I certainly do not want to say is that Natives should honor veterans any less. As a veteran from a long line of veterans, I see that acts of honoring are the greater part of what enables veterans to bear their own pains more easily. What all the other options for newer traditions I am pointing toward have in common is a goal of rescuing and selflessly helping other Native people. Too many Native people are living in combat zones already without having to seek out wars many Natives, perhaps even most, do not even believe in. There is no contradiction between honoring those who served before while seeking out and developing newer and better traditions. After all, isn't the fondest wish of all veterans that their children never have to do the same?

Appendix

TABLE 1 Nicknames of Military Vehicles

Coast Guard Ships

Official Name	Nickname(s)
Apalachee	"Apple"
Chaataqua	"Cha-cha," "Chat"
Chincoteague	"Chickenfeed"
Comanche	"Co-manch," "Pregnant Marshmallow"
Haida	"Haida Maru"
Klamath	"River Boat"
Lipan	"Dry Dock Warrior," "Limpin Along"
Modoc	"Mud Duck," "Mighty Mud Duck," "Ghost of the Oregon Coast"
Mohawk	"Mo-chicken," "Slo-hawk," "All Ahead Moped"
Mohican	"Mighty Mo"
Ojibwa	"OJ"
Onondoga	"Rolling O"
Seneca	"Six Boat"
Snohomish	"Snow Boat"
Ute	"Good Shoot Ute," "Ute R Rust," "Love Boat"
Winnebago	"Wind Bag," "Winnie Hoo Hoo," "H_2O Winnie"
Yankton	"Rock N Roll"

Army Aircraft

Official Name	Nickname(s)
Shawnee	"Flying Bananas"
Iroquois	"Huey"
Mohave	"Cross Eyed Monster," "Deuce"
Sioux	"Supercharged Sioux"
Tomahawk	"Hawk" (in the UK)

TABLE 2 Personnel and Equipment at Wounded Knee II

Government and Paramilitary Forces[1]

Law Enforcement "Troops"	Arms
155 FBI	155 M-16s, 88 shotguns, 155 handguns, 17 .30 caliber machine guns (mounted on APCS)
100 U.S. marshals (USM), including 65 in Special Operations Group (SOG)	80 M-16s, 20 M-1s with scopes, 20 shotguns, 100 handguns (plus the same .30 caliber guns available to FBI)
25–30 BIA	shotguns, handguns
10–15 Border Patrol	shotguns, handguns
50–75 Guardians of Oglala Nation (GOON)	shotguns, hunting rifles, handguns
100 Ranchers Association (RA)	shotguns, hunting rifles, handguns

Government and Paramilitary Supplies

>500,000 rounds of ammunition (including tracers and armor piercing)	APCS were used as bunkers by FBI various other government vehicles
flak jackets	2 F-4 surveillance planes
gas masks	1 surveillance helicopter
grenade launchers (for tear gas)	hotels used to house government forces
17 armored personnel carriers (APCS)	every other night

American Indian Movement (AIM) and Independent Oglala Nation (ION) Forces[2]

"Defenders" or "Occupiers"	
>600 who were in Wounded Knee altogether	147 whites (many outside Wounded Knee)
250–350 at Wounded Knee at any one time	9 Mexicans
40–125 AIM members	5 blacks
>301 American Indians	33 original Wounded Knee residents or "voluntary hostages"
180 Oglalas	possibly up to 42 government informers
160 Indians from 64 other tribes (most from Rosebud Reservation)	

Arms[3]

23 "HPS"	crossbows, bows, arrows, knives, Molotovs
25–27 .22s	
5–26 shotguns	2 wood dummies of .30 and .50 caliber machine guns
5–17 other hunting rifles	
13–14 handguns	3 plastic toy machine guns
1 M-1	dummy guns of pipe and wood
1 AK-47	3 "homemade bombs"
gun parts or unusable from museum	

AIM and ION **Supplies and Equipment**
For Building Bunkers

5,602 concrete blocks	1 John Deere loader
680 sacks of cement	1 tractor
30 tons of sand	1 Jacobson trench digger
21,000 feet of lumber	2 dump trucks

Other Supplies

250–2,770 rounds of ammunition	hundreds of backpacks filled with
9 horses	supplies smuggled in
50 chickens	2,500 gallons of gas
63 cows	gas siphoned from negotiators' cars
5 planeloads of supplies	1 U-Haul van
(no weapons or ammunition in them)	various private cars

Notes:

1. The figures for government forces come from Dewing, *FBI Files*, 13, 16, reel 21, from an unlabeled FBI paper. For the Ranchers' Association, see reel 19, Batesto Gebhardt memo, March 3, 1973. For GOON, see Lyman, *Wounded Knee 1973*, 22. The figures for ammunition are for *rounds fired only* and come from the attorney general's estimate in Zimmerman, *Airlift to Wounded Knee*, 335.

2. Estimates for AIM and ION forces come from Lyman's recall of the Red Cross estimate in *Wounded Knee 1973*, 72; Dewing, *FBI Files*, reel 21, interview with Alan Scofeld, March 21, 1973, arrest records in reel 25, April 30, 1973, another estimate on reel 25 dated August 10, 1973; Guy Frantze, interview by the author, June 6, 1973; and Rev. Paul Manhart's estimate according to Dewing, *FBI Files*, 106.

3. Unlike the list of government and paramilitary forces, where each group's arms are shown alongside the group, this list shows all the weapons known to be in Wounded Knee. The bombs were defused by U.S. marshals according to Dewing, *FBI Files*, reel 25, memo, May 26, 1973. No mention is made of what type of bombs they were. The list of weapons is from Dewing, *FBI Files*, reel 25, memo, May 8, 1973, as well as a handwritten note on the same reel; and Zimmerman, *Airlift to Wounded Knee*, 327. The high estimate of ammunition is from Dewing, *FBI Files*, reel 26, memo, May 8, 1973. The low estimate is from Akwesasne Notes, *Voices*, 78. The list of materials for bunkers is from Dewing, *FBI Files*, 102, 103.

Notes

Introduction

1. Black Lodge Singers, *Veterans Honor Songs*.

2. Milo Yellow Hair, "In the Spirit of Crazy Horse," *Frontline*, PBS/WETA, Boston, 1990.

3. Flint Institute of Art, *The American Indian and the American Flag*, 1, 5, 13; Heard Museum, "Stars and Stripes in Native American Art"; William Powers, "The American Flag in Lakota Art," *Whispering Wind*, August 31, 1996, 5.

4. Flint Institute of Art, *The American Indian and the American Flag*, 1, 5, 13.

5. Flint Institute of Art, *The American Indian and the American Flag*, 1, 5, 13; Andrew Metz, "Celebrating Their Service to the U.S.," http://www.newsday.com/nationalworl . . . /ny-stind0702,0,7982964.story?coll (accessed July 23, 2003); Russell, "Dead Indians," 2, 5.

6. Flint Institute of Art, *The American Indian and the American Flag*, 1, 5, 13; Canadian Press, "Aboriginals Come Out in Force to Protest Conditions in Canada," *The Guardian*, June 22, 2001, A5.

7. E-mails to the author. This Churchill supporter hardly did him credit. Her intent was more to shock than seriously argue, quoting from Maoists and being extremely childish by using elaborate descriptions of bodily functions and male genitalia. After she threatened to "expose" me repeatedly (for what, was never quite clear, other than not agreeing with Churchill on every single point as she demanded), I have not heard back from her or seen any sign of an exposé.

1. "Let's See Some of That Apache Know-How"

1. The first part of this section is based on *The Outsider*, directed by Delbert Mann, Universal Pictures, 1961. The rebuttals using examples from Hayes's own life and accounts from his fellow soldiers are based on Hemingway, *Ira Hayes*.

2. "Written by Stewart Stern," http://www.wga.org/journal/1998/0798/stern.html (accessed July 24, 2003).

3. This section is based on *Veronico Cruz*, directed by Miguel Pereira, Anchor Bay Studios, 1987.

4. A cross-section of the criticism of *Windtalkers* can be found at Rob Schmidt, "*Windtalkers*: No Guts, No Glory," http://www.bluecorncomics.com/windtlkr .htm (accessed June 30, 2002). Schmidt's essay also thoroughly covers the problems with historical accuracy and stereotyping in *Windtalkers*. I will not needlessly duplicate it.

5. Accounts of conflict between Pope's family and New Age people are based on e-mails from Red Sparrow Pope, a grandson of John Pope, to Trisha Jacobs, a Cherokee activist, in January and February 2003, available online at http:// users.pandora.be/gohiyuhi/frauds/frd0054.htm. This section as a whole is based on *Billy Jack*, directed by Tom Laughlin, Warner Studios, 1971.

6. "Amazing Story behind the Legend of Billy Jack," http://www.billyjack .combooks/legendbook.html (accessed February 19, 2003).

7. An amusing side note: from conversations with Maori activist Huhanna Hickey, I heard that *mokos* have to be earned in arduous trials of physical combat. Someone wearing a *moko* who did not earn it is likely to be attacked, even killed, by Maori gangs who wear *mokos*. If Beltran ever goes to New Zealand, he should hire very good bodyguards.

8. Larry Brody, "Tales from *Star Trek Voyager*," http://www.tvwriter.com/ startrek2.html (accessed March 12, 2003).

9. "Names," http://www.thewritechoice.net/names.htm (accessed March 12, 2003).

10. Rob Schmidt, "Native Veterans in Fiction," http://www.bluecorncomics/ fictvets.htm (accessed April 19, 2003).

11. This section is based on Tim Truman, *Scout*, issues 1–12; Truman, *Scout War Shaman*, issues 1–4; and "Indian Comics Irregular," http://groups.yahoo .com/group/IndianComicsIrregular (accessed January 24, 2003). The information on Truman's background comes from "Tim Truman," http://www.comicon.com/ truman/truman.htm (accessed November 13, 2002).

12. Norton, *Hosteen Storm*; Norton, *Lord of Thunder*; Norton, *The Sioux Spaceman*.

13. This section is based on *The Dirty Dozen*, directed by Robert Aldrich, MGM/UA Studios, 2001 special edition. The discussion of the Rain Dance edited out of the film can be found at "Clint Walker," http://www.classicimages.com/1999/ april1999/walker.html (accessed January 24, 2003).

14. *Powwow Highway*, directed by Jonathan Wacks, Anchor Bay Studios, 1989.

15. *Skins*, directed by Chris Eyre, First Look Pictures, 2002.

16. Momaday, *House Made of Dawn*; Silko, *Ceremony*.

17. Erdich, *Love Medicine*; Wong, *Love Medicine*.

18. Owens, *The Sharpest Sight*.

19. Red Eagle, *Red Earth*, 18, 20, 22, 35, 38, 49, 51, 57, 70, 76, 82, 96, 115, 130.

20. St. Pierre, *Of Uncommon Birth*, 12, 39, 48, 59, 77, 78, 92, 98, 105, 129, 130, 172, 175, 190, 192, 271, 274.

2. "They Kill Indians Mostly, Don't They?"

1. Roberts, *Northwest Passage*, 70.
2. Neillands, *Combat Zone*, 9, 11.
3. Rogers, *Journals of Major Robert Rogers*, 43–51.
4. Rogers, *A Concise Account of North America*, 12, 161, 210, 231, 233, 237.
5. Rogers, *Journals of Major Robert Rogers*, 67, 105, 165.
6. Rogers, *Journals of Major Robert Rogers*, 105, 106, 111.
7. Rogers, *Journals of Major Robert Rogers*, 105, 106.
8. Brumwell, *White Devil*, 188, 193–94; Gordon Day, "The Identity of the St. Francis Indians," http://htt.com/Abenaki/StFrancisIndians.html (accessed March 27, 2000); Galloway, *The American Revolution in Indian Country*, 66, 72.
9. Day, "Identity."
10. Brumwell, *White Devil*, 96. Brumwell's argument for Rogers's motive is unlikely, not the least of which because it was Ottawas, Pottawatomis, and Ojibwes that are the most likely candidates for scalping Rogers's brother's corpse. St. Francis was an Abenaki village.
11. Neillands, *Combat Zone*, 12.
12. Parkman, *Montcalm and Wolfe*, 1:446, 447, 451, 2:14, 264.
13. Parkman, *Montcalm and Wolfe*, 2:265.
14. Roberts, *Northwest Passage*, 70.
15. Roberts, *Northwest Passage*, 38, 71, 169.
16. Roberts, *Northwest Passage*, 38, 66.
17. Roberts, *Northwest Passage*, 73, 180.
18. Locke, *Intrepidity*, 576, 579.
19. Locke, *Intrepidity*, 572.
20. Cuneo, *Robert Rogers of the Rangers*, 107.
21. Cuneo, *Robert Rogers of the Rangers*, 49; Brumwell, *White Devil*, 228–30.
22. "Rogers' Rangers," http://www.toy-soldier.com/zzdemo/ts-21.htm (accessed February 13, 2000).

3. Before a Native Veteran Tradition Can Begin

1. Larry Evers and Phillip Molina, "Coyote Songs," http://www.richmond.edu/faculty/ASAIL/SAI.ns/d62.html (accessed September 21, 2000).
2. Evers and Molina, "Coyote Songs."
3. Painter, *With Good Heart*, 71, 306; Spicer, *The Yaquis*, 130, 173, 210.

4. Loewen, *Lies My Teacher Told Me*, 127–30; Nash, *Red, White, and Black*, 298–99, 310–19. Loewen and Nash discuss the failure of white reformers who believed in either coexistence or gradual assimilation and how the choice presented to Native groups gradually became one of either complete "instant" assimilation or permanent exclusion. Nash discusses how the choice offered by the British, exclusion or assimilation, became the pattern adopted by the United States for most of its history. Loewen actually goes further than I do and argues that assimilation efforts by both white reformers and Indians who tried to "civilize" themselves completely failed thanks to the intransigent hostility of most whites, leaving permanent exclusion as the only option left to Native people. Loewen does note that there was, however briefly, a significant minority of white opinion, such as the Whig Party, that favored just treatment for assimilated Natives during periods such as prior to forcible Indian Removal, but that they were always outnumbered, outmaneuvered, and outvoted by greater numbers of more hostile whites. Both Loewen and Nash show a great deal of cultural interchange between Natives and some whites, which the majority of whites regarded with loathing and the authorities devoted a great deal of effort to ending or controlling.

5. Deloria, *We Talk, You Listen*, 121–23. Deloria describes this as a process of white treatment of Native groups bringing about a widespread concern for sovereignty and tribal identity as *nations*. He does not use the term "nationalism." That is my own interpretation.

6. This is my own argument throughout this chapter based on an understanding of the writing of Deloria, Loewen, and Nash and seeing how their view applies to the subject of this chapter. Mestizo refers to someone of mixed Spanish and Indian ancestry. *Mestizaje* can refer to a mix of lineages or cultures.

7. Du Hart, *Yaqui Resistance and Survival*, 34; Radding, *Wandering Peoples*, 292.

8. Du Hart, *Yaqui Resistance and Survival*, 54; Taylor, *Drinking, Homicide, and Rebellion*, 22, 52, 165.

9. Knight, "Peculiarities of Mexican History," 115, 116, 118, 118n98.

10. Knight, "Peculiarities of Mexican History," 108, 138, 140.

11. Gossett, *Race*, 25–26. Arthur Toynbee argues the latter view, Hans Kohn the former.

12. Holm, *Strong Hearts*, 35–38.

13. It is difficult to prove a negative. But knowing that the Tlaxcalans had one of the strongest martial traditions that continued throughout the colonial period, I made an effort to find evidence of military societies among them and did not find any.

14. Meadows, *Kiowa, Apache, and Comanche Military Societies*, 38, 343. Meadows uses the term "military society" to describe the same societies I refer to solely as warrior societies. Both terms are used interchangeably throughout his book and in most other works on Native martial sodalities in the United States.

However, Natives in the United States use "warrior society" exclusively and works on Natives in Mexico use the term "military society" exclusively. This is why I use both designations.

15. Painter, *With Good Heart*, 304; Spicer, *Cycles of Conquest*, 396; Spicer, *The Yaquis*, 181, 182, 221.

16. Spicer, *People of Pascua*, 5, 258, 262, 263; Spicer, *The Yaquis*, 143, 174.

17. Parezo and Sheridan, *Paths of Life*, 156, 157.

18. Castile and Kushner, *Persistent Peoples*, 116, 125, 139, 140, 142, 144.

19. Crumrine, *Mayo Indians of Sonora*, 71, 134–37, 150.

20. Spicer, *The Yaquis*, 302.

21. Rachel Hays, "Cross-Border Indigenous Nations," http://www.irc.online.org.brdline/1996/b120/b129indi.html (accessed September 16, 2000).

22. Smith, *Borderlander*, 5, 57, 68, 70, 71.

23. Smith, *Borderlander*, 77, 136, 154.

24. Smith, *Borderlander*, 82, 136, 186, 222, 226, 227.

25. Hatfield, "Indians on the U.S.-Mexico Border," 148, 215; R. Smith, *Borderlander*, 230, 231; Spicer, *The Yaquis*, 23.

26. Dumond, *The Machete and the Cross*, 103, 133, 236; Joseph and Wells, *Summer of Discontent, Seasons of Upheaval*, 96, 210. *Cruzob* refers to the crosses that the insurgent Mayans prayed to. *Mestizos de buen hablar* means roughly "mixed-bloods who are well spoken or spoken well about." The intention behind the label is to imply these Mayans voluntarily gave up or left behind their Indian identity and are now thought of as no different than the *vecinos*. The essential point is that Mayans clearly recognized they were still in an unequal hierarchical relationship based on both class and ethnicity, no matter what the mestizos label tried to imply.

27. Thompson, *Patriotism, Politics, and Popular Liberalism in Nineteenth-Century Mexico*, 308, 309.

28. Campbell, *Zapotec Renaissance*; Du Hart, *Yaqui Resistance and Survival*, 85, 208; Hall, *Álvaro Obregón*, 19, 20.

29. Spicer, *The Yaquis*, 228–31, 235; Campbell, *Zapotec Renaissance*, 77, 78, 218; Du Hart, *Yaqui Resistance and Survival*, 211.

30. Du Hart, *Yaqui Resistance and Survival*, 86, 95; Spicer, *Cycles of Conquest*, 66, 67.

31. Juan Carlos Beas and Manuel Ballesteros, "Indigenous Movements and Magonismo," http://antap.oakland.edu/Anthap_1/Chiapas_News_archive/cn40317.txt (accessed September 21, 2000); McLoughlin, *After the Trail of Tears*, 123, 176, 184–85, 192–93, 214–15.

32. Centro de Investigaciones Economicas y Politicas de Accion Comunitaria, "Forced Displacement in Chiapas," http://flag.blackened.net/revolt/mexico/comment/displacement_nov98.html (accessed April 16, 2003); Andrew Reding, "Guatemala, Kaibiles, and the Massacre at Los Dos Erres," http://www.worldpolicy.org/globalrights/guatemala/kaibiles.html (accessed April 16, 2003).

4. Thunderbird Warriors

1. Anne Thundercloud (niece of Mitchell Red Cloud), e-mail interview by the author, April 5, 2002; Annita Red Cloud, "Visit to the USNS Red Cloud," http://www.hocakworak.com (accessed April 8, 2002) and Red Cloud, "USNS Red Cloud Makes Big Waves in San Diego," http://www.hocakworak.com (accessed April 8, 2002); Jake Tapper, "Mark Salter: 'The Voice of John McCain.'" http://www.salon.com.news.feature/1999/10.12/salter/print.html (accessed March 4, 2000); "USNS RED CLOUD LAUNCHING—Korean War Project," http://www.koreanwar.org/html/units/19ir_redcloud.htm (accessed March 4, 2000).

2. Rossignoli, *Army Badges since 1945*, 143; Jim Skinner, e-mail interview by the author, March 8 and 21, 2002, April 7, 2002.

3. "American Indian Mascots: Respectful Gesture or Negative Stereotype?" *Indian Country Today* 21, no. 8 (1991): A5. In one survey, 81 percent of Natives found mascots offensive; 10 percent did not.

4. Cornel Pewewardy, "Why Educators Can't Ignore Indian Mascots," http://members.tripod.com/earnestman/cornel.why.educators.htm (accessed March 1, 2002).

5. Mayer and Royer, *Selling the Indian*, xi.

6. Deloria, *Playing Indian*, 7, 8, 20, 26, 185, 186, 187, 191.

7. 45th Division Museum, Company C, 279th Regiment Mascot Display, Oklahoma City.

8. King and Springwood, *Team Spirits*, 319.

9. King and Springwood, *Team Spirits*, 146; "An Arapaho Mascot in Colorado?" *Wind River News* 17, no. 47: 1; Michael Stanley, "Arapahoe Dedication Friday in Denver," *Wind River News* 17, no. 49: 1.

10. Stedman, *Shadows of the Indian*, 240–52.

11. David Rider, "Indians and Animals: A Comparative Essay," http://members.tripod.com/earnestman/david_rider_essay.htm (accessed March 1, 2002).

12. "Chiefs Creed and Induction Certificate," http://www.airforcechiefs.org/creed.html (accessed July 22, 2000); "CMSgts Group-Exploitation of Native Peoples by the USAF," http://members.tripod.com/earnestman/cmsgts/cmsgts.p2.htm (accessed October 30, 2000); "In Name Only," http://members.tripod.com/earnestman/cmsgts/cmsgts.pg1.htm (accessed February 26, 2002); "NCR Chiefs Group Merchandise," http://www.cmsgt.net/ncr/merchandise.htm (accessed July 22, 2000); "Say No to USAF Mascots," http://www.thespike.com/article.htm (accessed November 14, 2000); Chuck Dineh to the author, June 8, 2004.

13. "Chiefs Creed and Induction Certificate"; "Our Red Earth Yahoo Club," http://messages.clubs.yahoo.com/clubs/ourredearth (accessed February 7, 2001); "Our Red Earth Messages," http://groups.yahoo.com/group/OurRedEarth (accessed April 6, 2001).

14. "Chiefs Creed and Induction Certificate"; Sam Lewin, "Air Force and

Indian Imagery," *Native American Times,* http://nativetimes.com/index.asp?act ion=displayarticlearticle_id6571 (accessed June 7, 2005).

15. Lott et al., *Almanac of Naval Facts,* 224.

16. "102nd Infantry Division," http://www.army.mil/cmh-pg/documents/eto-ob/102ID-ETO.htm (accessed January 25, 2000).

17. "26th Infantry Regiment Association," http://www.bluespader.org (accessed April 12, 2002).

18. Ministry of Supply and Services Canada, "Native Soldiers, Foreign Battlefields," http://www.vac-gcc.ca/historical/other/native/htm (accessed June 8, 1998).

19. Ted Hibbert (assistant curator, 45th Division Museum, Oklahoma City), interview by the author, July 9, 2000.

20. 45th Division Museum, Unit Patches Display, Oklahoma City.

21. Franks, *Citizen Soldiers,* 50, 51.

22. "Bushmasters," http://www.azng.com/153a/bushmasters.htm (accessed February 12, 2000); Franco, "Publicity, Persuasion, and Propaganda," 66.

23. "History of the 81st Brigade," http://www.washingtonarmyguard.com/81bde/history.htm (accessed February 26, 2002).

24. "Naval History and Photography," http://www.hazegray.org (accessed September 29, 2000); "National Association of Fleet Tug Sailors," http://www.nafts.com/images (accessed September 29, 2000); Naval Historical Center, "USN Ship Naming," http://www.history.navy.mil/faqs63-1.htm (accessed September 29, 2000).

25. "USS *Clark,*" http://navysite.de/ffg/FFG11.htm (accessed May 10, 2004).

26. Lenton, *British & Empire Warships of the Second World War,* 154, 164–77, 228, 234, 432, 462, 611, 633, 687.

27. "Naval Museum of Manitoba," http://www.naval-museum.mb.ca (accessed February 12, 2000); "Ship and Unit Badges," http://www.dnd.ca/navy.marcomn/badges.html (accessed February 12, 2000).

28. "Naval History and Photography"; "National Association of Fleet Tug Sailors"; Naval Historical Center, "USN Ship Naming."

29. "Naval History and Photography"; "U.S. Coast Guard Cutter Nicknames," http://www.uscg.mil/hq/g-cp/history/cutternicknames.html (accessed April 16, 2002).

30. "Aztec Club of 1847," http://www.walika.com/aztec.history.htm (accessed September 16, 2000); *Aztec Club of 1847 (Military Society of the Mexican War),* 9, 27; Executive Committee, "Annual Circular of the Montezuma Society."

31. Butler Miltonberger and James Huston, "134th Infantry Regiment Combat History of World War II," http://www.coulthart.com/134/chapter_1.htm (accessed April 30, 2004).

32. Diane Camurat, "The American Indian in the Great War," http://raven.cc.ukan.edu/~kansite/ww_one/comments/camurat1.html (accessed August 10, 1999).

33. Camurat, "The American Indian in the Great War."

34. Texas Military Forces Museum, 36th Division Association, "T-Patch," http://www.kwanah.com/txmilus/36division/archives/intro/tpatch.htm (accessed October 8, 2000); Neillands, *Combat Zone*, 11, 77.

35. "Air Combat II: Pilots of Fortune," *US News & World Report*, 1998.

36. "Shoulder Insignia," http://www.guard.bismark.nd.us/patch.htm (accessed October 16, 1998); "Peoria Air Guard History," http://www.ilpeor.ang.af.mil/history.htm (accessed August 25, 2000); Lieutenant Colonel George O'Bryan, e-mail message to the author, June 20, 2004.

37. "Aircraft Used in the Vietnam War," http://www.ov-1.com (accessed November 3, 2000).

38. "Nothing But Indians," http://www.ov-1.com/73rd_SAC/Indian.html (accessed November 3, 2000).

39. Dallas Massey Sr., "Message Given at Dedication Ceremonies for New Apache Longbow Helicopters," *Fort Apache Scout* 37, no. 19: 1; Massey, "Mcdonnell Douglas Says 'Things Look Good' at Apache Aerospace," *Fort Apache Scout* 33, no. 3: 3; Massey, "Chairman's Vision," *Fort Apache Scout* 37, no. 13: 2.

40. "Malibu Mirage: The Ultimate Piston Single," http://www.avweb.com/articles/malibu (accessed March 5, 2002); "The New Piper Aircraft Inc.," http://www.newpiper.com/hist.htm (accessed March 5, 2002); Clark, *The Piper Indians*, vi, 7; Piper, *The Story of Piper Aircraft*, 9, 10.

41. "73rd SAC Home Page," http://www.73rd_SAC/first.html (accessed November 3, 2000); http://www/geronimos.org/Page_4x.htm (accessed February 12, 2000).

42. Chinnery, *Vietnam*, 8, 12, 21, 42, 53, 55, 120, 123, 184; Spenser, *Whirlybirds*, 85, 172.

43. Gale Couret Toensing, "NORAD Drops Terms," *Indian Country Today*, http://www.indiancountry.com/content.cfm?id=1096411424 (accessed August 19, 2005).

44. Scheina, *Latin America*, 15, 34, 368.

45. Scheina, *Latin America*, 29, 38, 55, 351; Isauro Covilli, "The Poor Are My Teachers," http://www.sedos.org/english/Covilli.html (accessed April 12, 2002).

46. Scheina, *Latin America*, 15, 109, 351; "History of the Brazilian Air Force," http://www.rudnei.cunha.nom.br/FAB/eng (accessed April 12, 2002); "Aviacion Azteca," http://www.muti.net.mx/cultura/general/genesis/avazteca/avaztec.html (accessed March 5, 2002).

47. Scheina, *Latin America*, 35, 321; "History of the Brazilian Air Force."

48. Rossignoli, *Army Badges since 1945*, 153; Swanborough, *U.S. Military Aircraft since 1908*, 52, 57, 81, 99.

49. Rossignoli, *Army Badges since 1945*, 153; "History of the Brazilian Air Force"; "Aviacion Azteca."

5. The Super Scout Image

1. Benn, *Iroquois in the War of 1812*, 87, 123.

2. Britten, *The American Indian in World War I*, 152.

3. White, *The Middle Ground*, 144; Deloria, *Playing Indian*, 77.

4. Merrell, *Into the American Woods*, 151.

5. Riding In, "Six Pawnee Crania," 104, 105, 111, 114; Massey, "Message Given at Dedication Ceremonies," 1.

6. Benn, *Iroquois in the War of 1812*, 4, 43, 56, 70, 122, 147, 153, 158; Hauptman, *Iroquois in the Civil War*, 14.

7. Apess and O'Connell, *A Son of the Forest*, 25, 26, 30, 31.

8. Hauptman, *Between Two Fires*, x, xii, 24.

9. Hauptman, *Iroquois in the Civil War*, 29, 43, 44.

10. Parker, *The Life of General Ely S. Parker*, 100, 106, 111, 141. Parker was the grandnephew of Ely Parker, and became a state archaeologist for New York.

11. Hauptman, *Iroquois in the Civil War*, 14, 45, 61.

12. Hauptman, *Iroquois in the Civil War*, 64, 67, 69, 73, 109, 146; Hauptman, *Between Two Fires*, 151.

13. Hauptman, *Between Two Fires*, 151.

14. Hauptman, *Between Two Fires*, 22, 23; Hauptman, *Iroquois in the Civil War*, 30, 31.

15. Densmore, *Menominee Music*, 201.

16. Densmore, *Menominee Music*, 202, 203; Densmore, *Cheyenne and Arapahoe Music*, 49.

17. *Communication of the Delegation of the Cherokee Nation to the President of the United States*, 5.

18. Hauptman, *Iroquois in the Civil War*, 42, 43.

19. Hauptman, *Iroquois in the Civil War*, 106, 108, 111, 113, 114, 120.

20. Hauptman, *Iroquois in the Civil War*, 66, 76, 85.

21. Hauptman, *Iroquois in the Civil War*, 126, 135, 143.

22. Hoxie, *A Final Promise*, 4–11.

23. Hoxie, *A Final Promise*, 4–11.

24. Hoxie, *A Final Promise*, xii, xiv, 245.

25. Jon Ault, "Native Americans in the Spanish American War," http://www.spanamwar.com/NativeAmericans.htm (accessed April 30, 2004); "TR Takes Charge," http://americanhistory.about.com/library/prm/bltrtakescharge2.htm (accessed April 30, 2004).

26. Ault, "Native Americans in the Spanish American War"; Jon Ault, "Frank Brito of the Rough Riders," http://www.spanamwar.com/Brito.html (accessed April 30, 2004).

27. Ault, "Native Americans in the Spanish American War"; Hagan, *Theodore Roosevelt and Six Friends of the Indian*, 44.

28. Sean McEnroe, "Painting the Philippines with an American Brush: Visions of Race and National Mission among the Oregon Volunteers in the Philippine Wars of 1898 and 1899," http://www.historycooperative.org/journals//ohq/104.1/mcenroe.html (accessed May 1, 2004).

29. McEnroe, "Painting the Philippines with an American Brush."

30. McEnroe, "Painting the Philippines with an American Brush."

31. Graymont, *Fighting Tuscarora*, xxiv, 7, 31, 32, 44; North American Iroquois Veterans Association, "7th Annual Powwow," 4.

32. Graymont, *Fighting Tuscarora*, xxiv, 7, 31, 32, 44.

33. Britten, *The American Indian in World War I*, 26.

34. Dixon, "North American Indian Cavalry," 4, 9.

35. Holm, *Strong Hearts*, 30–64.

36. Holm, *Strong Hearts*, 30–64.

37. Lindemann, *American*, ix, x, 240, 313; Department of the Interior, Office of Indian Affairs, *The American Indian in the World War*, 2, 4.

38. Britten, *The American Indian in World War I*, 62, 63; Parman, *Indians*, 62.

39. Zissu, "Conscription, Sovereignty, and Land," 537–41, 549–51, 559–65; Britten, *The American Indian in World War I*, 66.

40. Sherow, "Fort Riley's Interaction with Native Americans," 15–17; Britten, *The American Indian in World War I*, 63, 70; Hale, "Going on the Great White Father's Warpath," 44, 47.

41. McCarthy, *Papago Traveler*, 68, 69, 74.

42. Eric Bonfield, "The Conscription Crisis among the Iroquois during World War I," http://iroquoisindians.freeweb-hosting.com/webdoc78.htm (accessed May 4, 2004).

43. Britten, "American Indians in World War I," 151; Farwell, *Over There*, 160.

44. Britten, "American Indians in World War I," 82; Farwell, *Over There*, 159.

45. Haycock, *The Image of the Indian*, 21, 44; James Dempsey, "Warriors of the King," *Canadian Business and Current Affairs*, section v.26 (50), March 27, 2000: 56.

46. Gordon Roy ([Ponca], U.S. Air Force [1957–77] and member of the Ponca Heyoshas), interview by the author, Sac and Fox Nation Annual Powwow, Stroud OK, July 6, 2000.

47. Boyd, *Kiowa Voices*, 65, 114.

48. Britten, "American Indians in World War I," 149, 150.

49. Dempsey, "Warriors of the King," 56.

50. Britten, "American Indians in World War I," 150.

51. Britten, "American Indians in World War I," 150.

52. Smith, *Pawnee Music*, 66.

53. Smith, *Pawnee Music*, 66.

54. Smith, *Pawnee Music*, 68.

55. Fenton, *Songs of the Iroquois*, 27. Incredibly, this book neglects to indicate which of the Six Nations Gibson belonged to.

56. Densmore, *Menominee Music*, 50, 51.

57. Prucha, *The Great Father*, 218, 275, 280, 286; Britten, "American Indians in World War I," 152.

58. Camurat, "The American Indian in the Great War"; Britten, "American Indians in World War I," 160.

59. Britten, "American Indians in World War I," 150, 151; Camurat, "The American Indian in the Great War."

60. Britten, "American Indians in World War I," 151.

61. Britten, "American Indians in World War I," 151; Sherow, "Fort Riley's Interaction with Native Americans," 1; Camurat, "The American Indian in the Great War."

62. Smith, *Pawnee Music*, 64.

63. Britten, "American Indians in World War I," 155.

64. Ministry of Supply and Services Canada, "Native Soldiers, Foreign Battlefields."

65. Britten, *The American Indian in World War I*, 104, 160, 171.

66. Britten, *The American Indian in World War I*, 1, 2; Dixon, *Chief Strong Wolf*, 4.

67. Britten, *The American Indian in World War I*, 109–15.

6. "Savages Again"

1. Bernstein, *American Indians and World War II*, 57.

2. Cowger, *The National Congress of American Indians*, 76.

3. Nash, *American West*, 128.

4. Bernstein, *American Indians and World War II*, 22.

5. Hurwitz and Simpson, *Against the Tide*, 2, 23; "Passing of Elders," http://www.dickshovel.com/eldes.html (accessed November 16, 2000); Eller, *Conscientious Objectors and the Second World War*, 32.

6. Bernstein, *American Indians and World War II*, 27, 112; Kluckhorn, *Navajo Witchcraft*, 282.

7. "Richard Frank Story," http://www.nativefederation.org/history/veterans/RichardFrankStory.html (accessed August 23, 2003).

8. Hutchinson, *Remembrances*, 27; "Royal Commission on Aboriginal People—Final Report," http://www.indigenous.bc.ca/v1/Vol1Ch12s1tos3.asp (accessed February 14, 2000).

9. Memorial to Fallen Veterans, Himdak Museum, Ak-Chin Reservation, Arizona, Fall 2001.

10. "Men of the Tundra: Alaska's Eskimos at War," http://www.alaskool.org/projects/ak_military/tundra.htm (accessed November 13, 2000); "Simon

Wiesenthal Center Multimedia Learning Online," http://motlc.wiesenthal.com/
gallery/pg43/pg0/pg43020.html (accessed November 13, 2000); "Alaska Native
Veterans Honored," http://www.tribalnews.com/local/11-8_vetrans.htm (accessed
July 24, 2003); "Draven Delkettie Goes to War," http://www.nativefederation
.org/history/veterans/DravenDelkettieStory.html (accessed August 23, 2003).

11. Franco, *Crossing the Pond*, 65; Nash, *American West*, 2, 241; Parman,
Indians, 115.

12. Roberts and Sasser, *One Shot, One Kill*, 36–37.

13. McDonald, *The Last Warrior*, 62, 72, 74, 75; Vogt, *Navajo Veterans*, 50,
51, 52, 65, 72, 77, 125, 130, 132, 135, 141, 147, 258, 265.

14. Johnson, *Navajos and World War II*, 56, 58, 59; Parman, *Indians*, 62.

15. Franco, *Crossing the Pond*, 140; Laurence Glass, "Short History of Indians
in the U.S. Military," 9, Box 1, Folder 7, American Indian File Collection, University
of Oklahoma, Norman; Rob Schmidt, "Indian Comics Irregular," http://groups
.yahoo.com/group/IndianComicsIrregular/message/81 (accessed April 4, 2001).

16. Hemingway, *Ira Hayes*, 1, 3, 48, 132.

17. Franco, *Crossing the Pond*, 65, 132; "Profile of Pte. Daniel Garneau,"
http://collections.ic.gc.ca/nativeveterans/soldier/dgarneau.htm (accessed April
7, 2004).

18. "First Warrior Shows Face of American Indian Veterans," http://mytwo
beads.com/FirstWarrior.html (accessed April 7, 2004).

19. Billie Bridenthal (daughter of William Freet [Miami], U.S. Army [1945–51]),
mail interview by the author, July 31, 2000; Donna Jones (daughter of Dewayne
Smead [Miami], U.S. Army Air Corps [1942–45]), mail interview by the author, February 2, 2000; Charles Richmond (chaplain, 45th Division, U.S. Army
[1942–53]), mail interview by the author, August 3, 2000.

20. Mirabal, *Taos Tales*, liner notes.

21. "The Power of Kiowa Song," http://www.uapress.arizona.edu/extras/kiowa/
kiowasng.htm (accessed October 20, 2000).

22. "The Power of Kiowa Song."

23. Meadows, *Kiowa, Apache, and Comanche Military Societies*, 132.

24. Meadows, *Kiowa, Apache, and Comanche Military Societies*, 132.

25. Meadows, *Kiowa, Apache, and Comanche Military Societies*, 132.

26. Howard, "Dakota," 113.

27. Lakota Thunder, *Veterans Songs*, lyric sheet.

28. Lakota Thunder, *Veterans Songs*.

29. Howard, "The Dakota Indian Victory Dance," 113.

30. Densmore, "The Songs of American Indians," 211.

31. Flint Institute of Art, *The American Indians and the American Flag*, 12.

32. Bulow, *Code Talkers*, 53.

33. Laurence Glass, "Short History of Indians in the U.S. Military," 30, Box 1,
Folder 7, American Indian File Collection, University of Oklahoma, Norman.

34. Hart, *American Warrior Songs for Indian Veterans*, lyric sheet.

35. *Honor the Earth Powwow*, lyric sheet.

36. Bryan Phelan, "Article—Dreaming of Victory," http://collection.ic.gc.ca/ nativeveterans/articles/article-dream.htm (accessed April 7, 2004).

37. Meadows, *Kiowa, Apache, and Comanche Military Societies*, 384.

38. Meadows, *Kiowa, Apache, and Comanche Military Societies*, 127, 128, 131, 132, 133.

39. Meadows, *Kiowa, Apache, and Comanche Military Societies*, 133, 343, 344, 389.

40. Hemingway, *Ira Hayes*, 43.

41. Hemingway, *Ira Hayes*, 47, 151.

42. Hemingway, *Ira Hayes*, 133, 158.

43. Hemingway, *Ira Hayes*, 133, 158.

44. Bulow, *Code Talkers*, 122; Urshel Taylor, "Ira Hayes," http://members .tripod.com/%7eShirleyGriffith/ira.html (accessed November 12, 2000).

45. Naval Historical Center, "Navajo Code Talkers, Fact Sheet," http://www .navy.history.mil/faqs/faqs61.2.htm (accessed April 17, 2001).

46. Marley Shebala, "No Ordinary Joe," *Navajo Times*, http://www.thenava jotimes.com/Business/business.html (accessed June 4, 2000).

47. Bernstein, "Walking in Two Worlds," 48–53; Hauptman, *The Iroquois Struggle for Survival*, 5, 6, 211, 213.

48. Franco, "Publicity, Persuasion, and Propaganda," 176.

7. The Half-Hidden Spirit Guide Totemic Mark

1. Lieutenant Commander Harold Lalonde ([Sault Ste. Marie Chippewa], son of Donald Lalonde, U.S. Air Force [1950–53]), e-mail interview by the author, March 25, 29, and 31, 1999.

2. The view of the New Deal for Indians, the effects of World War II and its aftermath on Native people, and the social backdrop of Native communities prior to, during, and after the Korean War in this section are based on numerous readings, among them Trafzer, *As Long as the Grass Shall Grow and the Rivers Flow*, and Philp, *Indian Self-Rule*.

3. Meadows, *Kiowa, Apache, and Comanche Military Societies*, 395.

4. Ministry of Supply and Services Canada, "Native Soldiers, Foreign Battlefields."

5. Tapper, "Mark Salter"; "USNS RED CLOUD LAUNCHING—Korean War Project."

6. "Notable People: Sioux City History," http://www.siouxcityhistory.org/ people/more.php?id=3_0_2_0_M (accessed April 4, 2003); United Auto Workers Fair Practices and Anti-Discrimination Department, "The Indian Who Never Got Home," 3, 10, 12, 15, 17, 20, 22, 24.

7. "Notable People"; Fixico, *Termination and Relocation*, 57.

8. "A Secret Army No More," http://members.tripod/Chiromara/061297.html (accessed February 2, 2000); "Congressional Record," http://members.tripod .com/Chiromara/conrec99.html (accessed February 25, 2000); "Covert Operations Recognized," http://members.tripod.com/Chiromara/06031999.html (accessed February 25, 2000).

9. Diane McLaughlin (daughter of Charles McLaughlin [Seneca], U.S. Air Force [1950–54]), e-mail interview by the author, March 14, 15, and 18, 1999.

10. "Reginald Winishut," http://www.firstwarrior.com/Gallery/reginald_wini shut.html (accessed April 7, 2004).

11. Meadows, *Kiowa, Apache, and Comanche Military Societies*, 134.

12. Meadows, *Kiowa, Apache, and Comanche Military Societies*, 134, 135, 136, 138; Boyd, *Kiowa Voices*, 72, 114.

13. Meadows, *Kiowa, Apache, and Comanche Military Societies*, 138, 139, 141; Boyd, *Kiowa Voices*, 104.

14. Meadows, *Kiowa, Apache, and Comanche Military Societies*, 147, 148.

15. Meadows, *Kiowa, Apache, and Comanche Military Societies*, 161, 163, 164, 166, 167.

16. Meadows, *Kiowa, Apache, and Comanche Military Societies*, 209, 225, 229, 230, 231.

17. Meadows, *Kiowa, Apache, and Comanche Military Societies*, 232, 235, 236.

18. Meadows, *Kiowa, Apache, and Comanche Military Societies*, 343, 344, 345.

19. Meadows, *Kiowa, Apache, and Comanche Military Societies*, 345.

20. Meadows, *Kiowa, Apache, and Comanche Military Societies*, 167.

21. Meadows, *Kiowa, Apache, and Comanche Military Societies*, 166.

22. Meadows, *Kiowa, Apache, and Comanche Military Societies*, 168.

23. Lakota Thunder, *Veterans Songs*.

24. Flint Institute of Art, *The American Indians and the American Flag*, 13.

25. Flint Institute of Art, *The American Indians and the American Flag*, 13.

26. Howard and Levine, *Choctaw Music and Dance*, 113.

27. *Winnebago Tribal Songs*, liner notes; Boyd, *Kiowa Voices*, xviii.

28. Neillands, *Combat Zone*, 11, 77.

29. "Native Americans in the Korean War," http://korea50.army.mil/history/ factsheets/native.shtml (accessed November 22, 2002); "USS *Clark*"; Kelen and Stone, *Missing Stories*, 36.

8. An American Ka in Indian Country

1. Magedanz, *South Dakotans*, 1–2.

2. Holm, *Strong Hearts*, 109–22, 129; Magedanz, *South Dakotans*, 67–68.

3. Birdwell, *A Hundred Miles of Bad Road*, 67, 125, 126, 134.

4. The background information in this section is based on my own interpretations of several works on this period. For Termination, see Fixico, *Termination and Relocation*. For economic factors, see Parman, *Indians*. See Philp, *Indian Self-Rule*, for firsthand accounts of how Native leaders and communities viewed Termination and the Red Power movement. For how relations between Native militants and traditionalists worked, see Deloria, *We Talk, You Listen*. For how Native individuals and communities established themselves in urban centers, see Margon, "Indians and Immigrants," 17–28.

5. Metz, "Celebrating Their Service to the U.S."; Birdwell, *A Hundred Miles of Bad Road*, 134.

6. "Richard Chagin's Story," http://www.nativefederation.org/history.veterans/RichardChaginStory.html (accessed August 23, 2003). For more on the forced relocation of Aleut Indians during World War II, see Kolhoff, *When the Wind Was a River*.

7. Lassiter, *The Power of Kiowa Song*, 89, 117, 118, 120, 123, 124; *New Grove Dictionary of American Music*, 4:635, 636.

8. Meadows, *Kiowa, Apache, and Comanche Military Societies*, 357, 359.

9. Meadows, *Kiowa, Apache, and Comanche Military Societies*, 346, 347.

10. Meadows, *Kiowa, Apache, and Comanche Military Societies*, 348.

11. Thomas Gallagher ([non-Native], U.S. Army [1953–57], member of the Lakota warrior society the Wild Horse Butte Tokalas), mail interview by the author, August 5, 1998.

12. Roy, interview.

13. A great number of books cover the history of AIM and its activities. See the books listed in the notes of the next chapter on Wounded Knee II for a start. See also their own history of themselves in "AIM History," http://www.aimmovement.org and http://www.dickshovel.com/aimhis2.html (accessed February 23, 2001).

14. "Haudenosaunee," http://www.sixnations.org/Threats_to_Traditional_Governments (accessed September 16, 2000); Sean Maloney, "PARAMETERS—U.S. Army War College Quarterly, Autumn 1997," http://carlisle.www.army.mil/usawc/Parameters/97autumn/maloney.htm (accessed September 30, 2000); Valma Blundell, "Reading Kanawake's Powwow as a Post-Oka Text," http://www.wlu.ca/~wwwpress/jrls/cjc/BackIssues/18.3/Blundell.html (accessed September 30, 2000).

15. "Haudenosaunee."

16. "AIM History"; "Election," http://www.nativecenter.com/election.htm (accessed February 23, 2001).

17. "Support Ts'Peten Defenders," http://www.finearts/uvic.ca/~vipirg/SISIS/GustLak/letter.html (accessed September 30, 2000).

18. "Haudenosaunee."

19. Hal Jack Johnson ([Tuscarora], U.S. Army [1950–58], commander of the North American Iroquois Veterans Association), North American Iroquois

Veterans Association Annual Powwow, Salamanca NY, interview by the author, August 16, 2000.

20. T. J. Grant, "Training on Rules of Engagement in Domestic Operations," http://www.cfsc.dnd.ca/irc/amsc/amsc1/014html (accessed September 30, 2000).

21. Holm, *Strong Hearts*, 31, 36–37, 38, 186.

22. Holm, *Strong Hearts*, 170.

23. Holm, *Strong Hearts*, 170.

24. Cummings, *Moon Dash Warrior*, 24, 75, 179, 210, 214, 216, 252, 259, 265.

25. Charles Ray Battiest ([Choctaw], U.S. Army [1964–67 and 1968–70]), mail interview by the author, October 15, 1998; Stephen Bowers ([Seminole], U.S. Army [1969–71]), mail interview by the author, March 23, 1999.

26. Roy, interview.

27. Steve Russell ([Cherokee], U.S. Air Force [1967–69]), San Antonio TX, interview by the author, August 8, 1998.

28. Betty Reid, "Blackening Rite Lightens Burden of Wartime Ghosts," *Arizona Republic*, August 19, 1993, NV-8.

29. Carrie Groeringer, "Possessions of a Warrior," *Indian Country Today*, May 25, 1994, B4.

30. Robert Sanderson, "Vietnam Powwow: The Vietnam War as Remembered by Native American Veterans," http://www.anpa.ualr.edu/digital_library/narra tives/SanViet.html (accessed April 10, 2004); "Bruce Heaton's Story," http://www .nativefederation.org/history/veterans/BruceHeatonStory.html (accessed August 23, 2003).

31. Sanderson, "Vietnam Powwow."

32. Holm, *Strong Hearts*, 169.

33. Alliance West and the Intertribal Veterans, *The Warrior's Edge*, liner notes.

34. Robertson, *Robbie Robertson*, lyric sheet.

35. "Hmong Seek More Recognition for Helping U.S.," http://www.csmonitor. com/durable/1998/05/21/p5s2.htm (accessed March 4, 2001); "The Forgotten Army," http://www.montagnards.org/The_Forgotten_Army.html (March 4, 2001); "Jim Morris Is Still Proud of His Service," http://www.thehistorynet.com/Vietnam/ Articles/04962_text.htm (accessed March 1, 2001); "Mountain People," http:// www.vietvet.org/mountain.htm (accessed May 15, 2002).

36. Stanton, *Green Berets at War*, 24, 39, 41; Lanning, *Inside the LRRPS*, 54, 89; Ninh, *The Sorrows of War*, 14.

37. Stanton, *Green Berets at War*, 24, 39, 41; "A Secret Army No More."

38. David Espey, "America and Vietnam: The Indian Subtext," http://www .english.upenn.edu/~despey/vietnam.htm (accessed August 25, 2000).

39. Jack Shulimson, "U.S. Marines in Vietnam, an Expanding War, 1966,"

http://www.army.milcmh~pg/books/Vietnamese/Sharpen/cho2.html#b8 (accessed May 8, 2004).

9. Bringing the War Home

1. Churchill, *COINTELPRO*, 243, 244.

2. Kitson, *Low Intensity Conflict*, 33, 50, 69.

3. Akwesasne Notes, *Voices*, 24; Lyman, *Wounded Knee 1973*, 37, 38; Dewing, *FBI Files*, reel 20, "AIM Assault on Roadblock 3," March 8, 1973. FBI agents reported ION members shooting and attempting to either assault or outflank their positions on one occasion. Different agents estimated that ten to forty Indians tried to catch them in a classic pincers-type assault. The calculation of the attack suggests it was not done impulsively out of anger. Given their limited weaponry and ammunition, an attempt to break out would have been suicidal. Any attempt to inflict casualties would have damaged their cause. Likely ION wished to test the federal agents' military abilities.

4. Dewing, *FBI Files*, reel 5, list of individuals captured at Wounded Knee II, dated June 13, 1973. Forty-two names are blacked out. Donald Parman, my advisor when I was getting my master's degree at Purdue, agreed with me the names blacked out very likely were those of informants or those who had plea-bargaining agreements. How many were informants before going to Wounded Knee and how many informed to avoid prosecution after being captured likely cannot be determined short of FBI agents or federal attorneys being willing to come forward and say.

5. Lyman, *Wounded Knee 1973*, 82; Dewing, "South Dakota Newspaper Coverage of Wounded Knee II," 54; Akwesasne Notes, *Voices*, 54.

6. The descriptions of the bunkers and Native defenses come from Lyman, *Wounded Knee 1973*, 25, 139; Dewing, *Wounded Knee*, 101, 102, 103, 133; Holm, *Strong Hearts*, 177, 178.

7. The descriptions of ION tactics come from Akwesasne Notes, *Voices*, 61, 67, 72, 76, 197, 198, 199; Dewing, *FBI Files*, reel 25; Guy Frantze, interview by the author, June 6, 1973.

8. Churchill, *COINTELPRO*, 245; Akwesasne Notes, *Voices*, 54, 72, 76, 197, 201; Zimmerman, *Airlift to Wounded Knee*, 236; Lyman, *Wounded Knee 1973*, 159.

9. Akwesasne Notes, *Voices*, 51, 76; Dewing, *Wounded Knee*, 147; Dewing, *FBI Files*, reel 14, airtel, June 19, 1975.

10. Akwesasne Notes, *Voices*, 61, 76; Churchill, *COINTELPRO*, 256; Dewing, *FBI Files*, reel 20, teletype, March 15, 1973, reel 25, memo, March 16, 1973, and reel 26, memo, May 8, 1973; Frantze, interview. There are dozens of such letters throughout the files, often passed along from congressmen. There are also angry editorials from newspapers across the country along the same lines throughout the files.

11. Akwesasne Notes, *Voices*, 61, 194, 196, 197, 198; Dewing, *Wounded Knee*, 133.

10. "Fighting Terrorism since 1492"

1. For one of the few descriptions of the war, see Nietschmann, *The Unknown War*; Marley Shebala, "Building a Community Heals War Scars," *Navajo Times*, August 1, 1996, A12.

2. Frank LePoine, "Legion Post Honors Dead Marines," *Indian Country Today*, November 2, 1983, 14.

3. Alexandra Gekas, "Tobacco Tax Reflects Forgotten Tribal Heritage," http://www.dailycardinal.com/news/2003/11/10/Opinion/Tobacco.Tax.Reflects.Forgotten.Tribal.Heritage-552856.shtml (accessed June 14, 2004); "Western Shoshone Defense Project," http://www.wsdp.org/brochure.htm (accessed June 14, 2004).

4. Crystal Holtz, "Mixed Reviews on the Gulf War," *News from Indian Country*, February 28, 1991, 20; Doug George-Kanetijo, "Learning the Bitter Lessons of Desert Storm," *News from Indian Country*, February 15, 1996, 14A; Armstrong Wiggins, "Kurds Are the American Indians of the Gulf," *Akwesasne Notes*, April 30, 1991, 25; "Project Indigenous Restoration Held in Toronto," *Akwesasne Notes*, June 31, 1991.

5. Katie McCarthy, "If We Stay, There Will Only Be More and More War Dead," *News from Indian Country*, February 15, 1991, 3.

6. Paul DeMain, "Troops on Their Way Home," *News from Indian Country*, March 15, 1991, 1.

7. James Hill, "Killed by Friendly Fire in 1991's Desert Storm," *News from Indian Country*, May 31, 1998, 22A.

8. N. L. Thomas, "American Indian Vet Plans Wheelchair Trek to St. Paul," http://www.yvwiiusdinvnohii.net/News2000/0200/MSUN000226VET.htm (accessed June 14, 2004).

9. Tsinajinnie, *Mother's Word*, liner notes.

10. "Veterans Honored at Powwow," *Char-Koosta News*, November 15, 1996, 1.

11. Jim Northrup, "Commentary," *News from Indian Country*, May 15, 1991, 20; "Endorse the Call to Action," http://home.earthlink.net/~npcboston/endrse65.htm (accessed June 14, 2004); "Food Supply to Indians Continues," *Native Nevadan*, March 31, 1992, 22.

12. "Native Intelligence: The Long View," http://www.bluecorncomics.com/naintel1.htm (accessed September 1, 2002); Joe Watson, "Token Arab," http://www.phoenixnewtimes.com/issues/2004-04-08/feature.html (accessed April 8, 2004).

13. Bevy Deer Johnston, "Elders Speak on September 11 Six-Month Anniversary," *News from Indian Country*, March 15, 2002, 17B; Frank King III, "Remembering 9-11 from a Native Perspective," *Native Voice*, September 25, 2002, 1.

14. "Native Intelligence."

15. "Native Intelligence."

16. Jack Forbes, "Right Wing Terrorism: Right Wing Response," *Windspeaker*, March 31, 2002, 5.

17. Alfred Taiaiake, "Toske, It's True, Understanding the Causes," *Windspeaker*, October 31, 2001, 5.

18. "Native Intelligence."

19. David Yeagley, "Comanche War Cry," http://www.badeagle.com/html/war_cry.html (accessed May 8, 2004). Originally published in *FrontPage Magazine*, September 14, 2002; David Yeagley, "American Indians Aren't Like Palestinians," http://www.badeagle.com/html/arent_pales.html (accessed May 8, 2004).

20. "Can an Indian Be a Patriot?" http://www.badeagle.com/html/indian_patriot.html (accessed May 8, 2004); Suzan Shown Harjo, "One Small and Unworthy Man," *Indian Country Today*, http://www.indiancountry.com/?1044632709 (accessed May 8, 2004). In Harjo's article, Comanche activist/educator Juanita Padapony challenged his claim to be Comanche or represent the tribe. Yeagley's ancestry was further challenged in "The Whisper," *Native American Times*, http://www.nativetimes.com/index.asp?action=displayarticle&article_id=6615 (accessed June 14, 2005). Yeagley threatened legal action and had the article removed, but it is still available at "Yeagley Isn't Indian," http://groups.yahoo.com/group/NatNews/message/38979 (accessed July 25, 2006) and "Author's Forum," http://www.bluecorncomics.com/yeagley.htm (accessed July 25, 2006). Yeagley describes hating being Indian on his own Web site in "Indians," http://www.badeagle.com/html/cultures_indians.html (accessed July 30, 2006): "Yeagley's Comanche mother did not raise her children (three boys and a girl) within Indian culture. She felt that culturally, socially, and professionally, this was a dead end. . . . She also disagreed with many Indian ways and customs. Therefore, her children were raised with the values of White Anglo-Saxon Protestants. . . . Yeagley was simply not taught Indian ways. Much of what he thought was 'Indian' came to him through his experience with whites. . . . Yeagley saw in the American Indian warrior stereotypes a theme that might provide a new impetus, a revival as it were, of much needed American Patriotism."

21. "Totem Pole Honoring Victims Set for Saturday," *Native American Times*, September 15, 2003, 3A.

22. Jim Kent, "Lakota and Brooklyn Students Share Feelings about 9-11," *News from Indian Country*, January 15, 2002, 12A; Jim Kent, "Mohawk Iron Workers to Be Honored at WTC Ceremony," *Native American Times*, April 1, 2002, 1; Johnston, "Elders Speak," 17B; "McCaleb Praises Indian Country," *Wind River News*, October 11, 2001, 1.

23. Jerry Reynolds, "Security Gets a Hearing," *Indian Country Today*, August 6, 2003, A1.

24. Reynolds, "Security Gets a Hearing"; Bruce Johansen, "Betting on Gaming," *Native Americas*, December 31, 2001, 28.

25. "Citizens for Personal Responsibility," http://www.bluecorncomics.com/stype5b4.htm (accessed November 8, 2005).

26. Jim Kent, "News," *News from Indian Country*, December 15, 2001, 12A; Mary Pierpoint, "News," *News from Indian Country*, November 7, 2001, A1.

27. "Slavin's Gallery," http://www.slavinsgallery.com/bean.htm (accessed June 16, 2004); "Armed with the Arrows of Defense," http://www.guthriestudios.com/NobleEagle.htm (accessed June 16, 2004).

28. Nathan Tohtsoni, "Reserves on Alert," *Navajo Times*, September 27, 2001, A1.

29. There are several things the reader should be aware of. I contributed to the first edition of an anthology with Churchill titled *They Call Us Indians*. Churchill later alienated the editor, Annika Banfeld, with childish and unprofessional behavior. To my relief and that of most of the other authors, he was removed from subsequent editions. I signed a petition supporting Churchill's free speech, even while disagreeing with him on many issues, especially his approach and worldview. I have worked briefly with American Indian Movement members in chapters in Arizona, Indiana, and Massachusetts, as well as the AIM Support Group of Northern Kentucky/Ohio, mostly on the issue of protecting Native ceremonies from New Age exploitation. I have never been an AIM member, though I have been often incorrectly identified as one.

30. Ward Churchill, "Some People Push Back," http://www.kersplebedeb.com/mystuff/s11/churchill.html (accessed June 1, 2006).

31. A copy of the brief filed against O'Reilly can be found at http://www.thesmokinggun.com/archive/1013043mackris1.html (accessed July 15, 2006). The death threats are described in "Joan Hinde Stewart Appears on CNN," http://www.hamilton.edu/news/wardchurchill/jhs_cnn.html (accessed July 15, 2006). See also Bob Newman, "Treason in the Teepee," http://www.mensnewsdaily.com/archive/m-n/2005/newman020606.htm (accessed February 6, 2005). Newman has also called for the executions of Howard Dean, John Kerry, and John Murtha as "traitors" for opposing the war and President Bush. Though Churchill's case may be the first time Newman has used race-baiting about Natives, he has a long history of preaching hatred of Latinos.

32. Ward Churchill, "Ward Churchill Responds to Criticism of 'Some People Push Back,'" http://www.kersplebedeb.com/mystuff/s11/ward_churchill_responds.html (accessed June 1, 2006).

33. Emma Perez, "A Neocon Test Case for Academic Purges," http://www.counterpunch.og/perez02282005.html (accessed February 28, 2005); John Mohawk, "Churchill Controversy Represents a Split in America," *Indian Country Today*, http://www.indiancountrytoday.com/content.cfm?id=1096410461 (accessed March 3, 2005).

34. For National AIM's view of the split, see "Background on U.S. Government War on AIM," http://www.aimovement.org/moipr/USVAIMbackground.html (ac-

cessed July 20, 2006). For Autonomous AIM's view, see "Autonomous AIM—The Real Thing," http://www.americanindianmovement.org/txaim/bellecourts.html (accessed July 20, 2006).

35. The revolutionary left may sometimes carry out actions that coincide with Native needs, such as the Zapatistas. But this is rare, especially in the United States, in part because American would-be revolutionaries are often themselves from the upper class, and although they are sometimes sincere, more often they are feeling alienated, are bored, or are "slumming" for a short time.

36. I briefly encountered Churchill the night before his speech at a concert held by the organizers. I was probably the only (other?) nonwhite person there. I saw him standing about ten paces away. He saw me and immediately took off the other way, then came back toward me and walked right by me, at the same time steadfastly refusing to look at me. I can only guess he confused me with someone he had problems with in the past and feared my trying to challenge him or debate him.

37. "Churchill 05," http://www.aimovement.org/moipr/churchill05.html (accessed July 20, 2006); Ann Coulter, "The Little Injun That Could," http://www.townhall.com/columnists/anncoulter/ac20050211.shtml (accessed February 11, 2005).

38. Ward Churchill, "Turning Quibbles over Footnotes into Academic Felonies," http://www.counterpunch.org/Churchill06142006.html (accessed June 14, 2006).

39. "Report of the Investigative Committee of the Standing Committee on Research Misconduct at the University of Colorado at Boulder Concerning Allegations of Academic Misconduct against Professor Ward Churchill," http://www.colorado.edu/news/reports/churchill/download/WardChurchillReport.pdf (accessed July 20, 2006). The most frivolous charge actually involves his ink sketch of a public domain photo that is more than 140 years old. Several of the supposed charges of fraud or plagiarism seem to be simple sloppiness, worth embarrassing any scholar into doing better but not worth ending anyone's career over. In one case Churchill is being held accountable for a publication's failure to include the byline of the original source. In possibly the most ridiculous charge, Churchill is accused of "misrepresentation" of the Dawes Act for what is simply a different opinion, albeit one I do not see as supportable. The legal opinion of some was that the worst case seems to be Churchill's plagiarism of Professor Fay Cohen's chapter on fishing rights in a book edited by Churchill's then-wife, Annette Jaimes, for whom he also admitted to ghostwriting an essay. Four other authors or professors also accuse Churchill of publishing their work without permission, which, in my view, is the most serious ethical lapse after the Cohen case. In some cases these incidents likely began as simple carelessness or forgetfulness, but his failure to correct them after all these years is clearly wrong.

40. Also of note is that this is not the first time Brown went after an AIM ac-

tivist he believed was not Native. Two of the five articles at his homepage are devoted to critiques of AIM leaders, namely Billy Tayac and Ward Churchill. Thomas Brown, "Ethnic Identity Movements and the Legal Process," http://hal .lamar.edu/~BROWNTF/PISCATAWAY.html (accessed July 1, 2006) even goes into an extensive "exposé" of Tayac's deceased family members. Brown removed his original article on Churchill, but a more measured version of it can be found at his homepage. See Thomas Brown, "Assessing Ward Churchill's Version of the 1837 Smallpox Epidemic," http://hal.lamar.edu/~browntf/Churchill1.htm (accessed July 1, 2006). The other articles posted at his homepage are on consumerism.

41. Jodi Rave, "Colorado Professor Fabricates Native History," http://www .missoulian.com/articles/2006/06/18/jodirave/rave18.txt (accessed June 18, 2006). It also should be noted that Rave's dislike for Churchill goes back to when she took one of his classes. Rave charges Churchill changed her grade from an A to a C because she disagreed with him.

42. "Yeagley Isn't Indian"; Harjo, "One Small and Unworthy Man." Yeagley frequently states on his own forum, "You're all much more Indian than me. So don't worry about that argument anymore." Yeagley's response to charges of his being an imposter is to point to his tribal enrollment. But fraudulent enrollments have happened before, most notably those of New Age exploiters Charles Storm and Brooke Schiavi, as well as many people listed on the Dawes Roll. Yeagley also produced his birth certificate when critics said he was adopted. But in closed adoptions, certificates are altered to show adopted children listed as birth children. It is possible that Yeagley could be adopted but never heard it from his adoptive parents. But it is very striking that Yeagley produces as "evidence" only written documents instead of doing what most Natives would do—discuss other Natives to whom they are related. The big mystery is why he does not ask his alleged blood relatives to speak out, including three brothers and a sister, or why they do not come forward themselves.

43. A comparison of photos strongly suggests that Yeagley either had plastic surgery or has dramatically altered his appearance in other ways. Compare his self-portrait to a photo of him on his introductory page on his Web site: "Dr. Yeagley's Biography," http://www.badeagle.com/html/biography.html (accessed July 15, 2006); "David Yeagley's Badeagle.com," http://www.badeagle.com (accessed July 17, 2006). His cheeks, cheekbones, and eyelids appear completely different. He also appears in his recent photos to be using makeup, which still does not hide how fair his skin tone is. He also grew his hair out and seems to be using hair straightener.

44. Huffer makes his living promoting bodybuilding, hunting, DVDs, pellet guns, and arthritis cures, and makes personal appearances promoting "Extreme Christianity." He variously claims to be three-fourths Menominee or Menominee/ Cherokee. Huffer is enrolled in the notorious Western Cherokee Nation of Arkansas and Missouri (WCNAM). For more on the WCNAM, see "Committee to Combat

Cherokee Frauds," http://cherokeeeldersociety.com/frauds.html (accessed July
15, 2006). Huffer also habitually wears a Plains Indian headdress that seems to
have been made by tribe Hollywood. For more on Huffer, see "Instinct Shooting,"
http://www.chiefaj.com (accessed July 1, 2006); Tony Reid, "Area Man Has
the Muscle to Back up Shooting Skills," *Herald and Review*, http://www.herald
-review.com/articles/2005/09/25/news/local_news/1010266.txt (accessed July
1, 2006); and http://users.pandora.be/gohiyuhi/articles/art00047.htm. Rita Ann
Suntz calls herself "Pale Moon Princess" and is variously identified as Cherokee,
Cheyenne, or Choctaw. Heading the American Indian Heritage Foundation at
http://www.indians.org, she once tried to promote the CIA as "an organization of
compassion and caring." See http://users.pandora.be/gohiyuhi/frauds/frd0082.htm
(accessed June 1, 2006); Koren Capozza, "Charity Scams: Making Big Business
Out of American Indian Poverty," http://www.arc.org/C_Lines/CLArchive/
story_web00_07.html (accessed June 1, 2006); and Adam Zagorin, "Remember
the Greedy: Story of Princess Pale Moon," http://www.yvwiiusdinvnohii.net/
articles/PaleMoon930816Greed.htm (accessed June 1, 2006).

45. Yeagley's claim of a PhD and title of doctor are deceptive, since he claims
expertise in history, Native cultures, and current affairs. His degree is in music.
Though his Web site describes him as "a published scholar," by his own account
he has a grand total of one scholarly article published in the United States. See
David Yeagley, "Jews," http://www.badeagle.com/html/cultures_jews.html (accessed July 15, 2006): "He has published only two academic papers in American
journals. In fact, both works are in the same journal, one of the more broad
minded, called the *Journal of the American Liszt Society*." His claims of being a
professor at Oklahoma State University (OSU) who was fired for promoting patriotism are largely false. He worked at OSU for a single semester as an adjunct,
teaching a single course. By his own description, and the quotes he provided from
two of his supervisors, he was fired for repeatedly falsely representing his own
views as that of his former university's. His supervisors actually did their best to
protect his position. What he did was the equivalent of a newly promoted army
corporal going to the press and falsely claiming to speak for the general. David
Yeagley, "I Was Fired for Being a Conservative Indian," http://www.badeagle
.com/html/fired.html (accessed July 20, 2006). "I was warned not to mention the
school name in articles or interviews, except with a disclaimer stating that my
views were independent. . . . 'This is it,' said Tim Faltyn, the new head of Arts
and Sciences. 'I can't protect you anymore. The administration has decided to
let you go.' The final ax fell in a meeting with Dennis, my supervisor. 'Yeagley,
you're creating a lot of bad PR.'" By any reasonable standard he is no scholar.
His main output is the essays he wrote for Horowitz's Web sites. For a man
who has been a student at universities for almost twenty-five years, his articles
seemingly do not reflect his long history in academia. Most are badly disjointed,
filled with one-sentence paragraphs with no logical progression and not much

thought or knowledge behind them, even taking into account his juvenile intent to shock. Often he does not even bother to use spell-check. His writing style comes across like that of a *National Inquirer* reporter who enjoys reading Aryan Nation pamphlets that try to sound like Sitting Bull. This is not surprising, since by his own admission he relates to his alleged heritage by the stereotypes about it. It is possible he could be deliberately dumbing down his writing for those on the far right he appeals to.

46. http://www.stormfront.org/forum/showthread.php?t=278379 (accessed July 15, 2006); "'White Race' Forum with No White People?" http://www.vnnforum.com/showthread.php?t=9721&goto=nextnewest (accessed July 15, 2006): "Dr. David Yeagley . . . has created a few new forums on his site. They all fall under the heading The White Race and include White Nations. . . . Dr. Yeagley has been somewhat sympathetic to our ultimate goals"; http://www.amren.com/0103issue/0103issue.htm (accessed July 15, 2006): "Indians to the Rescue! David Yeagley . . . thinks whites have gone soft and are giving the country away to foreigners"; David Yeagley, "Liberals Gamble Away Indians' Future," http://frontpagemag.com/Articles/ReadArticle.asp?ID=13399 (accessed July 15, 2006); http://www.badeagle.com/html/biography.html (accessed July 15, 2006): "Yeagley . . . wrote . . . a collection of seven epics, dedicated to Her Imperial Majesty [wife of the shah of Iran.]" For the first year, Badeagle.com was almost empty, an embarrassment considering the time and money he and Horowitz put into it.

47. Rob Schmidt, "Stereotype of the Month Contest," http://www.bluecorn comics.com/stype216.htm (accessed February 12, 2004).

48. Jim Kent, "Native Veterans Planning to Hold DC protest," *News from Indian Country*, May 15, 2002, 2A; Kent, "Lakota Hold Day of Prayer at Bear Lodge," *News from Indian Country*, December 15, 2001, 12B; Kent, "Lakota Elder Traces Family through Three Centuries," *News from Indian Country*, July 31, 2002, 10B.

49. Lucas Eastwood, "Patrolling Rugged Mountains of East Afghanistan," *Confederated Umatilla Journal*, December 31, 2002, 1.

50. A. A. Guenther, "Local Member Defends U.S. in Afghanistan," *Ft. Apache Scout*, May 17, 2002, 14.

51. Sam Lewin, "Member of Blackfoot Nation Killed in Afghanistan," *Native American Times*, November 1, 2003, 1A; David Ensor, "CIA: Two Dead in Afghan Ambush Were Agency Workers," http://www.cnn.com/2003/WORLD/asiapcf/central/10/28/cia.afghanistan (accessed November 1, 2003).

52. John Brown, "Our Indian Wars Are Not Over Yet: 10 Ways to Interpret the War on Terror as a Frontier Conflict," http://www.commondreams.org/views06/0120-20.htm (accessed January 20, 2006).

53. Shaheen, *Reel Bad Arabs*, 18, 505.

54. The five wars are the Filipino Insurrection, the Vietnam War, the War in

Afghanistan, and both Iraq wars. Schmidt, "Stereotype of the Month Contest"; James Pinkerton, "Fox News Expert Says U.S. Handling of Iraq Is Like Vietnam," http://altantaindymedia.org/newswire/display/27388/index.php (accessed April 8, 2004).

55. Jim Lobe, "Bush Circles Wagons, But Cavalry Has Joined the Indians," http://www.commondreams.org/headlines04/0510-06.htm (accessed May 10, 2004).

56. "Indian Leader Says War Funding Hurts Tribes," *Wind River News*, October 16, 2003, 8; Arvol Looking Horse, "A Comment on the War in Iraq," *Native Times*, April 19, 2003.

57. Sherman Alexie, "Relevant Contradictions," http://www.thestranger .com/2003-02-27/feature2.html (accessed March 5, 2003).

58. "Indian Leader Says War Funding Hurts Tribes," 8; Larry Adams, "No More Illegally Elected U.S. Presidents," *Ojibwe News*, January 9, 2004, 4; Dean Chavers, "Nobody Thanked Me," *Seminole Tribune*, July 4, 2003, 2.

59. Brenda Norrell, "Coal, Oil Interests Paved Bush's Road to Baghdad," *Navajo Times*, April 10, 2003, A1.

60. Tony Blackfeather, "Statement of the Tetuwan Oyate, Teton Sioux Nation Treaty Council against the United States Invasion of Iraq and Call for United Nations General Assembly Intervention," http://www.treatycouncil.org/new _page_57111112311121111.htm (accessed July 20, 2006).

61. Marl Shaffer, "War Brings Many Impacts on Navajos," *Navajo Times*, April 2, 2003, A8 (reprint of *Arizona Republic* article); Bill Donovan, "Shirley Blasts War in Iraq," *Navajo Times*, http://www.navajotimes.com/_content/blasts .php (accessed October 12, 2005).

62. Jennifer Baldwin, "Supporters March to Counter Anti-War Talk," *Navajo Times*, March 27, 2003, A1; Mary Pierpoint, "Haskell Veterans Hold Ceremony in Support of U.S. Troops," *Native Voice*, April 19, 2003, B3; "American Indians Fighting a Very Old War," *Indian Country Today*, March 5, 2003, A4.

63. Darryl Fears, "Conditions in Indian Country Are Worse Than in Iraq," *Washington Post*, February 17, 2005, A23; Megan Holland and Julia O'Malley, "Mother Blames Policy for Son's Iraq Injuries," *Anchorage Daily News*, http:// www.adn.com/news/military/story/7210503p-7122975c.html (accessed November 16, 2005).

64. Bryan O'Connor, "Cheyenne Perform Victory Dance to Honor Marine Tank Driver," http://www.billingsgazette.com/index.php?display=rednews/2003/07/03/ bu.../30-victory-dance.in (accessed July 6, 2003).

65. Gabriela Rico, "O'odham Pray: 29 from Tribe Called Up," *Tucson Citizen*, March 28, 2003, 1B; Dean Ferguson, "Ceremony Offers Blessing to Soldiers," *Lewiston Morning Tribune*, March 21, 2003, 5A.

66. "Warrior Died Serving 2 Nations," http://www.whiteearth.com/story7.htm (accessed May 10, 2003); "The Wings of an Eagle," http://www.tsalagi-atsilvsgi .net/Lakota_Warrior.html (accessed January 30, 2004).

11. "A Woman Warrior, Just Like Lozen"

1. Lynn Ducey, "Army Friendship Ends in Rejoice, Mourning," *State Press*, April 7, 2003, 1.

2. Before this becomes a side debate about the roles of gays in Native cultures, let me point to my earlier example of Lozen, who did marry and is remembered by Apaches as uncommonly beautiful and feminine. It has unfortunately become quite common for many non-Native gays to distort the history of Natives such as Lozen for their own agendas. For example, one exploitative site run by a New Age operator named Julia White (who poses as a "Cherokee Sioux elder") is aimed at non-Natives and distorts the life story of Lozen to make her appear to have been a lesbian. Even many urban Native gays have taken to calling themselves two-spirits when, traditionally, many two-spirits were not gay, and most gay Natives were never considered two-spirits. While it is understandable that non-Native gays look to Native cultures for models of less repressive societies, this should not be an excuse for ignoring facts.

3. Carrie McLeary, "Tribal Historian Tracks Crow Veteran Stories," *Indian Country Today*, November 17, 1997, B4.

4. Dawn Martin Hill, "Traditional Medicine in Contemporary Contexts," http://www.naho.ca/english/pdf/research_tradition.pdf (accessed June 14, 2004).

5. Foley, *Father Francis M. Craft*, 1, 2, 4, 17, 40, 100, 103, 122, 127, 129, 130, 131, 153.

6. Foley, *Father Francis M. Craft*.

7. Foley, *Father Francis M. Craft*.

8. Mark Shaffer, "Hopis Await Word on Fate of Missing GI," *Arizona Republic*, April 27, 2003, B1.

9. For accounts of the Anna Mae Aquash case, see "Anna Mae Pictou," http://www.dickshovel.com/annalay.html (accessed June 26, 2004). The most famous account of the Leonard Peltier case is Matthiesen, *In the Spirit of Crazy Horse*.

10. Arizona Indian Gaming Association, "Arizona Indian Gaming Tribes Honor Lori Piestewa," http://biz.yahoo.com/prnews030421/1am05_1.html (accessed May 25, 2003); Carmen Duarte, "Blanket Tribute to Piestewa," *Arizona Daily Star*, April 4, 2003, B1; "Lori Ann Piestewa Legacy Blog," http://www.nativeweb.org/weblog/piestewa (accessed April 15, 2004).

11. "Phoenix Editorial Column Inspired Name Change to Piestewa Peak," http://www.gannett.com/go.newswatch/2003/aprilnw0425-3.htm (accessed February 12, 2003).

12. "Piestewa Peak: Our Stand," *Arizona Republic*, April 28, 2003, B10; Robbie Sherwood, "It's Official: Piestewa Peak," *Arizona Republic*, April 18, 2003, A1.

13. "Support the Piestewa Peace Process," http://www.human2human.org/piestewa-peace.htm (accessed February 12, 2003); S. J. Wilson, "Is Piestewa

Peak a Partisan Issue?" http://www.navajohopiobserver.com (accessed April 15, 2004).

14. "Arizonans Divided on Squaw Peak Rename," *State Press*, April 30, 2003, 4; Wendy Godfrey, "Arizonans Support Name Piestewa Peak But Not Parkway Renaming," http://www.westgroupresearch.com/releases/piestewao504.html (accessed April 15, 2004).

15. "Letters," *Navajo Times*, April 8, 2003, 7.

16. "Piestewa Died Fighting Iraqis in Combat," http://ca.groups.yahoo.com/group/firstnationsgathering/message/3182 (accessed April 28, 2003); Osha Gray Davidson, "The Forgotten Soldier," http://www.rollingstone.com/politics/story/?id=6085435 (accessed June 4, 2004).

17. "Piestewa Died Fighting Iraqis in Combat"; Kristen Go, "Laughter Helps Piestewa's Family Cope," http://www.tucsoncitizen.com/local/7_22_03piestewa.html (accessed July 23, 2003).

18. "Piestewa Died Fighting Iraqis in Combat"; "Family of Dead POW blasts NBC," http://cnews.canoe.ca/CNEWS/World/Iraq/2003/12/31/301369-ap.html (accessed June 14, 2004).

19. Billy House, "Female Combat Debate Focusing on Piestewa," http://www.azcentral.com/12news/news/article/0310piestewa-invest10-CP.html (accessed March 23, 2004).

20. David Yeagley, "A Tribute to a Hopi Warrior," http://www.freerepublic.com/f-news/891001/posts (accessed April 11, 2003).

21. Robert Nelson, "Squaw Peeved," *Phoenix New Times*, April 17, 2003, 12.

22. Nelson, "Squaw Peeved."

23. Nelson, "Squaw Peeved."

24. "Letters," *Phoenix New Times*, May 8, 2003.

25. "Letters," *Phoenix New Times*, April 24, May 8 and 15, 2003.

26. Robert Nelson, e-mail messages to author, May 13 and 14, 2003, June 1 and 2, 2004.

27. Godfrey, "Arizonans Support Name Piestewa Peak But Not Parkway Renaming"; Terry Bledsoe, "Perfect Time to Give Landmark New Name," http://www.ahwatukee.com/afn/opinion/corner/030416c.html (accessed April 15, 2004); Richard Ruelas, "Adding up Numbers to Figure Out Events of 2003," http://www.azcentral.com/arizonarepublic/news/articles/1231ruelas1231z7.html (accessed April 15, 2004). One month later, the freeway was renamed from Squaw Peak Freeway to Piestewa Freeway by a vote of 5–2. One year later, in an effort to avoid controversy, the park name changed from Squaw Peak Park to Phoenix Mountains Park rather than Piestewa Park.

28. Godfrey, "Arizonans Support Name Piestewa Peak But Not Parkway Renaming"; Associated Press, "Businesses with 'Squaw' in Name Face Problems with Switch," *State Press*, April 23, 2003, 3.

29. Robbie Sherwood, "A Year Later, Piestewa Remembered," http://www

.azcentral.com/arizonarepublic/local/articles/0322piestewa22.html (accessed March 23, 2004); Debra Krol, "Piestewa Name to Stay on Peak," *Arizona Native Scene*, April 2004, 1.

30. Sherwood, "A Year Later, Piestewa Remembered."

31. "Lori Piestewa's Dream Come True," http://nativeunity.blogspot.com/ 2005/05/lori-piestewas-dream-come-true.html (accessed May 28, 2005).

32. Rene Gonzalez, "Pat Tillman Is Not a Hero," http://media.dailycollegian. com/pages/tillman_lobandwithdth.html?in_archive=1 (accessed April 30, 2004). Gonzalez's main point is that Tillman chose to join the war when Afghanistan did not threaten the United States. Many misinterpreted his article as a personal attack on Tillman's memory, and he received numerous death threats and other abuse. A sample of them, as well as incitement by pro-war people to harass Gonzalez and Gonzalez's follow-up response, is at http://djslybri.blogspot.com (accessed April 30, 2004). John Tranquillo, "Tillman Not Arizona's Only Hero," *State Press*, April 27, 2004, 4. Ironically, as time passed it became clear that Tillman felt far differently about the war than either pro-or antiwar opponents assumed. Tillman's fellow soldiers described a man who said, "This war is so fucking illegal," and named Noam Chomsky as his favorite author. War proponents Ann Coulter and Sean Hannity both replied, "I don't believe it," after hearing the news and attempted to assert that the story must have been fabricated. Actually the sources for the story were Tillman's mother and brother, and a member of his platoon. Tillman also became the center of another controversy when it was revealed that he had died from "friendly fire," mistakenly killed by fellow soldiers. His own parents were among those most strongly objecting to how his memory was being misused by war proponents. As far as I know, this has not led to any calls for the memorials to him to end or be changed. Dave Zirin, "Pat Tillman, Our Hero," *The Nation*, http://www.thenation.com/doc/20051024/zirin (accessed July 1, 2004); "Hannity, Coulter 'Don't Believe' That Tillman Liked Chomsky, Opposed War," *Media Matters*, http://mediamatters.org/items/200509290001 (accessed July 1, 2006); Robert Collier, "Family Demands the Truth," *San Francisco Chronicle*, http://www.sfgate.com/cgi-bin/article.cgi?f=/c/a/2005/09/25/MNGD7ETMNM1.DTL (accessed July 1, 2006).

33. Jodi Rave Lee, "Soldier's Death Helped Better America for Natives," http:// www.journalstar.com/native.php?story_id_41378 (accessed April 22, 2003).

Conclusion

1. Roy, interview. It is likely Roy referred to his extended family rather than a nuclear family.

2. "Prison Writings," http://www.wmich.edu/dialogues/texts/prisonwritings .html (accessed June 14, 2004).

3. Carrie McLeary, "Tribal Historian Tracks Crow Veteran Stories," *Indian Country Today*, November 17, 1997, B4; Jerome Theraud, "Rocky Boy Has Many

Serving," http://www.havredailynews.com/articles/2003/03/27/local_headlines/ rockyboy.txt (accessed June 14, 2004); Research Directorate, "Semiannual Race/ Ethnic/Gender Profile of the Department of Defense Forces," 12–17. The last source has statistics showing Natives numbering only 0.7 percent of the army compared to 2.2 percent of the coast guard and 0.8 percent of the military overall.

4. "Indians in the Military," http://www.bluecorncomics.com/military.htm (accessed June 14, 2004).

Bibliography

Archival Sources

Arizona State University, Labriola American Indian Data Center, Tempe
    Audio Collections
    Biographies
    Ephemera
    Small Manuscripts
    South Dakota Oral Histories
Arizona State University, Southwestern Collections, Tempe
    Biographies
    Ephemera
Indiana University, Bloomington
    Photo Collections
    Thomas K. Dixon Files
    World War I Questionnaires for Returned Native Soldiers
Library of Congress, Washington DC
    New England Native Veterans Project
Newberry Library, Chicago
    Chicago American Indian Oral History Project
    Edward Ayer Collection of Ethnology
    Elmo Scott Watson Papers
    Ely Parker Papers
    Murray Wax Papers
Purdue University, West Lafayette IN
    FBI Files on AIM and Wounded Knee II
University of Oklahoma, Norman
    American Indian File Collection
    Te Ata Fisher Collection
Women Veterans Memorial, Arlington VA
    Oral History Project

Bibliography

Published Sources

Akwesasne Notes. *Voices from Wounded Knee, 1973, in the Words of the Participants*. Rooseveltown NY: Akwesasne Notes, 1976.

Aleiss, Angela. "Prelude to World War II: Racial Unity and the Hollywood Indian." *Journal of American Culture* 18, no. 2 (1995).

Alliance West and the Intertribal Veterans. *The Warrior's Edge*. Portland OR: Shortwave Records, 1999.

Apess, William, and Barry O'Connell. *A Son of the Forest and Other Writings*. Amherst: University of Massachusetts Press, 1997.

Arbogast, Doyle. *Wounded Warriors: A Time for Healing*. Omaha: Little Turtle Publications, 1995.

Aztec Club of 1847 (Military Society of the Mexican War). London: Hanbury and Tomsett, 1928.

Banfeld, Annika, ed. *They Call Us Indians*. Goteborg: New World Foundation, 2004.

Belleranti, Shirley. "Code Talkers." *Westways* 75, no. 3 (1983).

Benavidez, Roy. *Medal of Honor: A Vietnam Warrior's Story*. Washington DC: Brassey's, 1995.

Benn, Carl. *Iroquois in the War of 1812*. Toronto: University of Toronto Press, 1998.

Bernstein, Alison. *American Indians and World War II: Toward a New Era in Indian Affairs*. Norman: University of Oklahoma Press, 1991.

———. "Walking in Two Worlds." PhD thesis, Columbia University, 1986.

Birdwell, Dwight. *A Hundred Miles of Bad Road*. Novato CA: Presidio Press, 2000.

Blacker, Irwin. *Irregulars, Partisans, and Guerillas*. New York: Simon and Schuster, 1954.

Black Lodge Singers. *Veterans Honor Songs*. Phoenix: Canyon Records, 1993.

Boyd, Maurice. *Kiowa Voices*. Fort Worth: Texas Christian University Press, 1981.

Britten, Thomas. *The American Indian in World War I: At War and At Home*. Albuquerque: University of New Mexico Press, 1997.

———. "American Indians in World War I: Service as a Catalyst for Reform." PhD thesis, Texas Tech University, 1994.

Brooklyn Editorial Collective. *Zapatista Documents of the New Mexican Revolution*. New York: Autonomedia, 1999.

Brumwell, Stephen. *White Devil: A True Story of War, Savagery, and Vengeance in Colonial America*. New York: De Capo Press, 2005.

Bulow, Nanette. *Navajo Code Talkers Reunion*. Salt Lake City: Western History Center, 1972.

Campbell, Howard. *Zapotec Renaissance: Ethnic Politics and Cultural Revivalism in Southern Mexico*. Albuquerque: University of New Mexico Press, 1994.

Cash, Joseph, and Herbert T. Hoover, eds. *To Be an Indian*. New York: Holt Rinehart, 1971.

Castaneda, Carlos, trans. *The Mexican Side of the Texas Revolution by the Chief Texas Participants*. Austin: Graphic Ideas, 1970.

Castile, George Pierre, and Gilbert Kushner, eds. *Persistent Peoples: Cultural Enclaves in Perspective*. Tucson: University of Arizona Press, 1981.

Chinnery, Phillip. *Vietnam: The Helicopter War*. Annapolis: Naval Institute Press, 1991.

Churchill, Ward. *Agents of Repression: The FBI's Secret Wars against the Black Panther Party and the American Indian Movement*. Boston: South End Press, 1988.

———. *The COINTELPRO Papers*. London: South End Press, 1990.

Clark, Bill. *The Piper Indians*. Blue Summit Ridge PA: Tab Books, 1988.

Communication of the Delegation of the Cherokee Nation to the President of the United States. Washington DC: Gibson Brothers, 1866.

Cowger, Thomas. *The National Congress of American Indians: The Founding Years*. Lincoln: University of Nebraska Press, 1999.

Crumrine, Ross. *Mayo Indians of Sonora*. Prospect Heights IL: Waveland Press, 1988.

Cummings, Delano. *Moon Dash Warrior*. Chapel Hill NC: Signal Tree Publications, 1998.

Cuneo, John. *Robert Rogers of the Rangers*. New York: Richardson and Steinman, 1959.

Deloria, Philip J. *Playing Indian*. New Haven: Yale University Press, 1998.

Deloria, Vine, Jr. *We Talk, You Listen: New Tribes, New Turf*. New York: Dell, 1970.

Densmore, Frances. *Cheyenne and Arapahoe Music*. Los Angeles: Southwest Museum, 1936.

———. *Menominee Music*. Washington DC: Smithsonian, 1932.

———. "The Songs of American Indians during the War." *Musical Quarterly* 10, no. 4 (1934).

Department of the Interior, Office of Indian Affairs. *The American Indian in the World War*. Bulletin 15. 1927.

Dewing, Rolland, ed. *The FBI Files on the American Indian Movement and Wounded Knee II*. Frederick MD: University Publications of America, 1986.

———. "South Dakota Newspaper Coverage of Wounded Knee II." *South Dakota Journal* 12, no. 1 (1973).

———. *Wounded Knee: The Meaning and Significance of the Second Incident*. New York: Irvington Publishers, 1985.

Dixon, Joseph. *Chief Strong Wolf: First American Indian in the War*. Philadelphia: n.p., 1923.

———. "North American Indian Cavalry: An Argument before the Committee on Military Affairs of the House of Representatives of the 65th Congress on June 25, 1917." Washington DC: GPO, 1918.

Donnelly, William. *Under Army Orders: U.S. National Guard during the Korean War*. Columbus: Ohio State University, 1998.

Du Hart, Evelyn. *Yaqui Resistance and Survival: The Struggle for Land and Autonomy, 1821–1910*. Madison: University of Wisconsin Press, 1984.

Dumond, Don. *The Machete and the Cross: Campesino Rebellion in Yucatan*. Lincoln: University of Nebraska Press, 1997.

Eller, Cynthia. *Conscientious Objectors and the Second World War: Moral and Religious Arguments in Support of Pacifism*. New York: Praeger, 1991.

Erdich, Louise. *Love Medicine*. New York: Holt, Rinehart, and Winston, 1984.

Executive Committee. "Annual Circular of the Montezuma Society." Richmond: Virginia Historical Society, 1855.

Farwell, Byron. *Over There: The United States in the Great War, 1917–1918*. New York: W. W. Norton, 1999.

Fenton, William. *Songs of the Iroquois*. Washington DC: Smithsonian, 1942.

Fixico, Don. *Termination and Relocation: Federal Indian Policy, 1945–60*. Albuquerque: University of New Mexico Press, 1986.

Flint Institute of Art. *The American Indians and the American Flag*. Flint MI: Flint Institute of Art, 1975.

Foley, Thomas. *Father Francis M. Craft, Missionary to the Sioux*. Lincoln: University of Nebraska Press, 2002.

Franco, Jere. "Bringing Them in Alive: Selective Service and Native Americans." *Journal of Ethnic Studies* 18, no. 3 (1990).

———. *Crossing the Pond: The Native American Effort in World War II*. Denton: University of North Texas Press, 1999.

———. "Publicity, Persuasion, and Propaganda: Stereotyping the Native American in World War II." *Military History of the Southwest* 22, no. 2 (1992).

Franks, Kenny. *Citizen Soldiers: Oklahoma's National Guard*. Norman: University of Oklahoma Press, 1988.

Galloway, Colin. *The American Revolution in Indian Country*. Cambridge: Cambridge University Press, 1995.

Gossett, Thomas. *Race*. Dallas: Southern Methodist University Press, 1970.

Gouveia, Grace. *Uncle Sam's Priceless Daughters: American Indian Women during the Great Depression, World War II, and the Post-War Era*. West Lafayette IN: Purdue University, 1994.

Graymont, Barbara, ed. *Fighting Tuscarora: The Autobiography of Chief Clinton Rickard*. Syracuse: Syracuse University Press, 1973.

Hagan, William. *Theodore Roosevelt and Six Friends of the Indian*. Norman: University of Oklahoma Press, 1997.

Hale, Frederick. "Going on the Great White Father's Warpath: Reaction to World War One on the White Earth Reservation." *European Review of Native American Studies* 111, no. 1 (1997).

Hall, Linda. *Álvaro Obregón: Power and Revolution in Mexico, 1911–1920*. College Station: Texas A&M University Press, 1981.

Hart, Mickey. *American Warrior Songs for Indian Veterans*. Gloucester MA: Rykodisc, 1997.

Hatfield, Shelly. "Indians on the U.S.-Mexico Border during the Porfiriato." PhD thesis, University of New Mexico, 1983.

Hauptman, Laurence. *Between Two Fires: American Indians in the Civil War*. New York: Free Press, 1995.

———. *The Iroquois in the Civil War*. Syracuse: Syracuse University Press, 1993.

———. *The Iroquois Struggle for Survival*. Syracuse: Syracuse University Press, 1985.

Haycock, Ronald. *The Image of the Indian: The Canadian Indians as a Subject and Concept in a Sampling of the Popular National Magazines Read in Canada, 1900–70*. Waterloo, Ontario: Waterloo Lutheran University, 1972.

Heard Museum. "Stars and Stripes in Native American Art." Fall 2002.

Heartbeat: Voices of First Nations Women. Washington DC: Smithsonian Folkways Recordings, 1995.

Hemingway, Albert. *Ira Hayes: Pima Marine*. New York: University Press of America, 1988.

Heth, Charlotte, ed. *Native American Dance: Ceremonies and Social Tradition*. Washington DC: National Museum of the American Indian, Smithsonian/ Starwood Publishing, 1992.

Holm, Tom. "Forgotten Warriors: American Indian Servicemen in Vietnam." *Vietnam Generation* 1, no. 2 (1989).

———. *Strong Hearts, Wounded Souls: Native American Veterans of the Vietnam War*. Austin: University of Texas Press, 1996.

Honor the Earth Powwow. Salem MA: Rykodisc, 1995.

Howard, James, and Victoria Lindsay Levine. *Choctaw Music and Dance*. Norman: University of Oklahoma Press, 1990.

———. "The Dakota Indian Victory Dance." *North Dakota History* 18 (January 1951).

Hoxie, Frederick. *A Final Promise*. New York: Cambridge University Press, 1984.

Hurwitz, Peena, and Craig Simpson. *Against the Tide*. New York: War Resisters League, 1984.

Hutchinson, Dave. *Remembrances: Metis Veterans*. Regina: Gabriel Dumont Institute, 1994.

Johnson, Broderick. *Navajos and World War II*. Tsaile AZ: Navajo Community College, 1977.

Joseph, Gilbert, and Allen Wells. *Summer of Discontent, Seasons of Upheaval: Elite Politics and Rural Insurgency in Yucatán, 1876–1915*. Stanford: Stanford University Press, 1996.

Josephy, Alvin. *Now That the Buffalo's Gone: A Study of Today's Americna Indians* . New York: Alfred Knopf, 1982.

Kelen, Leslie, and Eileen Hallet Stone. *Missing Stories: An Oral History of Ethnic and Minority Groups in Utah*. Cambridge: Cambridge University Press, 2002.

Kiczu, John, ed. *The Indian in Latin American History*. Wilmington DE: Scholarly Resources, 2000.

King, Richard, and Charles Springwood. *Team Spirits: The Native American Mascots Controversy*. Lincoln: University of Nebraska Press, 2001.

Kipp, Woody. "The Eagles I Fed Who Did Not Love Me." *American Indian Culture and Research Journal* 18, no. 4 (1994).

Kitson, Frank. *Low Intensity Conflict*. North Haven CT: Archon Books, 1971.

Kluckhorn, Clyde. *Navajo Witchcraft*. Boston: Beacon Press, 1944.

Knight, Alan. "Peculiarities of Mexican History." *Journal of Latin American Studies* 24, special edition (1992).

Knox, Donald. *The Korean War, Pusan to Chosin: An Oral History*. New York: Harcourt, Brace, and Jovanovich, 1985.

Kohn, Rita, and W. Lynwood Montell, eds. *Always a People: Oral Histories of Contemporary Woodland Indians*. Bloomington: Indiana University Press, 1997.

Kolhoff, Dean. *When the Wind Was a River: Aleut Evacuation in World War II*. Seattle: University of Washington Press, 1995.

Lakota Thunder. *Veterans Songs*. Bismarck ND: Makoche Records, 1999.

Lanning, Michael. *Inside the LRRPS*. New York: Ivy Books, 1988.

Lassiter, Luke. *The Power of Kiowa Song*. Tucson: University of Arizona Press, 1998.

Lenton, H. T. *British & Empire Warships of the Second World War*. Annapolis: Naval Institute Press, 1998.

Lindemann, Frank. *American: The Life Story of Great Indian*. New York: John Day, 1930.

Locke, Major John. *To Fight with Intrepidity: The Complete History of the U.S. Army Rangers*. New York: Pocket Books, 1998.

Loewen, James. *Lies My Teacher Told Me: Everything Your American History Textbook Got Wrong*. New York: Touchstone, 1996.

Lott, Arnold, et al. *Almanac of Naval Facts*. Annapolis: Naval Institute Press, 1964.

Lyman, Stanley. *Wounded Knee 1973: A Personal Account*. Lincoln: University of Nebraska Press, 1991.

Magedanz, Thomas. *South Dakotans in Vietnam: Excerpts from the South Dakota Vietnam Veterans Oral History Project, Pierre Area*. Pierre SD: Vietnam Era Veterans Association, Robinson Museum, 1986.

Margon, Arthur. "Indians and Immigrants: A Comparison of Groups New to the City." *Journal of Ethnic Studies* 4, no. 4 (1976).

Martin, Charles. "A Good One Is a Dead One: The Combat Soldier's View of Vietnam and the Indian Wars." *Kentucky Folklore Record* 26, no. 3–4 (1980).

Matthiesen, Peter. *In the Spirit of Crazy Horse*. New York: Penguin Books, 1992.

Mayer, Carter, and Diana Royer. *Selling the Indian: Commercializing and Appropriating American Indian Cultures*. Tucson: University of Arizona Press, 2001.

McCarthy, James. *A Papago Traveler: The Memories of James McCarthy*. Tucson: University of Arizona Press, 1985.

McDonald, Peter. *The Last Warrior*. New York: Orion, 1993.

McLoughlin, William. *After the Trail of Tears: The Cherokees' Struggle for Sovereignty, 1839–1880*. Chapel Hill: University of North Carolina Press, 1993.

Meadows, William. *Kiowa, Apache, and Comanche Military Societies: Enduring Veterans, 1800 to the Present*. Austin: University of Texas Press, 1999.

Merrell, James. *Into the American Woods: Negotiators on the Pennsylvania Frontier*. New York: W. W. Norton, 1999.

Mirabal, Robert. *Taos Tales*. Boulder: Silverwave Records, 1999.

Momaday, N. Scott. *House Made of Dawn*. New York: Harper Collins, 1968.

Nash, Gary. *Red, White, and Black: The Peoples of Early America*. New York: Prentice Hall, 1974.

Nash, Gerald. *The American West Transformed*. Bloomington: Indiana University Press, 1985.

Neillands, Robin. *In the Combat Zone: Special Forces since 1945*. New York: New York University Press, 1998.

New Grove Dictionary of American Music. 4 vols. London: Macmillan, 1986.

Nietschmann, Bernard. *The Unknown War*. New York: Rowman and Littlefield, 1989.

Ninh, Bao. *The Sorrows of War*. New York: Riverhead Books, 1991.

North American Iroquois Veterans Association. "7th Annual Powwow." Salamanca NY: North American Iroquois Veterans Association, 1999.

Norton, Andre. *Hosteen Storm: The Beastmaster*. New York: Ace Books, 1959.

———. *Lord of Thunder*. New York: Ace Books, 1962.

———. *The Sioux Spaceman*. New York: Ace Books, 1960.

Owens, Louis. *The Sharpest Sight*. Norman: University of Oklahoma Press, 1995.

Painter, Muriel. *With Good Heart: Yaqui Beliefs and Ceremonies in Pascua*. Tucson: University of Arizona Press, 1986.

Palmer, Laura. *Shrapnel in the Heart: Letters and Remembrances from the Vietnam War Memorial*. New York: Random House, 1987.

Parezo, Nancy, and Thomas Sheridan, eds. *Paths of Life: American Indians of the Southwest and Northern Mexico.* Tucson: University of Arizona Press, 1996.

Parker, Arthur C. *The Life of General Ely S. Parker, Last Grand Sachem and Grant's Military Secretary.* Buffalo: Buffalo Historical Society, 1919.

Parkman, Francis. *Montcalm and Wolfe.* 2 vols. New York: Little, Brown, 1937.

Parman, Donald L. *Indians and the American West in the Twentieth Century.* Bloomington: Indiana University Press, 1994.

Philp, Kenneth, ed. *Indian Self-Rule: First-Hand Accounts of Indian-White Relations from Roosevelt to Reagan.* Logan: Utah State University Press, 1986.

Piper, William Jr. *The Story of Piper Aircraft.* New York: Newcomen Society, 1970.

Prucha, Francis Paul. *The Great Father: American Indians and the United States Government.* Lincoln: University of Nebraska Press, 1985.

Purnell, Jennie. *Popular Movements and State Formation in Revolutionary Mexico: The Agraristas and Cristeros of Michoacán.* Durham: Duke University Press, 1999.

Radding, Cynthia. *Wandering Peoples: Colonialism, Ethnic Spaces, and Ecological Frontiers in Northwestern Mexico, 1700–1850.* Durham: Duke University Press, 1997.

Red Eagle, Phillip. *Red Earth: Two Novellas.* Duluth: Holy Cow Press, 1997.

Research Directorate. "Semiannual Race/Ethnic/Gender Profile of the Department of Defense Forces." Patrick AFB, FL: Defense Equal Opportunity Management Institute, 1999.

Richmond, Charles. "Religious Contributions of the Thunderbirds in the Korean War." 45th Infantry Division Museum, Oklahoma City.

Riding In, James. "Six Pawnee Crania." *American Indian Culture and Research Journal* 16, no. 2 (1992).

Roberts, Craig, and Roger Sasser. *One Shot, One Kill.* New York: Pocket Books, 1990.

Roberts, Kenneth. *Northwest Passage.* New York: Doubleday, 1936.

Robertson, Robbie. *Robbie Robertson.* New York: Medicine Hat Records, 1987.

Rogers, Roberts. *A Concise Account of North America.* Chicago: Newberry Library, 1869.

———. *Journals of Major Robert Rogers.* New York: Corinth Books, 1961.

———. *Journals of the Siege of Detroit.* Chicago: Newberry Library, 1840.

Ross, John. *Rebellion from the Roots: Indian Uprising in Chiapas.* Monroe ME: Common Courage Press, 1995.

Rossignoli, Guido. *Army Badges since 1945.* London: Blandford Press, 1973.

Russell, Steve. "Dead Indians." In *They Call Us Indians*, edited by Annika Banfeld. Goteborg: New World Foundation, 2004.

Scheina, Robert. *Latin America: A Naval History, 1810–1987.* Annapolis: Naval Institute Press, 1987.

Shaheen, Jack. *Reel Bad Arabs: How Hollywood Vilifies a People.* New York: Olive Branch Press, 2001.

Sherow, James. "Fort Riley's Interaction with Native Americans: 1853 through 1911 and 1911 through World War II." Fort Detrick MD: U.S. Army Medical Research and Materiel Command, 1999.

Silko, Leslie. *Ceremony.* New York: Viking Penguin, 1977.

Slotkin, Richard. "Dreams and Genocide: The American Myth of Regeneration through Violence." *Journal of Popular Culture* 5, no. 1 (1971).

Smith, F. D. *Pawnee Music.* Washington DC: GPO, 1929.

Smith, Ralph Adam. *Borderlander: The Life of James Kirker, 1793–1852.* Norman: University of Oklahoma Press, 1999.

Spenser, Jay. *Whirlybirds: A History of the U.S. Helicopter Pioneers.* Seattle: University of Washington Press, 1998.

Spicer, Edward. *Cycles of Conquest: The Impact of Spain, Mexico, and the United States on the Indians of the Southwest, 1533–1960.* Tucson: University of Arizona Press, 1962.

———. *People of Pascua.* Tucson: University of Arizona Press, 1988.

———. *The Yaquis: A Cultural History.* Tucson: University of Arizona Press, 1980.

Stanton, Shelby. *Green Berets at War: U.S. Army Special Forces in SE Asia, 1956–75.* Novato CA: Presidio Publishing, 1985.

Stedman, Raymond. *Shadows of the Indian: Stereotypes in American Culture.* Norman: University of Oklahoma Press, 1982.

Steele, Ian. *Warpaths: Invasions of North America.* Oxford: Oxford University Press, 1994.

Stone, Eileen. *Missing Stories.* Cambridge: Cambridge University Press, 2002.

St. Pierre, Mark. *Of Uncommon Birth: Dakota Sons in Vietnam.* Norman: University of Oklahoma Press, 2004.

Swanborough, Gordon. *U.S. Military Aircraft since 1908.* London: Putnam Books, 1971.

Taylor, William. *Drinking, Homicide, and Rebellion.* Stanford: Stanford University Press, 1999.

Thompson, Guy. *Patriotism, Politics, and Popular Liberalism in Nineteenth-Century Mexico: Juan Francisco Lucas and the Puebla Sierra.* Wilmington DE: Scholarly Resources, 1999.

Trafzer, Clifford. *As Long as the Grass Shall Grow and Rivers Flow: A History of Native Americans.* New York: Harcourt Brace, 2000.

Tsinajinnie, Delphine. *Mother's Word.* Phoenix: Canyon Records, 2001.

United Auto Workers Fair Practices and Anti-Discrimination Department. "The Indian Who Never Got Home." Detroit: Solidarity House, 1952.

Vogt, Evon. *Navajo Veterans*. Cambridge MA: Peabody Museum, Harvard University, 1951.

White, Richard. *The Middle Ground*. New York: Cambridge University Press, 1991.

Wilson, Arthur. *Korean Vignettes: Faces of War: 201 Veterans of the Korean War Recall That Forgotten War: Their Experiences and Thoughts and Wartime Photographs of That Era*. Portland OR: Artwork Publications, 1996.

Winnebago Tribal Songs. Taos NM: American Indian Soundchiefs, 1993.

Wise, Jennings. *The Red Man in the New World Drama*. New York: Macmillan, 1971.

Wong, Hertha Dawn. *Love Medicine: A Casebook*. Oxford: Oxford University Press, 1999.

Zimmerman, Bill. *Airlift to Wounded Knee*. New York: Swallow Press, 1976.

Zissu, Erik. "Conscription, Sovereignty, and Land: American Indian Resistance during World War I." *Pacific Historical Review* 64, no. 4 (1995).

Index

Abenaki Indians, 40–42
Adams, Larry, 202
Afghanistan, 175, 196–98, 221, 262n32
African Americans, 99–100
Agents of Repression, 166
Ak-Chin, 118
Akers, Donna, 208–9, 224
Alaska National Guard, 119
Albright, Madeline, 188
alcohol use, 120, 131
Alexie, Sherman, 21, 201
Alliance West, 158
Al Marayat, Salam, 200
Al Qaeda, 180, 184, 196
American Gulf War Veterans Association, 178
American Indian Council of Governments, 221
American Indian Graduate Students Association, 179
American Indian Movement (AIM), 2–3, 142–43, 152, 223, 251n3, 254n29; Ward Churchill and, 190–91; as a warrior society, 170–71; Wounded Knee II and, 166–70
American Indians and World War II (Bernstein), 7
American Indian Studies (AIS), 9–10
American Indian Veterans Association, 143
American Indian Veterans Memorial Organization, 176

American Legion (magazine), 133
American Legion (veterans group), 11, 106, 175
American Renaissance, 195
Amherst, Jeffrey, 40, 41
Anderson, Barbara, 177
Anderson, Kathy, 204
Andrews AFB, 71
Angie, Tracey, 186
Anglo-Americans: adoption of, by Native Americans, 44–45; and assimilation of Native Americans, 96–97, 238n4; attacks on Native Americans by, 40–42, 56; Manifest Destiny and, 66, 96–100; Mexican-American War and, 77–78; and need for Native American soldiers, 9–10; patriotic songs of, 12; view of, of Native Americans during colonial times, 39–42, 89; views of, of Native Americans in military, 101–6; and War Mother Societies, 129–30
Anquoe, Jack, 158
Anthony, Mary, 210
anthrax, 185–86
Apache Indians, 28, 55, 56, 57, 80, 197; ceremonies of, 142, 157; personal medicine of, 111, 122
The Apache Kid, 27
Apess, William, 91
Aquash, Anna Mae, 172, 211
Arabs, movie portrayals of, 199–200

Argentina, 83
Arizona Republic, 203, 214
Arlington National Cemetery, 138–39, 173
Army and Navy Union, 100
assimilation, 96–97, 102, 106, 112, 238n4
Attica Prison, 166
Attocknie, Joe, 151–52
Axtell, Horace, 122
Aztec Society, 77

Bad Hand, Howard, 4
Baker, Joe, 165
Banderas, Juan, 48, 54
Banfeld, Annika: *They Call Us Indians*, 254n29
Banks, Dennis, 142–43, 190, 192
Banyaca, Thomas, 117
Barse, Harold, 149
Battiest, Charles Ray, 155
Bean, Jerry, 186
The Beastmaster (Norton), 28–29
Beastmaster's Ark (Norton), 28–29
Begay, Sam, 156
Bell, Chriss, 99
Bellecourt, Claude, 143, 153, 190, 192
Bellecourt, Vernon, 190, 192
Beltran, Robert, 24, 35
Benavidez, Roy: *Medal of Honor*, 8
Benn, Carl, 87
Benson, Diane, 204–5
Benson, Latseen, 204–5
Bentzlin, Eric, 177
Bernstein, Alison, 6; *American Indians and World War II*, 7
Big Hole Massacre, 122
Billie, Jim, 67
Billy Jack, 22–24
Bin Laden, Osama, 180, 181
Birdwell, Dwight, 148, 149; *A Hundred Miles of Bad Road*, 8
Black, George, 108
Black, Joshua, 108
Blackbear, Ray, 111

Black Crow Lodge, 151–52
Blackening Way ceremony, 156
Blackfeather, Tony, 202–3
Blackfoot Indians, 197
Blackhawk, Andrew, 107
Black Lodge Singers, 1, 158–59
bloodletting, 109
Blue Coat, Barbara, 206
Boone, Daniel, 45
Boone, Pat, 21
Boot, Max, 198
Boudinot, E. C., 95
Boutwell, Leon, 67
Bowers, Stephen, 156
Bowlby, K. C., 104–5
Bow Leaders Society, 48–49, 53–54, 55
Bowley, Freeman, 96
Brazil, 83
Breuners, 221
Brito, Frank, 98
Brito, Joseph, 98
Britten, Thomas, 6, 9
Bronson, Charles, 30
Brown, Jacob, 91
Brown, Jim, 30
Brown, John, 198
Brown, Thomas, 192–93
Brumwell, Stephen, 42, 46
Brushel, Sam, 177
Buffalo Medicine Society, 145
Bureau of Indian Affairs (BIA), 116, 136
Burns, Michael, 74
Bush, George H. W., 176, 177
Bush, George W., 179–81, 185, 201–2, 216, 254n31
Bustancy, Don, 200
Butcher, 27
Butler, Marion, 138

Cajeme. *See* Leyva, José Maria
Camp, Carter, 166–68
Campbell, George, 46
Camurat, Diane, 6, 8
Canada, 73, 74, 75–76, 111, 118, 224, 228; draft resistance in, 104–5, 106;

lack of Termination effort in, 137; Red Power movement in, 154, 171; and Vietnam War, 150–51; warrior societies in, 107, 153

cannibalism, 46

Cannon Films, 200

Carimon, Jim, 107

Carlson, Patrick, 198

Carlson, William, 197–98

Carranza, Venustiano, 58

Cassavetes, John, 30

Catholicism, 48–50, 51–52

Cavco, 221

Center for Military Readiness, 216

ceremonies and personal medicine: and Korean War, 140; and Second Iraq War, 205–6; and Vietnam War, 154–58; and World War I, 109–11; and World War II, 118–22

Ceremony (Silko), 32, 62

Chakotay. See *Star Trek: Voyager*

Chalepah, Alfred, 142

Chaletson, Rose Chalepah, 142

Charis, Heliodoro, 58

Chavers, Dean, 202

Cherokee Indians, 4, 8, 22, 27, 52, 148, 224; ceremonies of, 156; and Civil War, 95

Cheyenne Indians, 110, 156–57, 177, 180, 183, 186, 205

Chief, Carmenlita, 211–12

Chief Plenty Coups (Crow), 102

Chile, 82–83

Chiles, Lawton, 145

Chilocco Indian School, 66

Chippewa Indians, 33, 121–22, 177

Chips, Ellis, 145

Choctaw Indians, 32–33, 208–9, 224

Christian Broadcasting Network, 200

Chumash Indians, 32–33

Churchill, Ward, 10, 180, 183, 235n7, 254n29, 255n36, 255n39; American Indian Movement and, 190–91; analysis of September 11, 2001, by, 187–89; and claim of Native American

identity, 191–92; critics of, 192–93; media attention on, 189, 195–96; *On the Justice of Roosting Chickens*, 187; supporters of, 189–90

Citizens for Personal Responsibility, 185

Civil War, U.S., 88, 92–96

Clark, James, 75

Clark, Jerome, 211–12, 214

Clark, Joseph, 146

Cleveland Indians (baseball team), 66–67

Clinton, Bill, 188

Clinton, Dewitt, 209

Code Talkers, Navajo, 20–21, 22, 113, 114–15, 120, 131–33, 211

Cohen, Fay, 255n39

Collier, John, 116, 119, 125, 136

colonialism, 9–10, 38–42, 224–25

Colville Reservation, 184

Comanche Indians, 53, 57, 182–83; David Yeagley and, 193–95; and War Mothers, 130; warrior societies of, 142, 151

Comanche Little Ponies, 151

comic books, 26–28

Common Dreams, 201

Communism, 163, 169

A Concise Account of North America (Rogers), 39–40

Congregation of American Sisters, 98, 209, 210

Congressional Committee on Military Affairs, 101

Cooper, Margaret, 177

Cortez, Miguel, 204

Coulter, Ann, 192

counterinsurgency (COIN), 164–70

Couric, Katie, 212

Cowan, Bill, 200

Coyote Society, 54

Craft, Francis, 209–10

Creek Indians, 103

Crockett, Davy, 45

Crossing the Pond (Franco), 8

Crow Creek Reservation, 147, 184

Crow Dog, Leonard, 168

Crow Indians, 102, 225
Cummings, Delano: *Moon Dash Warrior*, 8
Cuneo, John, 45–46
Curtis, Tony, 18, 131
Cusick, Nicholas, 92

dances. *See specific types of dances*
Dances with Wolves, 21
Dasheno, Walter, 177
Dawes Act, 96–97, 255n39, 256n42
Dean, Howard, 254n31
de Cabora, Santa Teresa, 55
DeCora, Lorelie, 167
de Lahontan, Louis: *Voyage*, 88
Delaware Indians, 94
Delkittie, Draven, 119
Deloria, Phillip, 66
Deloria, Vine, Jr., 139, 180, 227
Dempsey, James, 107
Densmore, Frances, 127
Diaz, Porfirio, 52
Dineh, Chuck, 70
The Dirty Dozen, 29–30
Disney, Walt, 69–70, 79
Dixon, Joseph, 33, 101–2, 112
Dokes, Jennifer, 214
Dominican Republic, 83, 175
Doniphan, Alexander, 56
Donnelly, Elaine, 216
Dowd, Gregory: *A Spirited Resistance*, 52
Doyeto, Martha, 124
draft, resistance to, 101–4, 117, 150
Draper, Teddy, 131
Draper, Tony, 18
Du Bois, W. E. B., 139
Ducheneaux, Wayne, 177
Duncan, Ray, 17, 111
Dunlay, Thomas: *Wolves for the Blue Soldiers*, 89
Dupris, Gerald, 204

Eastwood, Lucas, 197
Eddy, John, 112
Eisenhower, Dwight, 117

Empty Saddle ceremony, 141–42
Erdich, Louise, 227; *Love Medicine*, 32
Evans, David, 46
Extreme Makeover: Home Edition, 221
Eyre, Chris, 31

Falleaf, Captain, 94
Faltyn, Tim, 257n45
Falzone, Lori, 184
Fancy Dance, 106
Farmer, Gary, 31
Finch, Frederick, 71
Finnicum, Brenda, 210
Firestarter (King), 27
First Iraq War. *See* Gulf War
Fisher, Langburn, 156–57
Fiske, Emmett, 92
Fitzsimmons Army Medical Center, 16
Five Civilized Tribes, 59, 103
Fixon, Jess, 105
flags, 3–5
Flathead Indians, 178
Fool Bull, Richard, 110
Fools Crow, Frank, 110
Forbes, Jack, 180
Fox Network, 189, 200
Franciscus, James, 18
Franco, Jere, 133–34; *Crossing the Pond*, 8
Frank, Richard, 118
Franks, Trent, 208, 216
Freire, Paolo, 9
Fritz, Dennis, 71
Fulcher, John, 120

Galloway, Colin, 41–42
Gardner, Darrel, 146
Garneau, Daniel, 122
Gary, Joseph, 146
Gauthier, Joseph, 94
gays, 260n2
George, Samuel, 93
Geronimo (Apache), 80, 90
Ghost Dance, 145
Gibson, Simeon, 108

Gillette, Guy, 138
Gillette, Jodi, 180
Glyn, R., 111
Gossett, Louis, 200
Grand Army of the Republic, 93–96
Grand Coulee Dam, 184
Granger, Erastus, 90
Grant, Ulysses S., 89, 92
Graveret, Garrett, 96
Gray, Mike, 203
The Green Berets, 161
Green Corn Rebellion, 103
Greene, Graham, 31
Grinnell, George Bird, 98
Gros Ventre Indians, 5
Gruening, Ernest, 119
Guardians of the Oglala Nation (GOON), 166
Guatemala, 60, 223
Guenther, A. A., 197
Guevara, Che, 164–65
Gulf War, 176–79
Gumbs, Harriet, 179
Guthrie, John, 186

Haida Indians, 74
Haig, Alexander, 164
Hale, Albert, 221
Hall, Tex, 202
Hamilton University, 189
Hanson, Phil, 221
Harjo, Suzan Shown, 180, 183, 195, 253n20
Hastings, Hugh, 92
Hauptman, Laurence, 92
Hauq, Monique, 184
Hawk Eagle, Sheldon Ray, 205–6
Hayes, Ira, 18–19, 115, 121, 130–32, 212, 227
Heaton, Bruce, 157
Henderson, James, 103
Henderson, James, Jr., 177
Hethuska. *See* Ohomah Lodge
Hickey, Huhanna, 236n7
Hicks, D. L. "Pappy," 139, 160, 161

Hillerman, Tony, 27
Ho Chunk Indians, 62–63, 86–87, 107, 127–28, 138, 145
Hoffman, George, 160
Holcomb, Manuel, 114–15
Holder, Stan, 166–68
Holliday, Robert, 203
Holm, Tom, 154, 171, 225–26, 228; *Strong Hearts, Wounded Souls*, 6–7
Homeland Security Act, 184–85
Hope, Bob, 146
Hopi Indians, 53, 102, 117, 210
Horowitz, David, 182, 194, 196
Horse Capture, George, 5
House Made of Dawn (Momaday), 32
Huey Newton, 62
Huffer, John, 194, 256n44
Hughes, Cinda, 193–95
Hulligan, Rose, 203
A Hundred Miles of Bad Road (Birdwell), 8
Hussein, Saddam, 176, 188, 201, 205, 208

Imperial Grunts (Kaplan), 198
Independent Oglala Nation (ION), 166, 168–69
Indian Scouts, 89–92
Inouye, Daniel, 184
Intertribal Veterans, 158
Iraq War. *See* Gulf War; Second Iraq War
Iron Eagle, 200
Iroquois Indians, 52, 73, 83, 86; and Civil War, 92–96; draft resistance by, 104–5; flag songs of, 108; and War of 1812, 90–92; warrior societies of, 153
Isbell, Thomas, 98
Iwo Jima, 18–19, 115, 121, 130–32

Jackson, Andrew, 4
Jackson, Efiza, 183
Jacob, Don, 215
Jesuit organizations, 53–54
Johnson, Broderick, 120–21
Johnson, Christine, 205

Johnson, Frank, 94
Johnston, Phillip, 132
Jones, William, 94
Jorgenson, Krg, 99
Justice League of America, 26–27

Kahranah, Bernard, 151
Kaibiles, 60
Kaplan, Robert: *Imperial Grunts*, 198
Kassanovoid, Forrest, 151
Keams, Paul, 156
Kent State, 166
Kerchee, Melvin, 151
Kerry, John, 254n31
Ketari, Catherine, 210
Kickapoo Indians, 57
King, Frank, III, 179–80
King, Jimmy, 126
King, Martin Luther, Jr., 23–24
King, Stephen: *Firestarter*, 27
*Kiowa, Apache, and Comanche Military
    Societies* (Meadows), 8
Kiowa Black Leggings Society, 140,
    141–42, 143–44
Kiowa Gourd Clan, 106, 140–41, 151
Kiowa Indians, 8, 106; and War Mothers,
    129–30; warrior societies of, 140–42;
    war songs of, 123, 143–44
Kirker, James, 55–56
Kirkwood, Robert, 46
Kit Carson Scouts, 161–62, 200
Kitcheyan, Charles, 197
Kitson, Frank, 164–65
Knight, Alan, 51–52
Korean War, 53, 75, 106, 247n2; and
    ceremonies and personal medicine,
    140; flag and war songs and, 143–45;
    Native Americans' response to,
    137–40; Navajo Code Talkers in, 132;
    Red Power movement and, 135–36;
    and War Mothers, 130; and warrior
    societies, 140–43
Krug, Julius, 138
Kurds, 176
Kwakiutl Indians, 74

La Deuda Interna, 20
Lafayette Escadrille, 78–79
Laflesche, Joseph, 96
Lakota Indians, 4, 34, 104, 182, 197,
    209; ceremonies of, 109–110, 157–58;
    flag songs of, 107, 125–26; warrior
    societies of, 152; war songs of, 144
Lalonde, Donald, 135, 140
Lalonde, Harold, 135
Lamour, Louis, 28–29, 35; *Last of the
    Breed*, 28
Lance Society, 108
Larson, John, 224
Lassiter, Louis, 123
Last of the Breed (Lamour), 28
The Last Warrior (McDonald), 8
Latin America, 19–20, 82–84
Laughlin, Tom, 23, 35
League of Indigenous Sovereign Nations,
    70
League of Nations, 105
Leanna, Ray, 147–48
Lee, Spike, 21, 62
Leslie, Delfred, 210
Leyva, José Maria, 58–59
Liguori, Mary, 210
Lincoln, Abraham, 93
Lindemann, Frank, 102
Lindsay, Barbara, 194
Little Big Man, 20
Lobe, Jim, 201
Long, Larry, 186
Looking Horse, Arvol, 201
Lord of Thunder (Norton), 28–29
The Losers, 27
Lovato, Ernie Dogwolf, 157
Love Medicine (Erdich), 32
Low Intensity Conflict (Kitson), 164
low-intensity conflict (LIC), 164–70
Lowry, Henry Berry, 96
Lozen (Apache), 208
Lumbee Indians, 95–96
Lummi Indians, 184
Luwak, John, 108
Lynch, Jessica, 207, 212
Lyons, Oren, 185

MacArthur, Douglas, 126
Maccuddam, Pi, 117
Mackris, Andrea, 189
Manifest Destiny, 66, 96–100, 183
Manitoba Warrior Society, 153
Mann, Henrietta, 180
Maoris, 236n7
Marquin, Mateo, 58
martial races, 75–76
Martinez, A, 31
Martinez, Tony, 177
Marvin, Lee, 30
Masonic lodges, 100
Mattaponi Indians, 102–3
Mauldin, Bill, 121
May, Karl, 112
Mayan Indians, 57, 239n26
Mayo Indians, 53, 54–55
McCarthy, James, 104; *Papago Traveler*, 8
McCarthy, Joe, 196
McDonald, Peter, 120; *The Last Warrior*, 8
McLaughlin, Charles, 140
McNair Program, 224
Meadows, William, 123; *Kiowa, Apache, and Comanche Military Societies*, 8
Means, Bill, 143
Means, Russell, 180, 190
Medal of Honor (Benavidez), 8
medicine, personal. *See* ceremonies and personal medicine
Menominee Indians, 94
Merino, José, 56
mestizos, 50–51
Métis, 118
Mexican-American War, 77–78
Mexico, 13–14, 61, 223; indigenous names and symbols used in, 82; integration of Native groups in, 51–52; Mexican-American War and, 77–78; military service of Natives in, 48–50; revolution in, 57–58; states of, 55–60; use of Quirquismo by, 55
Meyers, Richie, 179

Micmaq Indians, 5
Miguel, Jasper, 214
Minnesota Peace Drum, 176
Mirabal, Robert, 123
Mohawk, John, 176, 190
Mohawk Indians, 159–60, 181
Mohawk Warrior Society, 53, 152–53, 173
Momaday, N. Scott, 13, 192, 227; *House Made of Dawn*, 32
Monk, Paul Joseph, 182
Montcalm and Wolfe (Parkman), 42–43
Montini, E. J., 214
Moon Dash Warrior (Cummings), 8
Mooney, James, 95
Moore, John, 42
Mopope, Jeanette Berry, 124
Morgan, Lewis Henry, 88
Morgan, Taylet, 66
Morrison, Samuel Eliot, 146
Mungie, Steve, 197
Murray, Charles, 71–72
Murtha, John, 254n31

Napolitano, Janet, 214, 218
Nash, Gerald, 115
National American Indian Housing Council, 204
National Congress of American Indians, 139, 146, 202
National Council of Churches, 167
National Indian Council, 137
National Liberation Front, 147, 160, 170
Native American Church, 141
Native American Gulf War Veterans, 178
Native Americans: assimilation of, 96–97, 102, 106, 112, 238n4; attacks on, 40–42, 56; as authors, 31–35, 35–36; ceremonies and personal medicine of, 109–11, 118–22, 140, 154–58; and citizenship, 116–17; and Civil War, 92–96; in comic books, 26–28; and counterinsurgency, 164–70; criticism of, of post-Vietnam U.S. interventions, 174–76, 201–6; Dawes Act and,

Native Americans (*cont.*)
96–97, 255n39, 256n42; draft
resistance by, 101–4, 117, 150; effects
of World War II on, 115–18, 134,
247n2; in fiction, 28–29, 31–35; and
flags, 3–5, 12–13; gay, 260n2; and
Gulf War, 176–79; legal and identity
questions concerning, 50–52, 114–18;
military ships named after, 62–63,
75–77; movie portrayals of, 16–26,
29–31, 43–44, 89, 131, 160–61;
names and symbols of, use of, 82–84;
national anthems of, 4; "natural"
abilities of, 111–12; and New Age
themes, 22–26; New Deal and, 88,
247n2; as pacifists, 101–2; and Pat
Boone Reflex, 18–22; portrayals
of Native Americans by, 30–35,
35–36; portrayals of, inaccuracy of,
35–36; portrayals of, positive, 29–30;
reactions of, to September 11, 2001,
179–86; religious beliefs of, 48–50,
51–52, 59–60, 121; and reservation
governments, 136–37; and reservation
system, 136–37, 149; sacred songs of,
12–13, 107–9, 123–29, 142, 143–45;
scalping practices of, 119–20; as
scouts, 16–18, 88–92; sports mascots
and, 63–65; stereotypes of, 63–69, 84,
133–34; and Super Scout Syndrome,
16–18; television portrayals of, 26–27;
warrior societies of, 52–55, 106–7,
129–30, 140–43, 151–54, 170–71,
178, 238n14; women's societies of,
129–30, 142. *See also* servicemen and
veterans, Native American
Native American Times, 194, 198
Native Voice, 204
Navajo Indians, 102, 120–21, 174, 202;
as Code Talkers, 20–21, 22, 113,
114–15, 120, 131–33, 211; draft
resistance by, 117; and Gulf War, 178
Navajo Times, 204, 215
navy: of Canada, 75–76; of Great Britain,
75; of United States, 62–63, 75, 76–77,
84

Neal, Richard, 177
Nelson, Robert, 217–19, 222
New Confederacy of the Iroquois, 88–89
New Deal, 88, 247n2
Newman, Bob, 189, 254n31
New Times, 217–20
Nickerson, Herman, 161–62
Nixon, Richard, 142, 148, 164
Noriega, Manuel, 174
Norrell, Brenda, 202
Norris, Chuck, 200
North American Aerospace Command
(NORAD), 81–82
North American Iroquois Veterans
Association, 100, 154
Northrup, Jim, 178
Northwest Passage (Rogers), 43–44, 45
Norton, Andre: *The Beastmaster*, 28–29;
Beastmaster's Ark, 28–29; *Lord of
Thunder*, 28–29

Obregón, Álvaro, 58
O'Bryan, George, 79
Of Uncommon Birth (St. Pierre), 34–35
Oglala Indians, 166, 168–69
Ohomah Lodge, 106, 151
Ojibwe Indians, 96, 111, 128, 153, 176
Okinawa, Battle of, 114, 126
Oliver, William, 139
Omaha Indians, 110, 126
Oneida Indians, 93, 153
One Nation, 195
One Year in Nam (Tecube), 8
On the Justice of Roosting Chickens
(Churchill), 187
Oorang Indians (football team), 67
Opata Indians, 58
Operation Noble Eagle, 186
Order of the Purple Heart, 211
O'Reilly, Bill, 189, 196
The O'Reilly Factor, 189
Ottawa Indians, 96
The Outsider, 18–19
Owens, Louis, 13, 31; *The Sharpest Sight*,
31, 32–33

Owl, David, 103
Oyler, Jimmie, 196

pacifism, 101–2, 117
Padapony, Juanita, 193–94, 253n20
Palmer, Gus, 124
Palmer, Lyndreth, 124
Pamunkey Indians, 95, 102–3
Panadis, Theophile, 41
Pan-Indianism, 143, 146
Panipakuxwe. *See* Falleaf, Captain
Papago Traveler (McCarthy), 8
Parker, Ely, 92–93, 94
Parker, Newt, 92
Parkman, Francis, 38, 42–43, 45, 46;
    Montcalm and Wolfe, 42–43
Parman, Donald, 224
Partido Liberal Mexicano, 59
Pataki, George, 185
patriotism, 2–5
Paughty, Linn, 145
Pawnee Indians, 90, 92, 110
Pegahmagabow, Francis, 111
Peltier, Leonard, 172, 211, 223
Perez, Emma, 190
personal medicine. *See* ceremonies and
    personal medicine
Peru, 82
Peter Pan, 70, 79
Peterson, Arthur, 100
Pettit, E. M., 93
Pewewardy, Cornel, 158
Pewewardy, Samuel, 158
Philippines, 98–100, 118
Piestewa, Lori, 175, 186–87, 198; death
    of, 207–8, 215–22; efforts to rename
    Squaw Peak after, 214–15, 217,
    220–21; Robert Nelson and, 217–20,
    222; tributes to, 207–8, 211–15
Piestewa, Percy, 217
Piestewa, Terry, 216
Piestewa Peace Foundation, 214–15
Piestewa Peak, 214–15, 217, 220–21
Pima Indians, 53, 54, 58, 131
Pine Ridge Reservation, 165

Piper, William, 80
Piper, William, Jr., 80
Piper Airplanes, 80
Platt, William, 99
Pollock, William, 97
Ponca Heyoshas, 106, 152
Pope, John, 22–23
Porter, Robert, 4
Potter, Jack, 165
Powers, William, 4
Powwow Highway, 30–31
Pratt, Richard, 98
Pratt, William, 33, 88
Predator, 16, 32, 112
propaganda, 130–34, 145–46, 160–62
pseudo-Indian images, 68–69, 77–78
pulp fiction, 28–29, 32
Pyle, Ernie, 121

Quirquismo, 55
Quiver, Elaine, 197

Rabayda, Michelle, 177
Ramon, Ed Humming Eagle, 157–58
Ranchers' Association, 166
Rasmussen, Keith, 131
Rave, Jodi, 193, 222
Reader's Digest, 133
Red Cloud, Annita, 62–63
Red Cloud, Mitchell, Jr., 62–63, 75, 138
Red Eagle, Phillip, 227; *Red Earth*, 33
Red Earth (Red Eagle), 33
Red Power movement, 59, 135–36, 148,
    154, 170, 249n4. *See also* American
    Indian Movement (AIM)
Redstar, Victor, 202
Regina Warriors Society, 153
Relocation, 137, 148–49
Renzi, Rick, 216
reservation system, 136–37, 149
Reverse Dance, 142
Rice, John, 21, 138–39
Richmond, Charles, 122
Rickard, Clinton, 93, 100
Rico, Gabriela, 205

Rides the Bear, Emma, 209
Riding In, James, 90
Rimsza, Skip, 214
Rind, Bacon, 110
Rios, Roy, 214
Roberts, Kenneth, 38, 43, 45, 46
Robertson, Robbie, 159–60
Rockne, Knute, 64
Rodeo Queens, 211
Rogers, Robert, 13, 37–42; *A Concise Account of North America*, 39–40; as Indian hater, 42–46; myths surrounding, 45–46; *Northwest Passage*, 43–44, 45; use of *savage* by, 40
Roosevelt, Franklin, 116
Roosevelt, Theodore, 97, 99
Rosebud Reservation, 119, 168
Rosenzweig, Seth, 20–21
Rotiskenrakete. *See* Mohawk Warrior Society
Rough Riders, 97–98, 111
Roy, Gordon, 152, 156, 223
Royal Canadian Mounted Police, 137, 153
Royce, Elvine Obamsawin, 41
Rumsfeld, Donald, 201
Russell, Steve, 4, 156, 224, 227

Said, Edward, 9
Sampson, Will, 29
Samuels, Ron, 200
San Manuel Band, 221
Sault Ste. Marie Reservation, 135
Savalas, Telly, 30
Scalp dances, 110, 120, 141, 151
scalping, 119–20
Scarborough, Joe, 189
Schaefer, Pauline Escudero, 28
Schiavi, Brooke, 256n42
Schmidt, Rob, 27
Schwarzenegger, Arnold, 16, 112, 200
Scout, 27–28
Scout War Shaman, 27
Second Iraq War, 175, 198–206. *See also* Gulf War

Seminole Indians, 57, 67, 103, 117, 184, 202
Seneca Indians, 92–93
September 11, 2001, 173–74, 175; Native American reactions to, 179–86; Ward Churchill and, 186–96
servicemen and veterans, Native American, 37–38, 73, 84–85, 223–28; academic study of, 224–25; and Civil War, 92–96; colonialism and, 9–10; and conflicts with Native groups, 19–20, 224; flag and war songs and, 12–13, 107–9; and Gulf War, 177–78; and Korean War, 137–40; Native American views on, 2–5; "natural" abilities of, 17–18, 111–12; in Philippines, 98–100; sacred songs and, 12–13; scalping by, 119–20; as scouts, 88–92; and Second Iraq War, 204–6; and Spanish-American War, 96–100; and sports mascots, 65–72; and Vietnam War, 148–51; and War of 1812, 90–92; warrior traditions and, 11–15; white conceptions of, 1; and World War I, 86–88, 101–6; writings on, 5–11. *See also* Native Americans; U.S. military
Seven Years' War, 38
Shaffer, Mark, 203
Shaheen, Jack, 199–200
The Sharpest Sight (Owens), 31, 32–33
Shea Homes, 221
Sherow, James, 103–4
Shirley, Joe, Jr., 203–4
Shore, Kevin, 177–78
Silko, Leslie Marmon, 13, 227; *Ceremony*, 32, 62
Simon, Stephen, 5
Sioux National Anthem, 145
Six Nations, 104–5, 133, 185. *See also* Iroquois Indians
Skiki Band, 110
Skinner, Jim, 63
Skins, 31
Smith, F. D., 110

Smith, Hamilton, 72
The Soldier's Letter, 99
songs, 12–13; flag, 12–13; and Korean
    War, 142–45; sacred, 12–13; and
    Vietnam War, 158–60; war, 123–29,
    143–45; and World War I, 107–9; and
    World War II, 123–29; 107–9, 123–29,
    142, 143–45
Sorvo, Brownie, 151–52
Southwick, Albert, 99
Spanish-American War, 87–88, 96–100
A Spirited Resistance (Dowd), 52
sports mascots, 63–72
Spy Buck (Shawnee), 56
Squaw Peak. *See* Piestewa Peak
Stallone, Sylvester, 161
Standing Bear v. Crook, 96
Standing Rock Reservation, 107, 119
Starkey, James, 182
Starr, Frank, 157
Star Trek: Voyager, 13, 24–26, 32, 35
Stedman, Raymond, 68
Stern, Stewart, 19, 35
Still Day, Rene, 202
Stop Loss program, 204–5
Storm, Charles, 256n42
St. Pierre, Mark, 227; *Of Uncommon
    Birth*, 35
Strand, Paul, 200
Strong Hearts, Wounded Souls (Holm), 6
Sun Dance, 109
Suntz, Rita Ann, 194
The Super Friends, 26–27
Super Scout Syndrome, 16–18, 89
Swanson, Bea, 176

Taiaiake, Alfred, 181
Tarahumara Indians, 53, 54, 56
Tardieu, Jean, 78
Tayebo, Louis, 123–24
Taylor, Maxwell, 161
Tecube, Leroy: *One Year in Nam*, 8
Tehda Puku Nu. *See* Comanche Little
    Ponies
Telfer, George, 99

Termination, 136–37, 142, 146, 148–49,
    249n4
Terrell, John, 56
Teton Sioux Nation Treaty Council,
    202–3
Tetuwan Oyates. *See* Teton Sioux Nation
    Treaty Council
Thenault, George, 79
They Call Us Indians (Banfeld), 254n29
Thomas, William, 95
Thompson, Jim, 153
Thornton, Russell, 193
Thunderbird Warriors. *See* U.S. Army
    45th Division
Tibbles, Thomas, 96
Tilfer, George, 99
Tillman, Pat, 221–22, 262n32
Titla, Mary Kim, 207–8
Tlaxcalan Indians, 53, 238n13
Tohono O'odham Indians, 55, 104, 117,
    205, 214
The Tomahawk, 104
Tomassi, John, 81–82
Tonori, Refugio, 58
Townsend, Kenneth, 6; *World War II and
    the American Indian*, 7–8
Tracy, Spencer, 43
True Lies, 200
Truman, Harry, 138
Truman, Tim, 27–28
Truscott, Lucian, 45
Tsinajinnie, Delphine, 178
Tsoodle, Fred, 141
Tucker, Gilbert, 75
Tuh Wi. *See* Black Crow Lodge
Tull, John, 177
Tulley, Julius, 174, 204
Turner, Frederick Jackson, 72
Tuscarora Warrior Society, 153
Tuwahi-Smith, Linda, 192
Twilight Zone, 25
Tyon, Thomas, 126

Umatilla Indians, 197
United Auto Workers, 139

United Spanish War Veterans, 100
U.S. Air Force, 78–82, 135
U.S. Army 45th Division, 65, 73–74, 85
U.S. Army Rangers, 45, 78
U.S. Coast Guard, 76
U.S. military: in Afghanistan, 175, 196–98, 262n32; "chiefs" and, 70–72; and Civil War, 88, 92–96; draft resistance and, 101–4, 117; and Gulf War, 176–79; Manifest Destiny and, 66, 96–100; and Mexican-American War, 77–78; Native Americans in, 37–38, 73; in Philippines, 98–100; post-Vietnam interventions by, 174–76, 201–6; Robert Rogers and, 42–47; and Second Iraq War, 175, 198–206; and Spanish-American War and, 96–100; and Stop Loss program, 204–5; symbolism and naming in, 62–63, 65–77, 84, 145–46; and War of 1812, 90–92; and World War I, 86–88, 101–6; at Wounded Knee II, 165–66. *See also* servicemen and veterans, Native American
U.S. National Guard, 78, 102, 104, 119, 138
USNS *Red Cloud*, 62–63, 75, 84, 138
USS *Delaware*, 84

Valdez, Linda, 214
Veronico Cruz, 19–20
veterans. *See* servicemen and veterans, Native American
Veterans Warrior Society, 178
Victory dances, 141, 145, 205
Vietnam Veterans Against the War, 170
Vietnam War, 79, 80–81, 106, 162; and ceremonies and personal medicine, 154–58; images of Native Americans and, 160–62; Native communities and, 147–51; Navajo Code Talkers in, 132; and warrior societies, 151–54; war songs and, 107–9; Wounded Knee II and, 166–70

Villa, Pancho, 98, 111
Vogel, Clayton, 132
Vogt, Evon, 120
Von Kleist, Joyce Riley, 178
Voyage (de Lahontan), 88

Walker, Clint, 29
Wallace, W. P., 75
Wall Street Journal, 198
Wandering Medicine, Lamar, 205
War Mother Societies, 129, 142
Warner, Volney, 164, 165
War of 1812, 90–92, 93
War on Terrorism/Long War. *See* Afghanistan; Second Iraq War
Warrior, Robert Allen, 91
warrior societies, 52–55, 238n14; and Gulf War, 178; and Korean War, 140–43; and Vietnam War, 151–54; and World War I, 106–7; and World War II, 129–30
Washburn, Winona, 206
Washington, Denzel, 200
Washington, George, 74
Watergate scandal, 163, 164
Watie, Stand, 95
Wayne, John, 160, 161, 200
Weaver, Jace, 91
White Calf, Henry, 126
White Eagle, Winslow, 145
White Earth Reservation, 177
Whitehorse, Charley, 130
Whitehorse, Roland, 124
White Horse Brigade, 106–7
Wicahpi Etan. *See* Bentzlin, Eric
Wiggins, Armstrong, 176
Wild Horse Butte Tokalas, 152
Williams, Heidi, 215
Wilson, Angela Cavender, 179, 224–25
Wilson, Dick, 166
Windtalkers, 20–21, 22, 30
Winishut, Reginald, 140
Winnebago Indians, 62–63, 86–87, 138, 145

Wolves for the Blue Soldiers (Dunlay), 89
women: societies for, 129–30, 142; as
  warriors, 208–10, 228–29
World War I, 86–88, 101–6; and personal
  medicine, 111; warrior societies after,
  106–7; war songs and, 107–9
World War II: and ceremonies and personal medicine, 118–22; draft resistance
  during, 116–17; effects of, on Native
  American communities, 115–18, 134,
  247n2; Native symbolism used in, 74;
  Navajo Code Talkers in, 114–15, 120,
  131–33; propaganda images during,
  130–34; Termination and Relocation
  after, 136–37, 249n4; warrior societies
  and, 53; war songs and, 123–29
World War II and the American Indian
  (Townsend), 7–8

Wounded Knee II, 163–70, 228; American
  Indian Movement and, 166–71
Wright, Asher, 92

Xavier, San Francisco, 1–2
X-Men, 27

Yaqui Indians, 1–2, 8, 22; Catholic
  religion of, 48–50, 51–52, 59–60;
  independence of, 58; in U.S. military,
  98; warrior societies of, 53–54, 55
Yeagley, David, 182–83, 193–95, 217,
  253n20, 256nn42–43, 257n45
Yellow Hair, Milo, 2–3
Yucipio, Román, 58

Zissu, Erik, 103
Zuni Indians, 102, 117, 119, 121